Family Pecan Trees

Family Pecan Trees

Planting a Legacy of Faith at Home

Carlos E. Asay

Deseret Book Company
Salt Lake City, Utah

Library of Congress Cataloging-in-Publication Data

Asay, Carlos E., 1926–
    Family pecan trees : planting a legacy of faith at home / Carlos
E. Asay.
       p. cm.
    Includes index.
    ISBN 0-87579-608-7
    1. Family—Religious life. 2. Parenting—Religious aspects—
Mormon Church. 3. Church of Jesus Christ of Latter-day Saints—
Doctrines. 4. Mormon Church—Doctrines. I. Title.
BX8643.F3A83   1992
248.8′45—dc20   92-15838
                                                     CIP

Printed in the United States of America

10   9   8   7   6   5   4   3   2   1

CONTENTS

CONTENTS

ACKNOWLEDGMENTS

I had the privilege of visiting with President Marion G. Romney in his office soon after the death of his wife. In the middle of our conversation, he directed my attention to a picture hanging on the wall. He asked, "Do you know who that angel woman is?" I responded, "That is your wife." With great emotion, he told me about his "beloved Ida" and extolled her many virtues. As he concluded the tender tribute to Sister Romney, he said, with a tear in his eye, "When I see her next, it will not be one moment too soon."

I, too, have a "beloved companion" — one who has been my "angel woman," inspiration, synergist, and lover for many years. I cannot remember when I didn't know her (we grew up together); and, it is difficult for me to remember when I didn't love her. Everything good and decent in my life, I relate to Colleen in one way or another. She is the one who is most responsible for making our home a heaven on earth. And, she is the one who encouraged me to write this book.

If I bring to this work any qualifications worthy of note, they are: I was born of goodly parents who planted in our home many of the "pecan tree" practices discussed within these pages; I married a saintly woman with strong faith who believed in the imperative need of perfecting and exalting practices at home; and my wife and I were blessed with children (Marcianne, James, Marcus, Brent, Clair, Timothy, and Carleen) who seemed to bring with them from another sphere of existence an inclination to love God and to serve each other.

I hope that what I have written within these covers, including many personal experiences, will give others a glimpse of marriage and family as I have experienced them and inspire an even greater attention to home and loved ones.

A story is told of a man who displayed family portraits in his office. One day a visitor asked about the pictures. "That's the jury," said the man. "These are the pictures of my family. Every once in a while I have to ask the question, 'What would they expect of me?' "

I relate to this story because I, too, proudly display pictures of my family in my office. They are both my judge and jury. Whenever I look at them, I am reminded of my first and foremost responsibilities, and of the need to plant and cultivate family "pecan tree" practices at home.

I acknowledge the professional assistance of my secretary, Margie McKnight, and my editor, Jack M. Lyon. Both have extended me valuable suggestions and ideas and expedited the completion of this writing project.

I also acknowledge the cooperation of many who have corroborated some of the experiences and materials included in this book. The list of those who have verified selected pages includes: Mark Benson (chapter 12), the C. Terry Graff family (chapter 13), the James R. Boone family (chapter 14), Henry Haurand (chapter 15), Dr. William G. Dyer and Dr. Phillip R. Kunz (appendix).

Admittedly, a number of the personal accounts used to explain or illustrate ideas in this book may be colored slightly by personal biases or shaded by fading memory. I have, however, tried to constrain my imagination and to rely heavily upon entries made in my personal papers at the time or soon after the experiences occurred in order to preserve the integrity of the book.

I do assume full responsibility for what is written, and I pray that no reader will be offended by what is printed. Rather, I hope that someone or many may be inspired by my thoughts about families and "pecan tree" practices to initiate actions that will strengthen the home and those who live in it.

PROLOGUE: WHAT ARE WE PLANTING?

*To every thing there is a season, and a time to every
purpose under the heaven ... a time to plant, and
a time to pluck up that which is planted (Ecclesiastes
3:1–2; emphasis added).*

The seeds of inspiration for this book were planted in my mind
and heart years ago when I read the following article:

> On the plains of Texas and Oklahoma, where trees
> are sometimes rare and precious things, there is a
> tradition that recognizes the responsibility of one gen-
> eration for the next.
> Rural homesteaders, once the house was built, the
> well dug and the first few crops harvested, would plant
> their "grandchildren grove."
> Laboriously, the farmer would read a score or more
> of seed catalogues and finally select a particular type
> of pecan tree. It had to be hardy and strong, able to
> withstand the deep winters and torrid summers of
> those dry plains. He would make his selection and
> send off carefully hoarded money.
> In due time, a tree, hardly larger than a switch,
> would arrive. The farmer would place roots of the dry
> and unpromising stick in water and then dig a hole,
> deep and wide. Tenderly, he would plant the tree,
> packing the soil firmly about its roots. Then he would
> water it, carrying bucketful after bucketful from his
> well.

If he did his job well, in the spring—wonders of all wonders—the stick would sprout leaves.

Over the years, he would plant others and carefully tend them. But it wouldn't be for his benefit, because pecan trees grow very slowly, inching their way upward.

To some it seemed folly, for the farmer would be dead and gone long before the grove he planted could provide substantial shade or a harvest of the sweet-meated nuts.

But there was a saying that explained: "Plant corn for yourself and pecans for your grandchildren."

. . . Some farmers felt work that went unrewarded for generations was a waste.

Instead of pecans, they planted plum trees that grew quickly and soon produced fat, juicy fruit. For a decade or two, the plum trees did well, but eventually their soft wood split, and from the roots sprouted plum bushes that eventually became a snarl of scraggly, unproductive branches.

. . . What are we coming to? Have we blinkered our vision to take in only the quick and easy, and the devil take tomorrow?

Just what are we planting, anyway? (Marvin Stone, "What Are We Planting?" *U.S. News and World Report*, June 13, 1977, p. 84).

One may conclude from the above account that the rural homesteaders of Texas and Oklahoma who planted "grandchildren groves" possessed a deep love for their families and a strict sense of responsibility for the rising generations. Such conclusion is strengthened by the knowledge that pecan trees do not begin to bear nuts until they are about five or six years old. "For another five years, they do not bear enough nuts to make them profitable. Only after the trees are about twenty years old does the owner receive return on his investment" (*World Book Encyclopedia* [Field Enterprises Educational Corporation, 1970], 15:198).

Obviously the rural pecan-tree growers of a hundred years

ago planted with the "eye of faith" focused upon children and grandchildren—the real fruits of the future (see Ether 12:19). They were schooled in patience, imbued with faith, and willing to make sacrifices. Otherwise, why would they content themselves with corn and carefully tend the "dry and unpromising stick" that would eventually provide others, not themselves, with shade and sweetmeated nuts?

We can learn much from the example set by the rural homesteaders of yesterday. They certainly had their priorities straight, because families came first. They cared more for posterity than "plums." They understood the law of the harvest, so they planted, watered, and cultivated, knowing that God would give the increase (see 1 Corinthians 3:6–8). They were even willing to forsake present comforts and conveniences in the hope that succeeding generations would enjoy a richer life as a result of their selfless actions.

But, we may appropriately ask, what about the rural and urban home-dwellers of today? What about you and me and our families? What are we coming to? That is the real issue! Have we blinkered our vision to take in only the quick and easy, and the devil take tomorrow? Just what are we planting, anyway, in the gardens we call home?

Family Responsibilities

Over the years, one modern prophet after another has reminded us of our family responsibilities. Said President Gordon B. Hinckley: "We come into this life as children of mortal parents and as members of families. Parents are partners with God in bringing to pass his eternal purposes with reference to his children. The family, therefore, is a divine institution, the most important both in mortality and in eternity" ("Why These Temples," *Ensign*, August 1974, p. 39). Elder Reed Smoot declared, "The strength of a nation is the home; the basis of the Church is the home; anything that interferes with the desire and love of home affects the nation and the Church" (*Confer-*

ence Report, October 1910, p. 70). President Harold B. Lee taught, "The greatest of the Lord's work you brethren will ever do as fathers will be within the walls of your own home" (*Ensign*, July 1973, p. 98). And President David O. McKay warned, "No other success can compensate for failure in the home" (*Conference Report*, April 1964, p. 5). These and other statements of inspired leaders make it perfectly clear that families are important and that parents have had, now have, and will forever have special responsibilities to fulfill in the rearing of children.

I wonder, however, whether the heads of modern-day families are listening to the pointed instructions given by the mouthpieces of the Lord. I wonder whether mothers and fathers are assuming full responsibility for the preservation of family and home. Soaring divorce rates, ever-increasing incidents of wife and child abuse, and other alarming statistics suggest that many parents have not only abdicated their responsibilities but also forsaken their guardian roles. Hence, the traditional family concept is being threatened seriously by many people, programs, and philosophies.

More than a few people in today's world ridicule marriage. Many popular programs undermine families and family unity. And some worldly philosophies invite young and old to do their own thing or what feels best without regard to others, including kith and kin. Such satanic influences have placed the family under siege and raised in the minds of all God-fearing people the question, What can we do to safeguard the family?

Too many of us, I fear, are lovers of our own selves, lovers of pleasure, and without natural affection or concern for others, particularly our own offspring. We go selfishly and foolishly on our way eating, drinking, and making merry, just as if tomorrow and children were not important. Though such deportment may bring a fleeting thrill or pleasure and fulfills prophecies made centuries ago by prophets of old, it will eventually curse the lives of future generations and incur the wrath of Almighty God. In the end, we will have offended the little ones and mocked the divine institutions of marriage and family (see 2 Timothy 3:1–7; 2 Nephi 28:6–7; Matthew 18:3–6).

The Purpose of This Book

The intent of this book is not to wave the white flag and acquiesce to the enemies of righteousness who regard the family as a passé organization. Quite the contrary! It is my feeling that the family must and can be preserved. This can be done by incorporating—planting, if you will—"pecan tree" practices and performances in our homes. I refer to practices and performances based upon the holy scriptures and rooted in the teachings of Jesus Christ. I refer to practices and performances that square with the admonitions of inspired prophets past and present. I refer to practices and performances that bind people together both physically and spiritually. I refer to practices and performances that bring joy into the lives of participants and that shower blessings upon those of succeeding generations. I refer to such "pecan tree" practices and performances as:

- Praying together
- Reading the scriptures
- Conducting family home evenings
- Giving and receiving priesthood blessings
- Bestowing names of significance
- Holding personal interviews
- Preserving cherished memories
- Using good humor
- Writing personal and family histories
- Organizing families and participating in family reunions
- Establishing wholesome family traditions
- Creating communication lifelines
- Rendering love and service at home
- Becoming involved in Church service

• Engaging in family and Church worship services
• Attending the temple

Each of these practices is based on righteous principles; each has welding power; and each, if planted, cultivated, and allowed to grow in a family garden, will bear a fruit "desirable above all other fruit." Yes, each will bear a fruit that is white, sweet, and capable of making participants happy (see 1 Nephi 8:10–12).

A Compilation

In many respects, this book is a compilation of thoughts about marriage, family, and home. Some of the thoughts are my own; some are the selected thoughts of Church leaders; and many of the thoughts are gleaned from the holy scriptures. By intent, each chapter includes some personal experiences to illustrate certain points and to provide a practical approach to the various subjects. Each chapter also includes suggestions and guidelines that may prove helpful to the reader in applying the perfecting and exalting practices proposed by the author.

Trees of Righteousness

The Prophet Isaiah spoke of one who would preach glad tidings, bind up the broken-hearted, proclaim liberty to the captives, and do other things to bless the lives of people. All of this was to be done so "that they [the people] might be called *trees of righteousness*, the planting of the Lord, that he might be glorified" (Isaiah 61:3; italics added).

I regard each "pecan tree" practice listed within these covers as a tree of righteousness. All are plantings of the Lord and will lead men and women to glorify God. And, if such practices are initiated and added upon, with the right spirit, they will produce righteous individuals and help immeasurably to perfect and exalt family units.

My list of "pecan tree" practices is not all-inclusive — only a dozen and four performances are mentioned. But the sixteen practices cited are basic, virtuous, understandable, and doable, even in single parent homes, and regardless of the size of house or the number of children.

It is my prayer that this book will help families plant the right crop and harvest the right fruit within their family garden plots. I hope that these suggestions will find proper rooting and bring about the cross-fertilization of other wholesome practices, so that it might be said of all family trees,

"I, the Lord, will cause them to bring forth as a very fruitful tree which is planted in a goodly land, by a pure stream, that yieldeth much precious fruit" (D&C 97:9).

INTRODUCTION: GOD AND FAMILY

For this cause I bow my knees unto the Father of our Lord Jesus Christ, of whom the whole family in heaven and earth is named (Ephesians 3:14–15).

A discussion about families and "pecan tree" performances would be superfluous if marriage and families were not divine institutions. But since "marriage is ordained of God" (D&C 49:15) and since we are members of "the whole human family of Adam" (Mormon 3:20), counsel concerning the preservation of these heaven-inspired arrangements is always timely and appropriate. Lest we forget, the Savior said in response to a question about the severance of a marriage and the break-up of a family: "What . . . God hath joined together, let not man put asunder" (Matthew 19:3–6).

We do "put asunder" sacred and important things when we forget marriage vows, neglect spouse and children, or fail to honor responsibilities of the home. In doing so, we offend Deity, for God wants laws obeyed, not broken; he wants parents to be united, not separated; he wants families welded together, not splintered; and he invites his sons and daughters to live after the manner of happiness, not after the manner of wickedness (see 2 Nephi 5:27). We must, therefore, do all within our power to prevent the fabric of the family from being torn asunder by ignorance, selfishness, or any other unholy practice or influence.

1

A Godly Concept

I once heard the host of a television talk-show ask a religious leader, "What scriptural evidence can you cite supporting your claim that the family is a godly concept?" The question was shocking to me because the answer to the question was so obvious and the scriptural evidences almost as plentiful as the stars in the heaven.

It seemed to me that the man was questioning, perhaps even mocking, something as basic and sacrosanct as motherhood, peace, love, or even God himself. And I wondered whether the glib host was a man of faith or whether he possessed even a cursory knowledge of the word of the Lord.

A search of the Standard Works of The Church of Jesus Christ of Latter-day Saints reveals some startling statistics about the words "family" and "families." These words are used 296 times in the Old Testament, once in the New Testament, 42 times in the Book of Mormon, 49 times in the Doctrine and Covenants, and 13 times in the Pearl of Great Price. By adding these numbers, we find that references to family and families are made *401* times in the scriptures.

These 401 references to family found in Holy Writ can be confusing to the reader unless the word and its various connotations are understood. The word generally refers to a married man and wife living under the same roof with children. It sometimes refers to a single parent, usually a widowed or divorced woman, with children to rear. Sometimes the word refers to a group of people related by ancestry or marriage. (In today's language, such groups are known as immediate and extended families.) The word is also used to distinguish people claiming descent from a common ancestor, tribe, or clan. In all instances, however, the contributors to the scriptures used the word *family* to describe special relationships existing between people who shared common interests, love, and family ties.

Here are but a few of the references to families found in the recorded word of God:

The Apostle Paul wrote of "the whole family in heaven and earth" (Ephesians 3:14–15). Members of this vast family are the offspring of the "Father of spirits," or God, the Eternal Father (Hebrews 12:9). Adam, Enoch, and Abraham were given knowledge concerning "all the families of the earth" (Moses 5:10; Moses 7:45; Abraham 2:11; 2 Nephi 2:20); hence, they knew something about "the whole human family of Adam" (2 Nephi 9:21; Mormon 3:20). The Prophet Amos spoke of the children of Israel as "the whole family which [God] brought up from the land of Egypt" (Amos 3:1). Other groups, such as the Lehites and Jaredites who were led to the Americas, had familial ties. Numerous references are made in the Old Testament to "the family of Judah" (Judges 17:7), "family of the Danites" (Judges 13:2), and other tribes. The epistles of the New Testament speak of Timothy and Titus as Paul's "own [sons] in the faith" (1 Timothy 1:2; Titus 1:4). Paul also addressed the Saints as brother and sister, suggesting a special brotherhood and sisterhood among the followers of Christ. Each of these references and many others associated with husbands, wives, and children leave little doubt that family is a God-inspired concept. In the words of a modern prophet, "The scriptures reveal the fact that the family is a divine and not a man-made institution" (Marion G. Romney, "Scriptures As They Relate to Family Stability," *Ensign,* February 1972, p. 57).

We find in the Bible Dictionary this convincing statement about families:

> The Bible is family oriented. The first man and woman — Adam and Eve — were a family. . . . The history of Israel begins with the family of Abraham. He is highly esteemed of the Lord as a father and teaches his children properly (Gen. 18:17–19). Family life is safeguarded with such divine commandments as Ex. 20:12, 14–17; 21:15–17. The frequent genealogical lists in the

3

scriptures give evidence of the importance that is placed on family. The book of Proverbs offers many instructions directed toward the family, such as Prov. 13:1, 22; 15:5, 20; 19:13, 26.

Jesus' teachings were directed to a family type of life, as in Matt. 5:45; 10:21; 13:57; 19:3–9; Mark 10:2–9; Luke 6:36; 15:31; John 19:27. The Lord frequently referred to his *Father*, and emphasized the "Fatherliness" of God. Paul and Peter gave much counsel about the duties of husbands and wives, parents and children (Eph. 6:1–4; Col. 3:18–21; 1 Pet. 3:1–7).

Latter-day revelation confirms all that the Bible teaches about the family and adds the most important truth that through the gospel of Jesus Christ the family can be sealed together in a permanent relationship for time and all eternity (D&C 132). [*Bible Dictionary*, pp. 670–71.]

Questions

Why would God declare, "It is not good that the man should be alone" and bring to Adam a wife known as "the mother of all living" if families were not important? (Genesis 2:18; 3:20). Why would God instruct a man to leave his father and mother and cleave unto a wife, if families were not essential? (see Abraham 5:18). Why would an apostle say, "Neither is the man without the woman, neither the woman without the man, *in the Lord*" if marriage and families were not part of the divine scheme? (1 Corinthians 11:11; italics added). Why would the Savior instruct us to address *"Our Father* which art in heaven" when we pray, if family relationships were not ordained of God? (Matthew 6:9; italics added).

Obligations of Family Members

Why would the Apostle Paul specify the obligations of family members if families did not serve God's purposes? Consider his counsel:

To wives: "Submit yourselves unto your own husbands, as

unto the Lord [or, as it is fit in the Lord]. For the husband is
the head of the wife, even as Christ is the head of the church:
and he is the saviour of the body. Therefore as the church is
subject unto Christ, so let the wives be to their own husbands
in every thing" (Ephesians 5:22–24; Colossians 3:18).

To husbands: "Husbands, love your wives [and be not bitter
against them], even as Christ also loved the church, and gave
himself for it; that he might sanctify and cleanse it with the
washing of water by the word, that he might present it to himself
a glorious church, not having spot, or wrinkle, or any such
thing; but that it should be holy and without blemish" (Ephesians 5:25–27; Colossians 3:19).

To husbands and wives: "Let every one of you in particular
so love his wife even as himself; and the wife see that she
reverence her husband" (Ephesians 5:33).

To children: "Obey your parents in the Lord: for this is
right [and well pleasing unto the Lord]. Honour thy father and
mother; (which is the first commandment with promise;) that
it may be well with thee, and thou mayest live long on the
earth" (Ephesians 6:1–3; Colossians 3:20).

One cannot read the above counsel without concluding
that families are important in the sight of God and that strong
family relationships must be preserved.

You will recall that Eli, an ancient high priest and judge,
suffered severe consequences "because his sons made themselves vile, and he restrained them not" (1 Samuel 3:13). Of
him it is written: "The blot on his character was his toleration
of the wickedness of his own sons" (*Bible Dictionary*, p. 663).

Those who fallaciously think that families and family responsibilities pertain only to a bygone day should review the
stern rebukes given modern-day Church leaders for failing to
take proper care of their families. Among other things, the Lord
has said: "I have commanded you to bring up your children
in light and truth. . . . You have not taught your children light
and truth, according to the commandments; and that wicked

5

one hath power, as yet, over you, and this is the cause of your affliction. And now a commandment I give unto you—if you will be delivered you shall set in order your own house, for there are many things that are not right in your house. . . . Your family must needs repent and forsake some things, and give more earnest heed unto your sayings, or be removed out of their place" (D&C 93:40, 42–43, 48).

Two Commandments

Two of the Ten Commandments, one-fifth of the tablet writings given to ancient Israel on Mount Sinai, had direct bearing upon the family unit. They are:

• "Honour thy father and thy mother: that thy days may be long upon the land which the Lord thy God giveth thee" (Exodus 20:12).

• "Thou shalt not covet . . . thy neighbour's wife" (Exodus 20:17).

At no time, down through the course of history, has God rescinded his words or softened the requirements as pertaining to the family. If anything, the expectations placed upon family members have risen as new threats to the endurance and stability of the family have surfaced. Fidelity in marriage, respect for parents, and family closeness will never become outmoded in the eyes of God for they are founded upon eternal principles. As summarized by President Marion G. Romney, "It is inconceivable that God would not have a plan and specifications for building the family, his most precious and enduring creation" ("Scriptures As They Relate to Family Stability," *Ensign*, February 1972, p. 57).

Family and Church

President Joseph F. Smith declared: "I want the young men of Zion to realize that this institution of marriage is not a man-made institution. It is of God. It is honorable, and no man who is of marriageable age is living his religion who remains

6

single. . . . Marriage is the preserver of the human race. Without it, the purposes of God would be frustrated; virtue would be destroyed to give place to vice and corruption, and the earth would be void and empty" (*Gospel Doctrine*, 5th ed. [Deseret Book Co., 1939], p. 272).

I emphasize these words of President Smith's: "No man who is of marriageable age is living his religion who remains single." Without marriage, there is no family; and, without family, there is no home. And, without the home, there is no "basis of a righteous life, and . . . no other instrumentality can take its place nor fulfill its essential functions," stated the First Presidency in 1960 (cited by Elder Harold B. Lee, in *Conference Report*, September 30, 1961, p. 79).

"The Church of Jesus Christ of Latter-day Saints," said Elder A. Theodore Tuttle, "is a family church. In its missionary work we seek to bring families into the Church. We teach the principles and perform ordinances that unite the family for eternity. Indeed, we may say that a prime purpose of this church is to perfect and exalt the family" (*Conference Report*, October 1972, p. 69).

Marriage, family, home, and true religion are so interrelated that it might be said that they are one and the same. All are godly concepts, and each one builds the others. They might be likened to a celestial room, wherein marriage is the doorway, family is the floor, home is the walls, and Church or religion is the ceiling. One cannot say to the other, "I have no need of you," for all the building "fitly framed together groweth unto an holy temple in the Lord" (1 Corinthians 12:21; Ephesians 2:21).

President Stephen L Richards provides this summary statement about family, Church, and God: "The home [or family] has an enlarged significance that is subordinate to nothing else in life, for it constitutes not only the source of our greatest happiness here in this life, but also the foundation of our exaltation and glory in the life to come. After all, it is essentially a religious institution. It has its origin in [a] religious ceremony. It is the fulfilment of [a] divine command. Its government is of a religious nature and the finest of its products are spiritual." (*Where Is Wisdom?* [Salt Lake City: Deseret Book Co., 1955], p. 193).

Journey and Home

Someone referred to life on earth as a journey and to death as a return home. Whether or not this someone was familiar with Holy Writ, he or she had it right. We are the spirit children of God, and we are members of his family. We have been sent to earth for the purpose of obtaining physical bodies, gaining experiences, and proving ourselves under the tutelage of parents and within the framework of a family unit (see Abraham 3:24–26). One day, however, all of us will die or experience a separation of our bodies and spirits, and our spirits will be "taken *home* to that God who gave them life" (Alma 40:11; italics added). The bitterness or sweetness of such return will be determined by our closeness to God, our acquisition of Christ-like virtues, and our faithfulness to family.

The purpose of the family is explained in the *Family Guidebook* — a publication of the Church:

> Because our Father in Heaven loves us, he wants us to become exalted as he is. To help us, he has given us a plan to follow based on divine laws of truth. Those who learn about the plan and follow it faithfully can someday become like our Father in Heaven and enjoy the kind of life he enjoys.
>
> Part of the plan was for us to leave heaven and come to earth. Here we gain a physical body, learn through experiences, and prove ourselves worthy to live again in the presence of God. We prove ourselves worthy by freely choosing to keep his laws. (See Abraham 3:24–25; 2 Nephi 2:27.)
>
> To help us prepare ourselves for life with him, our Heavenly Father has organized us into families. Fam-

8

ilies on earth are similar to the families that we will have in the celestial kingdom (*Family Guidebook,* p. 4).

God and family are inseparable and eternal (see appendix A, "The Latter-day Saint Concepts of Family"). They must not be legislated away or washed aside by waves of modern norms and the foolish practices of worldly people. Rather, they must be protected and preserved through "pecan tree" practices and other sanctifying performances that harmonize with the revealed word of God. It is our duty, our opportunity, and our joy to

> *"take especial care of [our families] from this time, henceforth and forever"* *(D&C 126:3).*

CHAPTER ONE

PRAYER

*Ye must pray always, and not faint; that ye must
not perform any thing unto the Lord save in the first
place ye shall pray unto the Father in the name of
Christ, that he will consecrate thy performance unto
thee, that thy performance may be for the welfare
of thy soul (2 Nephi 32:9).*

Soon after my return from the mission field, I was invited to
Church Headquarters to give a report and to receive my release
from full-time missionary service. The General Authority assigned to interview me was Elder Spencer W. Kimball of the
Council of the Twelve Apostles.

Elder Kimball greeted my wife and me warmly and shared
with us an hour of precious advice that established the foundation for our marriage. Among other things, he counseled us
to remain active in the Church, to accept opportunities to serve,
to pay our tithing, and to seek the full blessings of the gospel.
The instructional procedure he used was to express his love
and concern, teach us a principle, and then commit us to live
it. He didn't mince words nor was he timid in issuing his
charges.

He indicated that my post-mission adjustment would not
be easy. He also stressed the critical nature of the challenge
that my wife and I were facing as we sought to establish our
family unit.

Elder Kimball placed special emphasis upon the principle and practice of daily prayer in our home. Such practice, he said, would be the keystone in our lives, linking heaven with home. "You will bless the food at mealtimes, pray together morning and night at the bedside as a couple, and conduct family prayers at the beginning and close of each day when the children come. Won't you?" he pressed. We stated that we would do as he instructed. "But doesn't it become monotonous for a couple to pray together twice a day or more?" I asked. He was quick to rebuke me and stated that prayers need not be long and drawn-out conversations. "How do you and your wife do it?" I inquired. He responded, "I am the voice at the beginning of each day, my wife is the voice at the close of each day." Then, he winked at me and added, "That way she gets in the last word."

My wife and I concluded in the presence of one who would eventually become the president and prophet of the Church that we would accept the charge given and plant the "pecan tree" practice of prayer in our family garden. We have cultivated the practice over the years, and the "tree" has flourished and produced nourishing fruit for our children and us.

Few, if any, practices are more virtuous or efficacious than the conduct of prayers within a family circle. I say this because, as President Kimball taught, prayer is the means of linking heaven and home. Through prayer we invite the Lord to become a partner to our marriage and a contributing member of our family. Through prayer we can converse with God and receive needed inspiration. Through prayer we obtain views of our divine destiny and keep our eyes fixed upon eternal goals. Indeed, it is through prayer that we maintain our God-ward position and retain the fellowship of the right Spirit (see 2 Nephi 32:8).

Caring Parents

A caring parent would never send a child off to school in the morning or a son off to work without some warm, protective clothing upon his back. Yet how many parents see their young ones out the door without the protective covering of the Spirit?

I regard sincere prayer as a protective covering, especially to those who pray that they will "not be tempted above that which [they] can bear" (Alma 13:28). It is also a spiritual shield to those who pray that they will be led by the Holy Spirit, watched over by guardian angels, or borne "up as on eagles' wings" (D&C 124:18). Yes, those who pray at home are more inclined to measure their words, guard their thoughts, and tend their actions when in the world than those who simply cover themselves with hats and coats as they leave the house.

Caring parents would do all within their power to give their sons and daughters the edge in meeting the vicissitudes of life. But how many parents fail to make available to their children unseen powers and aids rallied through the Holy Spirit?

Sincere prayer is much like an escalator. It will lengthen your stride and accelerate your pace if you hold to the right, if you keep moving, and if you do your part. As someone put it, "You pray as if all depends on God and work as if all depends on you." Prayers can bring inspiration, the ministration of angels, gifts of the Spirit, and other powers and blessings. But if we or our children fail to exercise faith and bend the knees in humble supplication to God, we are left to our own limited and puny resources (see Mormon 2:26).

Caring parents have on hand a first-aid kit full of medicines and bandages so that minor physical wounds may be treated tenderly. Each day around the house seems to bring its share of skinned knees, scratched faces, and bruised elbows. But how many parents keep on hand the salves and disinfectants needed to heal the deeper injuries to the soul?

Sincere prayer is like a balm of Gilead. It emits spiritual, resinous juices that have a soothing and healing effect upon many family ills. Prayer can mend a broken heart, assuage troubled feelings, restore peace of mind, and knit souls together in a wonderful way. It is not to be borrowed occasionally or applied sparingly; it must be used daily so that its powers may both prevent and cure problems.

Caring parents encourage their children to participate in a regular exercise program, knowing that a "body fit is a help in keeping the mind pure" (William Osler, *A Way of Life* [New York and London: Paul B. Hoeber, Inc., 1937], p. 25). However, how many of these same parents help their offspring to maintain spiritual fitness?

In my view, sincere prayer is an aerobic exercise for the spirit or "inner man." It causes the "breath of life" within a person to stir with activity so that the spiritual muscles and pulse are strengthened (Genesis 2:7). It enables a purer form of adrenalin to run throughout one's system, sparking lofty thoughts and generating exhilarating feelings. Such prayer or "labor in the spirit," along with study, fasting, and other unseen exertions, keeps the spirit fit and benefits the whole soul (Alma 17:5).

Yes, prayer—sincere prayer—is a protective covering, an escalator, a balm of Gilead, an aerobic exercise for the spirit, and much more. As we so often sing:

> Prayer is the soul's sincere desire . . .
> Prayer is the burden of a sigh . . .
> Prayer is the simplest form of speech . . .
> Prayer is the Christian's vital breath . . .
> Prayer is the contrite sinner's voice . . .
>
> (*Hymns,* no. 145.)

I would add one more important definitive line: *Prayer is a "pecan tree" practice that must be planted in the lives of individuals and families!*

Divine Expectations or Charges

Soon after the organization of the Restored Church in 1830, the Prophet Joseph Smith received a revelation containing pointed instructions to parents. One of the instructions given

13

was this: "They shall . . . *teach their children to pray*, and to walk uprightly before the Lord" (D&C 68:28; italics added).

This charge from the Lord was simply a reiteration of a divine expectation stated to other people in earlier times. To the ancient Nephites Christ said: *"Pray in your families* unto the Father, always in my name, that your wives and your children may be blessed" (3 Nephi 18:21; italics added).

And, through Amulek, God instructed, "Call upon his holy name. . . . Cry unto him in your houses, yea, *over all your household, both morning, mid-day, and evening"* (Alma 34:17, 21; italics added).

Notice the all-inclusiveness of this injunction ("all your household") and the suggested frequency ("both morning, mid-day, and evening"). Such instructions remind us of the resolve expressed by the Psalmist: "Evening, and morning, and at noon, will I pray, and cry aloud: and he shall hear my voice" (Psalm 55:17).

These and similar scriptural references inform us that all parents are expected to establish houses of prayer wherein a steady stream of edifying conversations ascend heavenward (see D&C 88:119; 109:8).

Suggestions

In establishing a house of prayer and in planting the "pecan tree" practice of prayer in your family unit, perhaps these suggestions will be appropriate:

1. *Spirit.* Help your children understand that prayer comes from above and not from below. It is a godly action, as this scripture attests: "For if ye would hearken unto the Spirit which teacheth a man to pray ye would know that ye must pray; for the evil spirit teacheth not a man to pray, but teacheth him that he must not pray" (2 Nephi 32:8).

When Christ's disciple implored, "Lord, teach us to pray," he was wrought upon by the Holy Spirit, not some satanic influence.

14

2. *Model.* Serve as a consistent model before the children. Bless the food before each meal; conduct family prayers in a regular manner; and pray with your spouse at the beginning and close of each day. Children may or may not listen to your preachments about the necessity of prayer, but they will observe and remember the image of parents on their knees supplicating God for needed blessings.

One caution, however. If the model set is to be effective, it must be consistent. Otherwise, the observers [children] may be led to question motives and depth of faith.

On one occasion, I was invited to the home of a priesthood leader for the purpose of meeting the members of his family. The hour was late when we arrived at the house, well beyond the bedtime of the younger children. As we walked into the living room, I saw seven weary children, dressed in their Sunday clothes, waiting for their father and a stranger from Church headquarters (me). A quick glance about the room convinced me that no one was impressed by my entry and that most wanted to be elsewhere.

The father invited me to instruct the family. I did so in two or three short statements, knowing that the children were tired and bored to death by the formal proceedings. Afterwards the father announced that we would engage in the daily family prayer with Tommy serving as the voice. Slowly and awkwardly the group assumed the position of a kneeling prayer. All of a sudden, one boy about twelve years of age blurted out, "What is this all about?"

It was obvious that the family gathering and prayer was a staged performance to impress me. Therefore, the boy's spontaneous outburst blew the father's cover and revealed the hidden motive. I do not know what went through the minds of the children on that occasion. I do know, however, how I felt about the inconsistency of the model set and the feelings of disappointment in the father that entered my heart.

3. *Desire.* Build the desire to pray within the hearts of your

children. Do so with the conviction that God grants to men, women, and children "according to their desire" or "according to their wills" (Alma 29:4).

Who can really judge the merits of a half-hearted or even pressured prayer—one in which a recalcitrant child participates? Perhaps Enos once dozed through a family prayer or even murmured against his father when requested to pray. Who knows? However, no one questions the merits of the prayer voiced by Enos, the son of Jacob, when he wrestled in the spirit before God. His "soul hungered"; he sought a remission of his sins; he knelt and supplicated his Maker "all the day long" and into the night; and he responded to the words of his father "concerning eternal life" (Enos 1:1–4). Enos, like Christ's Nephite disciples, prayed mightily because he was "filled with desire" (3 Nephi 19:24).

Said Enos: "After I had prayed and labored with all diligence, the Lord said unto me: I will grant unto thee according to thy desires, *because of thy faith*" (Enos 1:12; italics added).

It is faith that opens the door of desire. Parents, therefore, must speak to their children about God, eternal life, the joy of the Saints, and other truths that appeal to craving spirits and the souls of believing men and women. In due time, the young ones will speak and think "prayers of faith" built upon desire and capable of reaching high into the heavens (see D&C 41:3; 42:14).

4. *Form.* Make certain that your children understand the form or pattern of prayer as taught by the Savior. We refer to that pattern as the Lord's Prayer (see Matthew 6:9–13 and 3 Nephi 13:9–13). Special emphasis should be placed upon what Christ taught about praying in secrecy, avoiding the use of vain repetitions, and guarding against all hints of hypocrisy.

I fear that occasionally we allow "Rameumptom-like" practices to encroach upon our family prayers. This occurs when we offer "the self-same prayer unto God," use boastful language, display self-righteous pride, and become more concerned about form than substance (Alma 31:12–23). Satan came among the Zoramites "and tempted them to worship him" by perverting their order of prayer. We must not permit him to do the same to us.

President John Taylor must have shocked his audience at a general conference when he pointed a finger at a man and asked, "Do you have prayers in your family?" The listener replied in a weak and barely audible voice, "Yes." "And when you do," added President Taylor, "*do you go through the operation like the guiding of a piece of machinery*, or do you bow in meekness and with a sincere desire to seek the blessing of God upon you and your household?" (*Journal of Discourses*, 21:118; italics added).

Proper and sincere prayers, free of stilted form and the workings of machinery, will enable us to meet the challenge of a modern prophet who said, "Endeavor to make your homes a little heaven, and try to cherish the good Spirit of God" (*Journal of Discourses*, 21:118).

5. *Personalize.* Teach your children to be more specific in their prayers. One shouldn't fault the adult or child who prays universally for "all the sick and afflicted." But the universal appeals should not be allowed to crowd out concern for the one. A prayer in behalf of "all truth seekers" or "the honest in heart" is certainly a boon to our missionary effort. Such will be heard and answered according to the will of the Lord. However, a petition in behalf of a Brother and Sister J. Brown who are being taught the gospel by elders Jones and Anderson personalizes the prayer and seems to focus the faith of the person or persons involved.

I have the feeling that Alma, the father, prayed specifically for his wayward son, not just for sinners everywhere. These are the words of the angel who confronted Alma the younger: "The Lord hath heard the prayers of his people, and also the prayers of his servant, Alma, who is thy father; for he has prayed with much faith concerning thee that thou mightest be brought

17

to the knowledge of the truth; therefore, for this purpose have I come to convince thee of the power and authority of God, that the prayers of his servants might be answered according to their faith" (Mosiah 27:14).

In Paul's epistle to the Colossians, we read: "Epaphras, who is one of you, a servant of Christ, saluteth you, always labouring fervently for you in prayers, that ye may stand perfect and complete in all the will of God" (Colossians 4:12).

These scriptures should serve to remind parents and others that prayer is a great activation or recovery tool. A wayward soul may be redirected; a prodigal son may be caused to "come to himself"; and members whom we think to be "less honourable," "uncomely," or "more feeble" in the faith may make needed changes in their lives, if we care enough to personalize our prayers in their behalf and if we muster sufficient faith (Luke 15:17; see also 1 Corinthians 12:14–27).

6. *God's will.* Remind your children that prayers are more than orders placed at the "take-out window" of the local fast-food restaurant. They are petitions made to an all-wise and loving Father in Heaven who knows what is best for us even before we ask. Hence, each prayer should be laced with words or thoughts indicating submission to divine will.

In the Lord's Prayer, this significant sentence is included: *"Thy will be done* in earth, as it is in heaven" (Matthew 6:10; italics added). In Gethsemane, the Savior prayed, "Father, *if thou be willing,* remove this cup from me: nevertheless not my will, but thine, be done" (Luke 22:42; italics added). If, therefore, Jesus sensed the need to bend his will to God, so should we.

The Lord loved Nephi and bestowed upon him great and almost unlimited powers. In the process of doing so, he promised: "All things shall be done unto thee according to thy word [or prayer], for thou shalt not ask that which is contrary to my will" (Helaman 10:5). What a tribute to a tireless minister of the gospel!

As you speak with your children about prayer and the need to petition God in the right way, read and discuss together these scriptures:

"Yea, I know that God will give liberally to him that asketh. Yea, my God will give me, if I ask not amiss" (2 Nephi 4:35).

"Ye ask, and receive not, because ye ask amiss, that ye may consume it upon your lusts" (James 4:3).

"He that asketh in the Spirit asketh according to the will of God; wherefore it is done even as he asketh" (D&C 46:30).

Teach your children to place their honest and heartfelt concerns before God whenever they pray. Encourage them to pray with faith, to seek the guidance of the Spirit, and to trust in the will of one who knows precisely what is right and best for them. Assure them that expressions of thanks for blessings received through the windows of heaven should be included with requests for added blessings.

7. *Friendship.* Assure your children that the Lord is their most important friend, and that prayer is one of the means whereby friendship with Deity is maintained.

Reference to God as an intimate friend might seem presumptive on our part, if it weren't for two facts: (1) The Lord declared to his apostles, "Ye are my friends" (D&C 84:63). He also entreated: "I shall call you friends, it is expedient that I give unto you this commandment, that ye become even as my friends in days when I was with them" (D&C 84:77); and (2), a friend is "one that seeks the society or welfare of another whom he holds in affection, respect, or esteem or whose companionship and personality are pleasurable" (*Webster's Third New International Dictionary*, p. 911). By definition, invitation, and command, we are morally bound to seek a special relationship or friendship with God.

In my youth, I had a special friend. I loved to be in his presence. His companionship was building to me in every respect, for he sought to do me good. He could be trusted, and there was no fault in his association. Additionally, our communications, verbally and nonverbally, were always uplifting. These and other aspects of our friendship knitted our souls together in a David and Jonathan fashion (see 1 Samuel 18:1).

However, I enjoyed, as a child and youth, a closer friendship with someone even greater than Joe. My parents introduced me to this "greater friend" when they taught me the rudiments of the gospel of Jesus Christ. The friendship grew as I attended Church services, engaged in service activities, and became acquainted with the holy scriptures. But the friendship really blossomed when I learned to pray regularly and receive answers to my prayers. God became and remains my acquaintance, confidant, and *friend*.

Said Elder Richard L. Evans, "He who has ceased to pray has lost a great friendship" (*Richard Evans' Quote Book* [Salt Lake City: Publisher's Press, 1971], p. 132). Yes, we do close the door on God, give him the silent treatment, and turn our backs to him when we stop praying. We must, therefore, guide our children in finding a friend in Jesus and our Heavenly Father through prayer.

8. *Hearts drawn out.* Help your children to understand the virtues of muted or silent prayers, and help them see the need to harbor an ongoing attitude of prayer.

Amulek's profound instructions about prayer included the following: "Ye must pour out your souls in your closets, and your secret places. . . . Yea, and when you do not cry unto the Lord, let your hearts be full, *drawn out in prayer unto him continually* for your welfare, and also for the welfare of those who are around you" (Alma 34:26–27; italics added).

A modern revelation contains this direction from the Lord: "I command thee that thou shalt pray vocally *as well as in thy heart*; yea, before the world as well as in secret, in public as well as in private" (D&C 19:28; italics added).

While visiting his "other sheep" in America he commanded the multitude "that they should not cease *to pray in their hearts*" (3 Nephi 20:1; italics added).

We read of a people who were persecuted by wicked rulers and even killed if found praying to God. Therefore, an alternative to the audible and observable prayer was adopted. The record reads, "Alma and his people did not raise their voices to the Lord their God, *but did pour out their hearts to him;* and he did know the thoughts of their hearts" (Mosiah 24:12; italics added).

All of these scriptural accounts teach us that prayer is more than a mouth-to-ear communication. It is also a heart-to-heart or mind-to-mind proposition. In the words of James Montgomery:

> Prayer is the soul's sincere desire,
> Uttered or unexpressed,
> The motion of a hidden fire
> That trembles in the breast.
>
> Prayer is the burden of a sigh,
> The falling of a tear,
> The upward glancing of an eye
> When none but God is near.
>
> (*Hymns*, no. 145.)

Perhaps the sweetest and most effective prayers are these:

• When a child, lost and all alone, cries out for help.

• When a young man or woman confronted with strong temptation allows his or her heart to be drawn out for strength to resist.

• When a mother prays in her heart for a son or daughter living in a faraway place who is faced with a serious crisis.

• When a father lies in a hospital bed with a serious illness and pours out his heart to God for more time and another chance.

A child is never too young to hear of such prayers. Help the little ones learn early in life the virtues of silent prayers. For when a heart is drawn out to God a soul is united with heaven.

9. *Sanctification.* Speak with your children about the sanc-

tifying influence of prayer. Help them to understand that prayer is the "spiritual soap" used in washing away sins and in making a person humble, clean, and saintly. It is to be used daily to keep one free of the things of the world so that the Holy Ghost may be received and retained.

Your children should know and appreciate the meaning of this inspired verse from the Book of Mormon: "Nevertheless they [a persecuted people] did fast *and pray oft*, and did wax stronger and stronger in their humility, and firmer and firmer in the faith of Christ, unto the filling their souls with joy and consolation, yea, even to the purifying and the sanctification of their hearts, which sanctification cometh because of their yielding their hearts unto God" (Helaman 3:35; italics added).

I have always been intrigued by the accounts of the resurrected Christ praying with the children and his disciples on the American continent. As the children prayed, angels descended "and encircled those little ones about, and they were encircled about with fire; and the angels did minister unto them" (3 Nephi 17:24). Was this incident not symbolic of protection and purification that can come to one, young or older, who seeks sanctification through prayer?

In the second instance, Christ's disciples prayed steadfastly, without ceasing. He, Christ, smiled upon them, "and behold they were white, even as Jesus" (3 Nephi 19:30). Once again, one wonders whether there is a type or shadow in this occurrence. Is it not possible that the "whiteness" that came upon the disciples symbolizes the light and goodness — even sanctification — that accompanies a closeness to the Savior attained through fervent prayer?

10. *Real intent.* Emphasize to your children that they must pray with real intent; otherwise words are hollow, and the effort is in vain.

This is what Mormon taught regarding this principle: "If [a person] offereth a gift, or prayeth unto God, except he shall do it with real intent it profiteth him nothing. For behold, it is not counted unto him for righteousness. . . . And likewise also is it counted evil unto a man, if he shall pray and not with real intent of heart; yea, and it profiteth him nothing, for God receiveth none such" (Moroni 7:6–7, 9).

Remember always that the promise of gaining a testimony of the Book of Mormon is predicated upon prayer "with a sincere heart," "with real intent," and with "faith in Christ" (see Moroni 10:4).

Let not your prayers be hindered by less than an earnest appeal to God Almighty. But rather let the "hidden man of the heart" be revealed by your honest and sincere prayers (see 1 Peter 3:4, 7).

11. *Cry unto God.* Follow the instructions on prayer that Alma shared with his son Helaman. Note especially what he said about thoughts, affections, thanks, and other aspects of continuous communication with God: "Cry unto God for all thy support; yea, let all thy doings be unto the Lord, and whithersoever thou goest let it be in the Lord; yea, let all thy thoughts be directed unto the Lord; yea, let the affections of thy heart be placed upon the Lord forever. Counsel with the Lord in all thy doings, and he will direct thee for good; yea, when thou liest down at night lie down unto the Lord, that he may watch over you in your sleep; and when thou risest in the morning let thy heart be full of thanks unto God; and if ye do these things, ye shall be lifted up at the last day" (Alma 37:36–37).

The eleven suggestions above may seem too obvious and too simple to the gospel scholar and sophisticated reader, for they are certainly not new or original thoughts of the author. Each suggestion, however, is rooted in the scriptures and identified as a prerequisite to efficacious prayers. And all of the suggestions given must be heeded if the "pecan tree" practice of prayer is to be planted and allowed to grow in your home.

Closing Thoughts

Years ago, Elder F. D. Richards issued this statement in the Tabernacle on Temple Square in Salt Lake City: "I wish to exhort the Saints to frequent their closets more than they do; to neglect not their prayers night and morning, and in the season thereof fail not to bow the knee and call your sons and daughters around you. If you do this, by and by your sons and daughters will rise up and call you blessed; if you do not they will get cold and depart from truth and the faith of the living God, and that will bring the greatest sorrow you can conceive of' (*Journal of Discourses*, 26:172).

Sometimes parents become frustrated in their efforts to help children establish the habit of prayer. Occasionally the modeling, preaching, and pleading seem to fall on deaf ears. But parents must not become discouraged or relaxed in fulfilling this expectation of the Lord. As one sage observed, the years show much that the days never can see. What may appear to be a failure today may emerge a success tomorrow. What was only a seedling yesterday may become a full-fledged plant in a few short days.

Better Next Time

Allow me to illustrate this point with a personal experience — one that reminded me that parental teachings do surface under certain and sometimes unlikely circumstances.

While attending a stake conference, the stake president invited me to speak with the Primary children. His counselor escorted me into the room where the youngsters met. I took my seat and watched the group assemble in an orderly and reverent manner under the watchful eyes of caring teachers. Into the room they streamed — children of various sizes, colors, and dress from the metropolitan area.

One young man walked through the door and caught my eye. He looked as if he had just gotten out of bed. A shoe was untied; the shirt tail drooped out of his trousers; the collar of the shirt was up on one side and down on the other; and his hair appeared to have been combed with a wash cloth.

I judged that the lad would pose a challenge to some sweet

instructor that morning. Two teachers apparently felt the same way, for they planted themselves on either side of the boy.

As the meeting began, the coordinator invited the unkempt lad to offer the opening prayer. Without a moment's hesitation the boy stepped forward, folded his arms, and bowed his head. The kind coordinator moved to his side and asked, "May I help you?" "No," he responded emphatically, "I'll do it myself."

Then, after a brief pause, the boy began to pray. The form of prayer was correct, the language was proper, the Spirit was present, and the boy seemed filled with desire. Obviously, caring parents had taught the young man how to speak with "the tongue of angels" (2 Nephi 32:2).

In the middle of the prayer, however, the lad said something that caught our attention. Said he, "Heavenly Father, bless us that we will be better next time than what we will be today."

That was fair warning, I thought to myself. Yet I was happy to exit the meeting early, leaving the challenge to the officers and teachers of the Primary organization. These officers and teachers understood, as I did, the thought the boy was trying to express — that we must strive to improve our behavior week to week and meeting by meeting.

Despite the minor "glitch" in the boy's prayer, any parent would have been proud of his effort. He demonstrated that he was no stranger to prayer and that the "pecan tree" practice of prayer was thriving in his family garden. I am confident that this boy will "go into the mount oft" as he grows to maturity and find victory and glory through his "diligence, faithfulness, and prayers of faith" (1 Nephi 18:3; D&C 103:36). Moreover, I am confident that he will rise up and call his father and mother blessed for teaching him about God, prayer, and the other things that matter most.

Lest we forget, it was the humble, vocal, and simple prayer of a fourteen-year-old boy that ushered in the Dispensation of the Fulness of Times (see JS–H 1:14–20). It was the great Intercessory Prayer of the thirty-three-year-old Savior that prepared his disciples and all Saints, including Saints in the latter days, for their ministries. And it is the prayers of the righteous that will prepare all of us to overcome the "cares of this life" and meet the challenges of the future. As the Master warned:

> *Watch ye therefore, and* pray always, *that ye may be accounted worthy to escape all these things that shall come to pass, and to stand before the Son of man (Luke 21:36; emphasis added).*

CHAPTER TWO

SCRIPTURE STUDY

These words, which I command thee this day, shall be in thine heart: *and thou shalt* teach *them diligently unto thy children, and shalt* talk *of them when thou sittest in thine house, and when thou walkest by the way, and when thou liest down, and when thou risest up (Deuteronomy 6:6–7; emphasis added).*

A classic American poem includes these lines:

> I had a Mother who read me the things
> That wholesome life to the boy heart brings—
> Stories that stir with an upward touch,
> Oh, that each mother of boys were such!
> You may have tangible wealth untold;
> Caskets of jewels and coffers of gold.
> Richer than I you can never be—
> For I had a Mother who read to me.
>
> ("The Reading Mother" by Strickland Gillilan,
> in *Best Loved Poems of the American People*,
> selected by Hazel Felleman [Garden City, N.Y:
> Doubleday & Co., 1936], p. 376.)

Let me state the last stanza once again but modify the last line:

> You may have tangible wealth untold;
> Caskets of jewels and coffers of gold.

Richer than I you can never be —
My mother read the scriptures to me.

Reading — A Magic Carpet

One writer referred to reading and poetry as a "magic carpet" upon which we may ride to faraway places and meet a multitude of people. Said he: "Here is a magic carpet on which one may ride back to childhood days, into the realm of fancy, through eerie castles, across uncharted seas and in spiritual places. For company, there are mothers, wives, sweethearts; there are men of God and worshippers; there are heroes, heroines, martyrs, laborers, schoolmasters, and a goodly company of folk who laugh" (Edward Frank Allen, introduction to *Best Loved Poems of the American People*).

Rich indeed are those who fellowship with the great minds of the past through good literature. They are unfettered by the barriers of time, distance, or social status, and, like royalty, can summon wise counselors to their side by reading the printed page. They can crawl into the minds of scholars, join the safaris of explorers, sit in the midst of sages, and, like those of unlimited means, gain a world of vicarious experiences by reading the best books. Yes, they who read place in their treasure chest of knowledge the jewels of thought and gems of wisdom mined and polished by others through the ages.

The real riches, however, are not found in the learnings and experiences of men. "Real" riches are obtained from God — the source of all knowledge and truth. Said the Lord, "If ye seek the riches which it is the will of the Father to give unto you, ye shall be the richest of all people, for ye shall have the riches of eternity" (D&C 38:39). Such riches — "the riches of eternity" — are deposited in the holy scriptures and are found by those who read the scriptures and live accordingly.

The translators of the King James Version of the Bible prefaced their work with these and other poignant thoughts: "Among all our joys, there was no one that more filled our hearts, than the blessed continuance of the preaching of God's sacred Word among us; *which is that inestimable treasure, which excelleth all the riches of the earth; because the fruit thereof extendeth itself,* not only to the time spent in this transitory world, but directeth and disposeth men unto that eternal happiness which is above in heaven" (second paragraph; italics added).

All of the scriptures, including the Holy Bible and Book of Mormon, constitute "that inestimable treasure," bear a "fruit" in the lives of those who read and live by the divine concepts contained therein. A world-renowned surgeon who personally tapped the treasure of Holy Writ counseled: "As the soul is dyed by the thoughts, let no day pass without contact with the best literature of the world. Learn to know your Bible, though not perhaps as your fathers did. In forming character and in shaping conduct, its touch has still its ancient power. Of the kindred of Ram and sons of Elihu, you should know its beauties and its strength. Fifteen or twenty minutes day by day will give you fellowship with the great minds of the race, and little by little as the years pass you extend your friendship with the immortal dead. They will give you faith in your own day. Listen while they speak to you of the fathers. But each age has its own spirit and ideas, just as it has its own manners and pleasures" (William Osler, *A Way of Life,* pp. 37–38).

Reasons for Scripture Study

There are many reasons why parents should and must plant the "pecan tree" practice of scripture reading in their family gardens. I shall cite some of these reasons in answer to some questions.

Do you want your children to obtain eternal life—the greatest gift of all? Then you must help them know and worship the true and living God. The Savior said: "This is life eternal, that they might know thee the only true God, and Jesus Christ, whom thou hast sent" (John 17:3).

What better way is there of getting acquainted with God than through the scriptural accounts of his dealings with prophets, seers, and revelators as recorded in Holy Writ?

Each prophet testified of God, the Father, and God, the Son. Each was a witness sent to prove revealed truth, just as Nephi verified the words of Isaiah and Jacob (see 2 Nephi 11:2–6).

Do you want your children to come unto Christ? If so, you must get them into the scriptures. "I told the brethren," said Joseph Smith, "that the Book of Mormon was the most correct of any book on earth, and the keystone of our religion, and a man would get nearer to God by abiding by its precepts, than by any other book" (Introduction to the Book of Mormon). It is through the Book of Mormon and the other scriptures that we come to the knowledge of our Redeemer and the very points of his doctrine so that we "may know *how* to come unto him and be saved" (1 Nephi 15:14; italics added).

Do you want your children to hear the voice of God and know his words? Such is made possible through the scriptures. This is what the Lord promised: "These words are not of men nor of man, but of me; wherefore, you shall testify they are of me and not of man; for it is my voice which speaketh them unto you; for they are given by my Spirit unto you, and by my power you can read them one to another; and save it were by my power you could not have them; wherefore, you can testify that you have heard my voice, and know my words" (D&C 18:34–36).

Scripture reading is like a daily interview with the Lord, providing the reader studies with real intent and listens to the whisperings of the Holy Spirit. The voice of the Lord came into the mind of Enos, whereby Enos received intelligence and truth that changed the course of his life. The same can happen to us and our children by feasting upon the word of God (Enos 1:1–10).

Do you want to provide your children spiritual protection

against the evils of our day? If this is your desire, you must equip them with the "whole armor" of God, including:

- Loins girt about with truth.
- The breastplate of righteousness.
- Feet shod with the preparation of the gospel of peace.
- The shield of faith.
- The helmet of salvation.
- The sword of the Spirit (see D&C 27:15–18).

These and other protective elements are made available through the scriptures. Such armor makes one "strong in the Lord, and in the power of his might," said Paul (Ephesians 6:10). However, what good is the shield, helmet, or sword, if they are not placed upon our young ones?

Do you want to provide your children with a flawless compass, even a Liahona, to guide them through life? This is also possible if you get them into the scriptures. Alma said to his son Helaman: "It is as easy to give heed to the word of Christ, which will point to you a straight course to eternal bliss, as it was for our fathers to give heed to this compass, which would point unto them a straight course to the promised land. And now I say, is there not a type in this thing? For just as surely as this director did bring our fathers, by following its course, to the promised land, shall the words of Christ, if we follow their course, carry us beyond this vale of sorrow into a far better land of promise. And now, my son, see that ye take care of these sacred things, yea, see that ye look to God and live. Go unto this people and declare the word, and be sober" (Alma 37:44–45, 47).

A similar thought is expressed in another scriptural reference: "Whosoever will may lay hold upon the word of God, which is quick and powerful, which shall divide asunder all the cunning and the snares and the wiles of the devil, and lead the man of Christ in a strait and narrow course across that everlasting gulf of misery which is prepared to engulf the wicked — and land their souls, yea, their immortal souls, at the

31

right hand of God in the kingdom of heaven, to sit down with Abraham, and Isaac, and with Jacob, and with all our holy fathers, to go no more out" (Helaman 3:29–30).

Do you want your children to garnish their thoughts with virtue (see D&C 121:45–46)? There is no better way of doing this than helping them program their minds or "personal computers" with revealed and recorded truths. It is written: "My thoughts are not your thoughts, neither are your ways my ways, saith the Lord. For as the heavens are higher than the earth, so are my ways higher than your ways, and my thoughts than your thoughts" (Isaiah 55:8–9).

Anyone who has been exposed to pornographic literature or suggestive and carnal conversation knows how critical it is to replace the evil thought with something better. It is, therefore, essential that our children become involved in a continuous process of garnishing their thoughts with virtue so they may block the negative cues and bring out the positive impulses.

Do you want inspired help in instructing and correcting your children? Moses, Peter, Paul, and many others, even the Savior himself, will assist you, if you get your children into the scriptures. Paul taught Timothy, his young protégé: "All scripture is given by inspiration of God, and is profitable for doctrine, for reproof, for correction, for instruction in righteousness: That the man of God may be perfect, throughly furnished unto all good works" (2 Timothy 3:16–17).

The warnings and instructions given Laman and Lemuel about the need for faith, prayer, patience, and other virtues never become outdated. They are as applicable to our children in today's cities as they were to Lehi's children as they wandered in the desert many years ago.

Do you want to prepare your children to say and do that which is right and true? Once again, encourage them to search the scriptures, for it is recorded: "Neither take ye thought beforehand what ye shall say; but treasure up in your minds continually the words of life, and it shall be given you in the very hour that portion that shall be meted unto every man" (D&C 84:85).

Concerning his recorded truths, Nephi wrote, "The words which I have spoken shall stand as a testimony against you; for they are sufficient to teach any man *the right way;* for *the right way* is to believe in Christ and deny him not; for by denying him ye also deny the prophets and the law" (2 Nephi 25:28; italics added).

Nephi also wrote that "the words of Christ will tell you all things what ye should *do*" (2 Nephi 32:3; italics added). In a world where the rightness and goodness of things have become obscured by evil-designing people, it is imperative that our children look to the scriptures for direction. If a parent truly loves a child, he or she will not rest until the child's hand has grasped firmly the "rod of iron" or "word of God" spoken of by the ancient prophet Lehi (1 Nephi 8:19; 11:25).

Do you want your children to know the purposes of God and the means by which those purposes will be realized? If so, get them into the scriptures.

How frequently we quote, "This is my work and my glory— to bring to pass the immortality and eternal life of man" (Moses 1:39). But how infrequently we take the time to explain the meaning of the words *immortality* and *eternal life.* Unless our children understand God's avowed purpose and the plan by which this purpose will be accomplished, their purposes may conflict with God's, and their plans lead them in the wrong directions. God's purpose should be our purpose; his work should be our work; and all of us should be invested in furthering the "divine cause."

We should follow the example set by Adam and Eve. Of them it is recorded, "[They] blessed the name of God, and they made all things known unto their sons and their daughters" (Moses 5:12).

Said Elder Richard L. Evans: "It is an act of greatness and

heroism to hold a family together, to set before them an example, to teach them in ways of truth, to live a life of consistency, to provide necessities, to nurse and serve in sickness, to wash, to cook, to clean, to make, to mend, to counsel, to love, to understand, to pray, to be patient, and to do the thousand other unnamed things that it takes to rear a family, to make a house a home—and to do it every day, sometimes without seeming gratitude—and to lead a family righteously unto eternal life. And since it is our Father's purpose to bring to pass the immortality and eternal life of his children, what could better be our purpose as parents?" (*Conference Report*, October 1964, p. 136).

Do you want your children to walk in the footsteps of Jesus and accept him as a standard of conduct for their lives? We read of a group, a fictitious group, who accepted the motto: "What would Jesus do?" Their aim or goal was "to act just as He would if He was in our places, regardless of immediate results. In other words, we propose to follow Jesus' steps as closely and as literally as we believe He taught His disciples to do."

Sheldon, in his fascinating book *In His Steps*, tells of the reformation of many lives as individuals live by the Savior's words. Some who were worldly became saintly; some who were unhappy found joy and peace of conscience; and some who lived aimlessly found purpose and reason for living. These blessings can be gained by our children and us when we take the Savior at his word and seek to live as he lived and strive to become more like him.

It has not been my intent to bury the reader with questions and reasons pertaining to the need for scripture study in our homes. Most of us understand perfectly well the value of God's recorded word. But do our children have the same understanding? Many do not. So, why not discuss the reasons I have cited with your family members, and add other related justifications for searching the scriptures that may come to mind.

Such discussion may prove enlightening to the more reluctant and skeptical ones and prepare the soil for the planting of the "pecan tree" practice of scripture study in your home.

Suggestions

Clever and caring parents do many things to help their children develop a love for God's holy word. Here are but a few ideas:

1. *Example.* Set the example for the little ones by reading in their presence. Let them see you with scriptures in hand. Demonstrate openly to them your high regard for the Bible, Book of Mormon, and other Standard Works of the Church. In time, they will be led to do what they have seen you do. Remember, an open book in hand draws the young ones to your side much faster than the closed, dust-covered text resting high upon the library shelf.

2. *Environment.* Create a scriptural environment in your home. This can be done by placing the sacred books on tables, exhibiting scripture-based pictures on the walls, and referring to biblical maps or charts that stir conversation. These actions will not only whet the reading interests of the children but also add to the feeling of reverence within the house.

3. *Conversation.* Do what the ancients did — speak openly of the Savior as the only "way [or] means whereby salvation can come unto the children of men" (Mosiah 3:17).

"For we labor diligently to write, to persuade our children, and also our brethren, to believe in Christ, and to be reconciled to God; for we know that it is by grace that we are saved, after all we can do. And we talk of Christ, we rejoice in Christ, we preach of Christ, we prophesy of Christ, and we write according to our prophecies, that our children may know to what source they may look for a remission of their sins" (2 Nephi 25:23, 26).

Who will question or doubt your love for God's word if you talk about it when you sit in the house, walk by the way, retire at night, or awake in the morning (see Deuteronomy 6:6–7).

Small talk around the dinner table about the weather or the next ball game has its place. These trivial and transient subjects, however, must not be permitted to push aside the weightier and prevailing matters about Christ, the gospel, and our prospects for eternal life.

4. *Read together.* President Marion G. Romney told this story:

> I remember reading it [the Book of Mormon] with one of my lads when he was very young. On one occasion I lay in the lower bunk and he in the upper bunk. We were each reading aloud alternate paragraphs of those last three marvelous chapters of Second Nephi. I heard his voice breaking and thought he had a cold, but we went on to the end of the three chapters. As we finished he said to me, "Daddy, do you ever cry when you read the Book of Mormon?"
>
> "Yes, Son," I answered. "Sometimes the Spirit of the Lord so witnesses to my soul that the Book of Mormon is true that I do cry." "Well," he said, "that is what happened to me tonight." ("The Book of Mormon," *Improvement Era*, May 1949, p. 330.)

The emotional impact of such an experience not only draws children closer to believing parents but also imbues a love for the scriptures. Perhaps in time they will forget what was read on that occasion. However, they will never forget how they felt when reading with their parents the words of Nephi about baptism, angels, prayer, and Christ.

5. *Read and relate.* Most children are introduced to the holy books while sitting on the laps of parents and listening to the stories of David and Goliath, Samuel's call, Jonah and the whale, and other accounts. In the process, listening leads to thumbing the pages, and thumbing the pages leads to mouthing the words. Eventually, the mouthing of the words turns to reading independent of the lap and parents.

Parents who love both children and the scriptures will be blessed to read with feeling. Furthermore, they will be blessed with the gift of story-telling, making the pages of the book come alive. "You are not just telling them [the children] bedtime stories," said one man, "you are telling them they are worth your time" (David Bly, "The Mind's Eye," *Deseret News*, May 5, 1991, A-27).

6. *Personalized scriptures.* Few gifts are appreciated more by youngsters than personalized scriptures, especially if they are used often in family gatherings. Children want a book of their own—one they can mark and use in their own distinct way. Most birthday or Christmas gifts are perishable items. They fade or break or slip away somewhere very quickly. But it is not so with a Bible, Book of Mormon, or Triple Combination. These copies of Holy Writ gain value with every red line or other personal touch identifying a favorite passage or meaningful verse.

7. *Meal appetizer.* Many of our meals begin with the serving of an appetizer, usually a fruit or drink. Why not change the pace and begin with a scripture appetizer? A verse or two of reading will enliven the dinner conversation and perhaps even make the food more palatable.

Try this experiment: Type on several 3x5 cards this scripture: "Jesus answered and said unto her, Whosoever drinketh of this water shall thirst again: but whosoever drinketh of the water that I shall give him shall never thirst" (John 4:13–14). Place the card in each glass on the table. Read the card and discuss briefly John 4:1–26 before serving and eating the meal.

8. *Brief devotional.* Some families conduct a brief devotional in the evening along with their evening meal. It is purposely kept simple and consists of a hymn, scripture reading, and prayer. Those who do this nourish their children spiritually as well as physically and create special family bonding to the scriptures.

Brevity and simplicity must be kept in mind in planning

these devotionals, especially if young children are involved. A formal or drawn-out ritual could sour a teenager against the practice.

9. *Seek answers to questions.* When confronted with perplexing problems, too many people take the easy course by racing to friends or priesthood leaders for answers. In the process, they become dependent upon others and miss the thrill of discovering truths on their own. Those who go into the mount oft, as Nephi did, to pray or read will be shown "great things" (1 Nephi 18:3). They will also stretch their souls and receive exhilarating experiences. All of us may climb a Mount Sinai or Mount Nebo and find treasures of knowledge by seeking answers to questions through the scriptures.

Said a modern prophet: "*I say that we need to teach our people to find their answers in the scriptures....* But the unfortunate thing is that so many of us are not reading the scriptures. We do not know what is in them, and therefore we speculate about the things that we ought to have found in the scriptures themselves. I think that therein is one of our biggest dangers of today" ("Find the Answers in the Scriptures," *Ensign*, December 1972, p. 3; italics added).

President Harold B. Lee knew that drinking directly from the fountain of truth was better than sipping from sources down the hill that have been polluted or diluted along the way.

10. *Scripture games.* Use your creativity in planning family home evenings and other gatherings by spicing the activities with scripture-based games. Scripture chases, like those used in the seminary program, appeal to the more competitive ones. Others may enjoy an exercise called "Stumping Mother and Father"—an exercise wherein the children ask questions or cite references that the parents cannot identify or answer. The idea is to make searching the scriptures interesting and fun so that children will go to the well and drink of the "living waters" on their own.

11. *Nightcap.* Many people drink warm milk or some other

soothing beverage at bedtime. Often, this drink is sipped while in bed just before falling asleep. Why not substitute a page or two of scripture for the drink as a nightcap? By doing so, lofty thoughts will be planted in the mind for the subconscious to mull over during the night. A lofty thought can be very soothing and nutritional to the soul.

12. *Applying the scriptures.* How many times have parents heard a son or daughter complain, "Let's not read the scriptures. They deal with people of an ancient day and are boring." When complaints of this nature are voiced, it is likely that the parents have failed to do what Nephi did. Said he: "I did liken all scriptures unto us, that it might be for our profit and learning" (1 Nephi 19:23).

A woman may read section 25 of the Doctrine and Covenants and say, "How wonderful for Emma." But if that same woman substitutes her name for Emma's and her husband's name for Joseph's, the scripture takes on a new world of meaning. And if she takes the time to list the instructions given and the blessings mentioned, the section becomes a personal guide for living. Thus it is with other portions of scripture applied to us and our times (see D&C 25:1–16).

13. *Right way of reading.* One of the great scholars of modern times was Ralph Waldo Emerson. It was his view that the right way of reading included: (1) "creative" reading, and (2) going directly to the source. Creative reading, in Emerson's mind, was a combination of reading and pondering, whereby a person reads between the lines, looks for hidden meanings, and allows new thoughts to emerge. Here are his words: "One must be an inventor to read well. . . . There is then creative reading as well as creative writing. When the mind is braced by labor and invention, the page of whatever book we read becomes luminous with manifold allusion. Every sentence is doubly significant, and the sense of our author is as broad as the world" (*The Works of Ralph Waldo Emerson*, "The American Scholar," p. 559).

39

In reference to the need to go directly to the source, Emerson wrote: "When he [the reader] can read God directly, the hour is too precious to be wasted in other men's transcripts of their readings" (*The Works of Ralph Waldo Emerson*, "The American Scholar," pp. 558–59). A good commentary on the scriptures serves its purpose; but there is no substitute for the revealed word of God preserved in Holy Writ.

Closing Thoughts

In this chapter, I have attempted to do three things: (1) Establish in the mind of the reader that the Holy Scriptures are a treasure of inestimable value; (2) cite reasons why parents should engage in scripture reading with the family; and (3) suggest a few steps that parents may take to plant the practice of scripture reading in the home.

Why is all of this so very important? Let's refer to two American prophets, one ancient and one modern, for the answer.

The one, who lived about 600 B.C., wrote, "I did read many things unto them [his people] which were written in the books of Moses; but *that I might more fully persuade them to believe in the Lord their Redeemer*" (1 Nephi 19:23; italics added).

The one who lived in the nineteenth century declared: "Search the scriptures — search the revelations which we publish, and ask your Heavenly Father, in the name of His Son Jesus Christ, to manifest the truth unto you, and if you do it with an eye single to His glory nothing doubting, He will answer you by the power of His Holy Spirit. *You will then know for yourselves and not for another. You will not then be dependent on man for the knowledge of God;* nor will there be any room for speculation. No; for when men receive their instruction from Him that made them, they know how He will save them. Then again we say: Search the Scriptures, search the Prophets and learn what portion of them belongs to you and the people of the [twentieth] century" (*Teachings of the Prophet Joseph Smith*, pp. 11–12; italics added).

Those who plant and cultivate the "pecan tree" practice of scripture study, and who practice it honestly and consistently, will be persuaded to believe in Christ, and, they will obtain an independent and abiding knowledge of God. Yes, they will open "caskets of jewels" and "coffers of gold" in the form of saving truths.

They will also testify:

> *My soul delighteth in the scriptures [the things of the Lord], and my heart pondereth them, and writeth them for the learning and the profit of my children. Behold, my soul delighteth in the things of the Lord; and my heart pondereth continually upon the things which I have seen and heard (2 Nephi 4:15–16).*

CHAPTER THREE

FAMILY HOME EVENINGS

*Go ye unto your homes, and ponder upon the things
which I have said, and ask of the Father, in my name,
that ye may understand, and prepare your minds
for the morrow, and I come unto you again (3
Nephi 17:3).*

How would you like to be 99 percent or even 100 percent
successful in rearing your children? Such phenomenal success
is realistic and within your reach, according to three latter-day
prophets. President Wilford Woodruff promised, "Ninety-nine
out of every hundred children who are taught by their parents
the principles of honesty and integrity, truth and virtue, will
observe them through life" (*Discourses of Wilford Woodruff*,
pp. 266–68). Said President Joseph F. Smith, "Not one child in
a hundred would go astray, if the home environment, example
and training, were in harmony with the truth in the gospel of
Christ, as revealed and taught to the Latter-day Saints" (*Gospel
Doctrine*, p. 302). President Harold B. Lee summarized: "If you
will have your Family Home Evenings and teach your children
in the home, the promise has been made that there won't be
one in a hundred that will ever go astray. And if you will see
to it that as the Home Teachers visit every home every month
and do what the Home Teachers are supposed to do, you will
have a strength in the raising of your family that will be far
beyond any pulling power to the opposite" (BYU Sixth Stake
Quarterly Conference, April 27, 1969).

Knowing of such wonderful and far-reaching statements made by presidents of the Church, who would be so foolish as to ignore this "pecan tree" practice with a promise? The practice is simply gospel instruction in the home by loving and caring parents; the promise is righteous children who will remain faithful. The overall result will be family unity and happiness in this life and eternal joy in the life to come.

Instructions of the First Presidency

To help fathers and mothers fulfill their divine responsibilities at home, the First Presidency made this announcement in 1915:

> We counsel the Latter-day Saints to observe more closely the commandment of the Lord given in the 68th section of the Doctrine and Covenants (verses 25–28). . . .
>
> To this end we advise and urge the inauguration of a "Home Evening" throughout the Church, at which time fathers and mothers may gather their boys and girls about them in the home and teach them the word of the Lord. They may thus learn more fully the needs and requirements of their families; at the same time familiarizing themselves and their children more thoroughly with the principles of the Gospel of Jesus Christ. . . .
>
> If the Saints obey this counsel, we promise that great blessings will result. Love at home and obedience to parents will increase. Faith will be developed in the hearts of the youth of Israel, and they will gain power to combat the evil influences and temptations which beset them. (*Messages of the First Presidency*, pp. 337–38.)

Over the years, the family home evening program has been reannounced and reemphasized many times by Church leaders. The First Presidency wrote in the *Family Home Evening Resource Book* in 1983: "We live in a time when selfishness, violence, immorality, and every other form of unrighteousness

43

increases unrestrained in most of the world. The family is being assailed on every side. It is with deep concern that we urge you as parents to gather your children around you and build love, loyalty, and companionship in your homes. You are responsible to teach your children to walk uprightly before the Lord.

"Hold family councils. Talk to your children in personal parent interviews. Read the scriptures together. Enjoy playing together. Have family prayers. Hold family home evenings. But above all, be a worthy example."

Lest we think that Church leaders are less than fully committed to the family home evening program, we should review the instructions given in the *General Handbook of Instructions*. Note the following: "Parents are to hold a weekly family home evening to teach and strengthen their families. Stake and ward leaders are to reserve Monday evenings for families and keep those evenings free of stake and ward meetings and activities. Monday family home evenings may include instruction in gospel principles, in addition to gospel study on Sunday, learning Church hymns and songs, and family activities. The Church provides lessons and other materials for families to use in their family home evenings" (*General Handbook of Instructions*, March 1989, pp. 2–6).

It shouldn't be necessary to review other official announcements pertaining to the conduct of family home evenings. The counsel received from Church leaders about this "pecan tree" practice is voluminous and consistent over the years. Therefore, those who believe that leaders are inspired will comply with instructions received and become "doers of the word, and not hearers only, deceiving [their] own selves" (James 1:22). Otherwise, the promised blessings associated with the program will be forfeited and the welfare of children placed in jeopardy.

Considerations

It is not an easy thing to conduct a successful family home evening, especially if several children of varying ages are involved. Anyone who says it is easy has probably never done it or has extremely high tolerance for confusion, unexpected emergencies, and other distractions. Like anything else of value, success can be achieved if the right price is paid in terms of planning, preparation, and honest effort.

If my own performance as a father in conducting family home evenings had been impeccable, it would be easy for me to propose a "things to do" list. (I am not suggesting that I have failed as a father. Thanks to a wonderful wife and children naturally inclined toward righteousness, things have turned out quite well despite my shortcomings.) I shall, therefore, mention some considerations based primarily upon the statements of those we sustain as prophets, seers, and revelators. Regard the following thoughts as only a beginning. Other and perhaps even better ideas may surface as you seek to faithfully hold home evenings with your family.

1. *Preparation during the week.* Elder Boyd K. Packer gave this advice some time ago:

> The father can improve family home evenings by drawing close to his children during the week, by making it a habit to tuck them in bed every night, to talk with them, to listen to them, and turn his heart to them.
>
> I learned a great lesson from one of the Brethren a few years ago—one that has meant much to our family.
>
> "I leave my briefcase at the office," he said.
>
> I didn't know what he meant, but he explained further.
>
> "When I have work to do I may stay at the office even until midnight, but when I go home my briefcase is left at the office. When I am home, I am home and available to my children."

45

We have tried to follow this example in our family. It is difficult to follow, but it is possible. To follow it as a rule, with the necessary exceptions, is infinitely better than to have made no rule at all. If the father will do this, every evening can be something of a family home evening ("How the Priesthood Can Help Improve Family Home Evenings," December 1968, p. 4).

2. *Essentials/Flexibility.* The essential elements of a family home evening and the need for flexibility are stressed in these instructions:

> Parents, draw your children around you and, with great love, teach them about the Savior and his commandments. Help them to develop individual strength and commitment to keep the laws of God. Build lasting unity in a setting of learning and fun.
>
> In conducting family home evenings, be flexible so that you may be guided by the Spirit. Let prayer, music, the scriptures, and brotherhood be the essentials of your home evenings. . . .
>
> We promise again that as you faithfully plan and hold quality family home evenings, you will gain strength to withstand the temptations of the world and will receive many blessings which will help qualify you to enjoy your families through eternity in the Celestial Kingdom (Spencer W. Kimball, N. Eldon Tanner, Marion G. Romney, *Family Home Evening,* 1978, p. 2).

3. *Home-based.* President Spencer W. Kimball had this to say about home-based activities: "Regarding our home evenings, an evening home with the family or an evening out to some place of interest with your family only partly solves the need of the home evening. Basically important is the teaching of the children the way of life that is vitally important. Merely going to a show or a party together, or fishing, only half satisfies the real need, but to stay home and teach the children the gospel, the scriptures, and love for each other and love for their parents is most important" (*Conference Report,* October 1977, p. 4).

4. *Atmosphere of love.* David O. McKay, who referred to home as "a bit of heaven" and who pictured "heaven to be a continuation of the ideal home," stressed the importance of love: "Homes are made permanent through love. Oh, then, let love abound. Though you fall short in some material matters, study and work and pray to hold your children's love. Establish and *maintain your family hours* always. Stay close to your children. Pray, play, work, and worship together" (*Conference Report*, April 1967, p. 135; italics added).

Prior to our move abroad on a Church assignment, a well-meaning friend approached me and asked, "Don't you hate the thoughts of leaving home?"

"No," I answered. "I'm taking my wife with me."

Home is where your love is. So long as you are accompanied or surrounded by those who love you and whom you love, you are home. It is not so much a place as it is a way of loving and living.

5. *Parental inspiration.* Speaking of the need for inspiration and the adaptation of Church-prepared materials to meet the unique needs of families, President Kimball counseled: "The Home Evening Manual is replete with good suggestions, but it should never replace inspired parental development with regard to what should be done in a particular evening to meet particular needs. If we will feed our families from the *gospel garden at home*, then what they get from Church meetings can be a rich supplement, but not their only diet" (*Ensign*, May 1978, p. 5; italics added).

6. *Participation.* On one occasion the chief priests and scribes expressed concern to Jesus about the words spoken by children in the temple. The Savior responded, "Have ye never read, Out of the mouth of babes and sucklings thou hast perfected praise?" (Matthew 21:16). "Perfected praise" can be heard in family home evenings when children are allowed to speak, sing, or pray. At the same time, lasting impressions and

truths are planted in the minds of the young, for much is learned and lodged by doing.

7. *Family councils.* For many years, Church members have been urged by priesthood leaders to hold family council meetings. Such meetings are usually held in conjunction with family home evenings and, if properly conducted, can "strengthen family ties, assure the children that they really belong, and convince them that their parents are interested in their welfare as well as in their problems" (Elder Mark E. Petersen, "Turning the Hearts of Family Members to the Family," *Relief Society Magazine*, October 1976, p. 727).

Of this type of family gathering, President Spencer W. Kimball said: "Concerning the governing of our families, we have been correctly taught that the family council is the most basic council of the Church. Under the direction of the father and mother, who should also counsel together, family councils may discuss family matters, discuss family finances, make plans, and support and strengthen family members. The Brethren have stated that an atmosphere of listening, honest communication, and respect for the opinions and feelings of others is vital to the success of these meetings" (*The Teachings of Spencer W. Kimball*, ed. Edward L. Kimball [Salt Lake City: Bookcraft, 1982], pp. 343–44).

8. *Model.* The Family Guidebook contains a simple outline of a weekly family home evening. It is worth quoting in full:

> Under the direction of the father, the family should hold a regular family home evening each week. The Church has kept Monday evening free of other activities so that families can be together to hold family home evening.
>
> As patriarch of his home, the father presides (acts as president and gives direction) at the family home evening. The father (himself) conducts or appoints a family member to conduct the home evening.
>
> The father either teaches the lesson or delegates the teaching of the lesson to his wife or to children

who are old enough. Everyone who is old enough should be given opportunities to participate. Small children can help in such ways as leading the music, quoting scriptures, answering questions, holding pictures, passing out refreshments, and praying.

Wherever there is a family, home evenings can be held. A family may consist of one individual or of a man and his wife; it may include children and other relatives. Whatever the individual situation, each family will be blessed by holding (as they hold) home evenings.

If the father is absent from the family, the mother should assume the leadership and should carry out the family home evening responsibilities.

The following suggests a sample home evening program:

Opening song (by family)

Opening prayer (by a child)

Poem or scripture reading (by a family member)

Lesson (by father, mother, or an older child)

Activity (a game led by a family member and played by all of the family)

Closing song (by family)

Closing prayer (by family member)

Refreshments

A family can hold a home evening in many other ways. Any activity that brings the family together and strengthens their love for each other, as well as fostering righteous living, fills the function of a family home evening. Such activities include reading the scriptures, discussing the gospel, sharing testimonies, performing a service project, singing together, going on a picnic, playing a family game, hiking, and others. All home evenings should include prayer (*Family Guidebook*, pp. 7–9).

9. *Resource book.* To help parents plan and conduct family home evenings, the Church has published a resource book, which contains thirty-seven lessons and many other helpful hints and instructional materials. It was prepared for use by

all families, including single adults, couples, single-parent families, and families with children of all ages.

I quote two paragraphs from the introduction to the resource book printed under the caption "The Responsibility of Parents":

> In the home, parents and children learn together to apply the gospel's teachings in their lives. You teach your children all day, every day whether you realize it or not. They pick up your habits, your prejudices, and your values from what you do as well as from what you say. The Lord has called you to be a parent, and he knows you can do it. You are part of his plan for his children.
>
> Don't expect perfection from your children or from yourself all at once. Strive with your children to improve your lives little by little, step by step, line upon line each day. This book has been assembled to help you in your awesome responsibility as a parent. (*Family Home Evening: Resource Book* [Salt Lake City: The Church of Jesus Christ of Latter-day Saints, 1983]).

These considerations may seem less important to parents who were raised in the pre-television and pre-video years, for there was a time when the activities of families were of necessity more home-centered. In a former day, each evening was spent at home, in the house, with parents and siblings. All activities, or nearly all, were homemade and held close to the hearth.

But times have changed. Many intrusions have been made upon the home, not the least of which is the electronic media. Moreover, society has become more mobile, and many influences have emerged that tend to pull youngsters out of the home and away from parents, even in the crucial formative years. Such conditions, if not checked, will weaken family ties and result in the demise of the most important organization of all—the family.

Learning the Hard Way

We all have a tendency to take certain things for granted until we are shocked into a realization of their importance. Such was the case with me and the need to hold regular family home evenings. The shock occurred when I was serving as a full-time mission president with my wife and seven children, ages five to eighteen.

I began the mission assignment with the firm resolve that I would serve with all my heart, might, mind, and strength, so that I might stand blameless before God (see D&C 4:2). I determined that I would go whenever and wherever someone needed me, and that I would not lose one missionary.

Once in the mission field, I was soon caught up in a whirlwind of activities. There was a continual round of zone conferences and missionary interviews to hold; an endless number of stake conferences to attend; and many, many firesides, cottage meetings, and training sessions. Each day was scheduled to the limit and beyond, leaving little or no time for the family.

My conscience bothered me for neglecting my wife, sons, and daughters. However, I rationalized away my errant behavior by telling myself that I was doing the Lord's work and shepherding his divinely called representatives.

One day I returned to the mission home from a long trip. My wife met me in the garage and indicated to me that we were slated to attend a "Back-to-School" program that evening in an elementary school where three of our children attended. "I'm too busy," I protested. "I have other commitments tonight."

My wife bristled slightly and stated firmly, "No, you have been neglecting the children, and you must go with me tonight for their sakes!"

Reluctantly, I canceled an appointment and accompanied my wife to the school. We went into the auditorium, where a brief orientation meeting was held. We were then instructed to visit each home room and view the work done by our children. In my organized way, I said, "Honey, you take one room and I'll take another. Then we will meet together in the third and last room." I was determined to get out of the school as soon as possible.

When we met at the third room, the teacher told us that there were two exhibits for us to see—one at the desk and one at the bulletin board. "You take the desk," I instructed my wife, "and I'll look at the board, and then we are out of here." I could not have been more impatient or selfish in my desires.

I quickly inspected a drawing made by our son. Then I glanced toward the desk, where my wife stood looking at a paper written by our boy. She stood there crying in the midst of the crowd. I rushed to her side and asked, "What is wrong?" She didn't say a word—just pointed to the paper on the desk. I read the following:

Essay—My Life
By —— Asay

I am a *dumb* boy.
I belong to a *dumb* family.
I live in a *dumb* house.
I go to a *dumb* church.

More lines followed, each punctuated by the word *dumb*. I felt as if someone had struck me over the head with a baseball bat. How very nearsighted I had been! How very negligent I had been as a husband and father in fulfilling my most important priesthood responsibilities.

I returned home from that sobering experience with the determination that I would do whatever was necessary to erase the word *dumb* from my son's vocabulary. I determined that I would hold regular family home evenings once again and reinstate other family "pecan tree" practices that I had pushed aside or placed in limbo.

Moreover, I initiated the practice of being home on Monday afternoons to receive the children as they returned from school.

I did so in casual clothes so that they would be assured that our family home evenings would not be disturbed or preempted by meetings or appointments of less significance.

I like to think that I have succeeded with the son who suffered from my negligence. I like to think that he and all of our children have been blessed by my example and teachings, including those presented in family home evenings. Perhaps the word *dumb* is in their vocabulary, but I hope that none are chained or burdened in their personal lives by its negative connotations.

Closing Thoughts

Anyone who is tempted to neglect the teaching and training of children in the home through family home evenings or other means should heed the following warning: "Parents are under obligation most solemn to instruct, train, and provide for their children. If they are indifferent or negligent and the children become evil or wicked, the parents are held responsible" (Heber J. Grant, Anthony W. Ivins, J. Reuben Clark, Jr., *Messages of the First Presidency*, June 17, 1933, p. 318).

On the other hand, those who do plant the "pecan tree" practice of family home evenings and who teach their children properly will nearly always reap success. This success has two parts. The first part relates to the future of each child, as expressed in this verse: "Train up a child in the way he should go: and when he is old, he will not depart from it" (Proverbs 22:6). The second part relates to the feelings children will forever harbor about home as expressed in the lyrics of a hymn: "There is my home, the spot I love so well, whose worth and beauty pen nor tongue can tell" (*Hymns*, no. 37).

What parent does not want a child to "turn out right?" What parent does not want a child to carry sweet memories of home? What parent does not long to declare:

I have no greater joy than to hear that my children walk in truth (3 John 1:4).

CHAPTER FOUR

PRIESTHOOD BLESSINGS

*My son, be faithful in Christ; and may not the things
which I have written grieve thee, to weigh thee down
unto death; but may Christ lift thee up, and may his
sufferings and death and the showing his body unto
our fathers, and his mercy and long-suffering, and
the hope of his glory and of eternal life, rest in your
mind forever (Moroni 9:25).*

In another place, I have written:

Soon after my eighteenth birthday, I felt the weight
of my father's hands upon my head as he gave me a
special blessing. This was occasioned by my entrance
into the military during World War II. My father antic-
ipated my apprehensions about leaving home and becoming involved in the business of fighting. So in the
blessing he gave me reassurance. He also admonished
me to rely upon the Lord and to keep the commandments. Specifically, he told me to live the Word of
Wisdom (avoid the use of tobacco and alcohol) and
to maintain the moral standards of the Church. Then
he promised me that if I would do all of these things,
I would return home safe, whole, and unstained by
the world.

Throughout my stint in the army, the words of my
father remained vivid in my mind and heart. Many times
I was enticed to live less than the Latter-day Saint kind
of life. But, each time temptation presented itself, the
promise of returning home safe and well resounded

in my ears. I wanted to draw claim upon the blessings cited by my father. In due time the pronounced blessings and more were mine; I had written my own blessing. (Carlos E. Asay, *In the Lord's Service* [Salt Lake City: Deseret Book, 1990], p. 13).

The last blessing my father gave me occurred soon after I received my call as a General Authority of the Church. The calling had come unexpectedly, and I was bothered by feelings about my worthiness to serve and my ability to function properly in the assignment given me. So, I sought out my father and asked him to give me a blessing. I knew that through him I could receive the reassurances that I so desperately needed at the time.

He placed his hands upon my head and pronounced a healing blessing. Among other things, he reminded me that I had been "called of God, by prophecy, and by the laying on of hands by those who are in authority, to preach the Gospel and administer in the ordinances thereof" (Fifth Article of Faith). Though I have continued to harbor feelings of inadequacy to this time, my father's words did give me the confidence to go forward in my calling.

Church Practice

My father's blessings were given me in accord with established Church practice. For many years, Church leaders have taught that Melchizedek Priesthood holders may give blessings of comfort and counsel to family members. These blessings may be given sons and daughters on special occasions, such as when they go to school, go on missions, get married, or enter military service. A family may record a father's blessing for family records, if the parents desire, but it is not preserved in Church records.

Said President Spencer W. Kimball concerning this practice: "A child leaving to go away to school or on a mission, a wife suffering stress, a family member being married or desiring

56

guidance in making an important decision—all these are situations in which the father, in exercise of his patriarchal responsibility, can bless his family" (*The Teachings of Spencer W. Kimball*, ed. Edward L. Kimball [Salt Lake City: Bookcraft, 1982], p. 506).

I recall a tender moment a few years ago when one of our sons was being married. The night before the temple marriage, within the sanctity of our home and in the presence of family members, I gave him a father's blessing. His wife-to-be was present and cried openly as she witnessed the proceedings and listened to the words spoken. Afterwards, she explained that she had never received such a blessing and wondered if I would give her one also. I was happy to oblige her, knowing that she was worthy of the finest of all blessings.

A Pecan Tree Practice

Men who love their families and who understand their patriarchal responsibilities do not hesitate to bless their wives and children. They know that this family "pecan tree" practice welds, binds, and blesses the lives of those who receive and those who give. It is a means whereby the father expresses a love divine and invokes heavenly influences to surround those who constitute his first and foremost responsibility.

In one publication, the responsibility of the father is defined as follows: "The father is the patriarch of the family and has important responsibilities that are his alone. He is the head of his home and the leader of his family. He should lead and guide them with humility and kindness rather than with force or cruelty. . . . He should set a good example for his family by keeping the commandments. . . . He should *also share the blessings of the priesthood with the members of his family.* When a man holds the Melchizedek Priesthood he can share these blessings by naming and blessing babies, administering to the sick, baptizing children, and *giving special priesthood blessings and ordinations*" (*Gospel Principles*, pp. 228–29; italics added).

57

We often use such expressions in our conversations as "bless your heart," "blessings to you," "may the Lord bless you," and other commonplace statements. Sometimes the words slip off the tongue without much forethought. Mostly, however, the intent is good and the feeling sincere. Those who respect the power of the priesthood do more than repeat a hackneyed stream of words; they become involved in a stream of efficacious blessings.

Said Elder F. D. Richards: "Every one in all the Church should be filled with a spirit of blessing. The authority of the Priesthood should cause a gushing forth from the fountain of the heart, a bubbling forth of streams of blessing, of consolation, of comfort and of rejoicing, each should try to help and benefit the other in every possible way" (*Journal of Discourses,* 26:100).

Other Types of Blessings

We may not appreciate fully the "streams of blessing" spoken of by Elder Richards until we list all the blessings and ordinances that may be performed by worthy priesthood holders as authorized by Church leaders. Over and beyond the blessing of comfort and counsel already discussed, other blessings include naming and blessing children, baptizing, confirming, administering the sacrament, conferring the priesthood and ordaining to an office, consecrating oil, administering to the sick (anointing with oil and sealing the anointing; see James 5:14–16), dedicating graves, and dedicating homes.

Specific and detailed instructions pertaining to all of the ordinances and blessings listed above are included in more than one Church publication. General instructions, however, that should be heeded by all who perform such ordinances and blessings relate to matters such as worthiness, guidance by the Holy Spirit, receiving proper authorization, and following established procedures.

All of these blessings benefit members of families, particularly when a father is able to bless his own. But in single parent homes where a father or worthy priesthood holder is absent, a home teacher, member of a bishopric, or some other priesthood bearer may be invited to assist with the blessings. When the priesthood holder pronounces his blessing in a spirit of love and genuine concern for the welfare of others, there is "a gushing forth from the fountains of the heart," as promised by Elder Richards.

Honest Desire

Abraham sought the blessings of the patriarchal order or of his fathers. His record states: "I sought for the blessings of the fathers, and the right whereunto I should be ordained to administer the same; having been myself a follower of righteousness, desiring also to be one who possessed great knowledge, and to be a greater follower of righteousness, and to possess a greater knowledge, and to be a father of many nations, a prince of peace, and desiring to receive instructions, and to keep the commandments of God" (Abraham 1:2).

Father Abraham reminds us that desire, honest desire, helps to make blessings efficacious. He desired greater knowledge, more righteousness, added instructions, and stronger obedience. He also wanted to become a father of nations and a prince of peace. Ultimately, he received all that he sought because his heart was right and the realization of the blessing conformed with the will of the Lord. So will it be for all who seek with honest desire similar priesthood blessings.

Obedience

All who plant the "pecan tree" practice of priesthood blessings must bear in mind and teach others the relationship of law, obedience, and blessings. An oft-quoted scripture is, "There is a law, irrevocably decreed in heaven before the foundations of this world, upon which all blessings are predicated—And when we obtain any blessing from God, it is by obedience to that law upon which it is predicated" (D&C 130:20–21).

A companion verse gives added insight: "For all who will have a blessing at my hands shall abide the law which was appointed for that blessing, and the conditions thereof, as were instituted from before the foundation of the world" (D&C 132:5).

> We do, in fact, write our own blessings by the way we live and serve. Blessings do not come to us automatically and simply because hands have been placed upon our heads and beautiful words spoken. Blessings flow from the divine source and are channeled to mortals when laws are honored and when lives are made to harmonize with the will of Deity" (*In the Lord's Service*, p. 10).

The Lord gave ancient Israel a choice. He said: "Behold, I set before you this day a blessing and a curse; a blessing, if ye obey the commandments of the Lord your God, which I command you this day: and a curse, if ye will not obey the commandments of the Lord your God, but turn aside out of the way which I command you this day, to go after other gods, which ye have not known" (Deuteronomy 11:26–28).

Whenever we participate in a priesthood blessing, we should keep in mind the sons of Lehi:

> All of them — Laman, Lemuel, Sam, Nephi, Jacob, and Joseph — were extended blessings. All of them, I suspect, felt the weight of their father's hands upon their heads. Their ears received the sounds from his voice as blessings were spoken. Still, they were left with their agency — the right to choose good or evil, the right to pen or erase their own blessings. Lehi warned his eldest sons: "If ye will hearken unto him [Nephi] I leave unto you a blessing, yea, even my first blessing. But if ye will not hearken unto him I take away my first blessing, yea, even my blessing, and it shall rest upon him" (2 Nephi 1:28–29).

Despite the warning, the eldest sons rejected the Spirit of God because their hearts were hard and their minds were blinded to the truth. They lost their privileges and were cursed. The other sons heeded their father's counsel, followed a path of righteousness, and retained the greater privileges (*In the Lord's Service*, p. 12).

Important Obligation

More than 150 years ago, missionaries were instructed, "In whatsoever house ye enter, and they receive you, leave your blessing upon that house" (D&C 75:19). Such instruction has been followed by thousands of modern-day representatives of the Lord as they have sought to acknowledge hospitality extended and to repay acts of kindness shown them by pronouncing blessings upon receptive households. But, at the same time, one wonders whether fathers have taken these instructions seriously enough and whether they are leaving *their* blessings upon *their* homes in accord with *their* sacred obligations and privileges.

"Every man," said God, "who is *obliged* to provide for his own family, let him provide, and he shall in nowise lose his crown" (D&C 75:28; italics added). This scripture reminds us that heads of families must meet the temporal and spiritual needs of family members. Women and children do have claim upon their husbands and fathers "for their maintenance" or temporal well-being (D&C 83:2, 4). After all, one who fails to provide for those of his own house has "denied the faith, and is worse than an infidel" (1 Timothy 5:8).

Yet, what about the higher needs? the spiritual needs? I speak of the needs that come from deep within one's soul and that yearn for proper gratification, the needs filled not by food, shelter, or clothing, but by expressions of love and concern, exemplary living, and the bestowal of priesthood blessings.

We are told that women and children have feelings that are "tender and chaste and delicate before God." For some reason, they seem more spiritually inclined and drawn toward the good. So, when men become involved in iniquitous living, they easily break "the hearts of [their] tender wives, and [lose] the confidence of [their] children" (Jacob 2:7, 35). But when men pray and attend to all family duties, including the obligation to bless their homes, wounded souls are healed and happiness reigns supreme (see D&C 20:47–51).

A Concluding Word

Something wonderful and indescribably beautiful happens when a father blesses a son or daughter, or a home teacher blesses a person within the confines of a home. A transfusion of virtue takes place between the one who is voice and the one who is addressed, if both are attuned to the influence of the Holy Spirit. Moreover, hearts are softened and souls are knitted together as God's power is used to change or direct the lives of loved ones.

It is a powerful thing when a father blesses a daughter and gives such counsel as "give heed to the word of Christ . . . look to God and live" (Alma 37:44, 47). It is a tender thing when a father blesses a faithful son and gives such commendation as, "I trust that I shall have great joy in you, because of your steadiness and your faithfulness unto God" (Alma 38:2). It is a sobering thing when a father blesses a rebellious child and pleads, "Let these things trouble you no more, and only let your sins trouble you, with that trouble which shall bring you down unto repentance" (Alma 42:29). It is a touching thing when a father blesses a righteous son or daughter who faces a serious challenge and says, "I recommend thee unto God, and I trust in Christ that thou wilt be saved; and I pray unto God that he will spare thy life" (Moroni 9:22). And, it is a building thing when a father blesses a young son or daughter and warns, "Let no man despise thy youth. . . . Neglect not the gift that is in [you]. . . . Save thyself, and them that hear [you]" (1 Timothy 4:12–16).

Priesthood is the power and authority of God delegated to man on the earth for the purpose of saving souls. It is, therefore, a means whereby priesthood holders may reach out to all in the name of the Lord and perform redeeming services, such as the pronouncement of blessings. If a priesthood holder fails to share his sacred powers with members of his family and others, as called upon, it is doubtful whether he deserves the privilege of representing Deity. He must, therefore, plant the "pecan tree" practice of priesthood blessings in his family garden and cultivate it carefully.

He who holds the priesthood and uses it to bless his family

shall be like a tree planted by the rivers of water, that bringeth forth his fruit in his season; his leaf also shall not wither; and whatsoever he doeth shall prosper (Psalm 1:3).

CHAPTER FIVE

NAMES OF SIGNIFICANCE

A good name *is rather to be chosen than great riches* (Proverbs 22:1; *emphasis added*).

A good name *is better than precious ointment* (Ecclesiastes 7:1; *emphasis added*).

"I hate my name!" exclaimed a young lady sitting onstage at a family reunion. She sobbed, "People mispronounce it, misspell it, and often make jokes about it. I'm going to have it changed to something that is easier to say and more pleasing to hear." Other feelings of disgust for her name were vented by the actress as she performed before a large audience of relatives.

Located on the set behind the young lady was a large tree with a person sequestered within the branches. This person asked, "Why do you criticize your family name?"

Somewhat startled by the talking tree, the girl blurted out, "Because it embarrasses me at times and makes me the brunt of snide remarks."

Said the hidden voice, "How much do you know about your name, its origins, and the people who bore it?"

In the ensuing dialogue between the tree and the girl, it was revealed that the complaining young lady knew little about her surname. Moreover, she acknowledged openly that her knowledge of the family tree, including its roots and branches, was woefully lacking.

For the next several minutes the Asay family history was

acted out on stage before the young lady and a very interested group of spectators. The man in the tree served as the narrator, and a cast of actors, young and old, assumed the roles and played the parts.

One scene centered upon the earliest known beginnings of the Asay family in the state of New Jersey. Another scene highlighted those who forsook family and friends and embraced the restored gospel of Jesus Christ. This chapter of the family history was a wrenching one to watch and to contemplate as great personal sacrifices were made by Grandfather and Grandmother Asay. Still another scene depicted the adventures and harsh life experienced by our forebears in emigrating westward to Utah and participating in pioneer settlements. More scenes followed in sequence as the Asay story was told in word and song.

Throughout the dramatization, tribute was paid to those who had gone before and who had distinguished the Asay name. It was demonstrated that our grandfathers and grandmothers had glorious views of the future — views that prompted them to plant family pecan trees for the good of succeeding generations. It was emphasized that our forebears possessed love, faith, goodness, and other rare virtues and strengths of character. It was proven that the Asay name was more than a strange combination of four letters of the alphabet with heavy accent on the first "a." Asay was the name of a God-fearing, family-oriented, fun-loving, Christian-living, and foresighted people.

When the curtain fell at the close of the drama, a rather subdued and teary-eyed young lady was seen on stage. One could observe that she had repented many times over of the rash statements made earlier about her name. She expressed gratitude not only for the name but also for the parade of ancestors who had provided her such a rich heritage. Like many of us, she had complained and criticized out of ignorance. Not until she knew the facts about her people and their glorious

65

past did she understand who she really was. And with that understanding, her name became a significant and precious possession.

Scriptures and Names

It is significant that "Adam gave names to all cattle, and to the fowl of the air, and to every beast of the field" while in the Garden of Eden (Moses 3:20). He also called his helpmeet "Woman, because she was taken out of man" (Moses 3:23). Later, according to the record, Adam called his wife's name Eve. He did not refer to her as "Ma," "dame," "madame," "it," or some other trivial or meaningless designation. He gave her that noble name of *Eve*, for it means *"the mother of all living"* (Moses 4:26; italics added).

The inspired pattern established by Adam in giving names of significance to others is well-established in the scriptures. For example, God changed Abram's name to Abraham when he was made a father of many nations (see Genesis 17:1–8). Sarai's name was changed to Sarah after she was blessed and told that she would be a "mother of nations" (Genesis 17:16). Joseph and Mary were commanded to name their son Jesus, "for he shall save his people from their sins"(Matthew 1:21). It was also revealed that others would call Christ's name "Emmanuel, which being interpreted is, God with us" (Matthew 1:23). And, so it has been with many, many others down through the stream of sacred and secular history.

Though all of Adam's children may not have received names of significance, many have, and it has made a difference. It made a difference in the lives of Helaman's sons, Nephi and Lehi. We read:

> They remembered the words which their father Helaman spake unto them. And these are the words which he spake:
> Behold, my sons, I desire that ye should remember to keep the commandments of God; and I would that

66

ye should declare unto the people these words. Behold, I have given unto you the names of our first parents who came out of the land of Jerusalem; and this I have done that when you remember your names ye may remember them; and when ye remember them ye may remember their works; and when ye remember their works ye may know how that it is said, and also written, that they were good.

Therefore, my sons, I would that ye should do that which is good, that it may be said of you, and also written, even as it has been said and written of them (Helaman 5:5–7).

The record attests that Nephi and Lehi did pattern their lives after their forebears or namesakes and did bring honor to the names given them.

A Good Name

A modern illustration of the profound influence that a good name may have upon a person is provided by President George Albert Smith, the eighth president of the Church. Said he:

> A number of years ago I was seriously ill. In fact, I think everyone gave me up but my wife. With my family I went to St. George, Utah, to see if it would improve my health. We went as far as we could by train, and then continued the journey in a wagon, in the bottom of which a bed had been made for me.
>
> In St. George we arranged for a tent for my health and comfort, with a built-in floor raised about a foot above the ground, and we could roll up the south side of the tent to make the sunshine and fresh air available. I became so weak as to be scarcely able to move. It was a slow and exhausting effort for me even to turn over in bed.
>
> One day, under these conditions, I lost consciousness of my surroundings and thought I had passed to the Other Side. I found myself standing with my back to a large and beautiful lake, facing a great forest of trees. There was no one in sight, and there was no

boat upon the lake or any other visible means to indicate how I might have arrived there. I realized, or seemed to realize, that I had finished my work in mortality and had gone home. I began to look around, to see if I could not find someone. There was no evidence of anyone's living there, just those great, beautiful trees in front of me and the wonderful lake behind me.

I began to explore, and soon I found a trail through the woods which seemed to have been used very little, and which was almost obscured by grass. I followed this trail, and after I had walked for some time and had traveled a considerable distance through the forest, I saw a man coming towards me. I became aware that he was a very large man, and I hurried my steps to reach him, because I recognized him as my grandfather. In mortality he weighed over three hundred pounds, so you may know he was a large man. I remember how happy I was to see him coming. I had been given his name and had always been proud of it.

When Grandfather came within a few feet of me, he stopped. His stopping was an invitation for me to stop. Then — and this I would like the boys and girls and young people never to forget — he looked at me very earnestly and said:

"I would like to know what you have done with my name."

Everything I had ever done passed before me as though it were a flying picture on a screen — everything I had done. Quickly this vivid retrospect came down to the very time I was standing there. My whole life had passed before me. I smiled and looked at my grandfather and said:

"I have never done anything with your name of which you need be ashamed."

He stepped forward and took me in his arms, and as he did so, I became conscious again of my earthly surroundings. My pillow was as wet as though water had been poured on it — wet with tears of gratitude that I could answer unashamed.

68

I have thought of this many times, and I want to tell you that I have been trying, more than ever since that time, to take care of that name. So I want to say to the boys and girls, to the young men and women, to the youth of the Church and of all the world: Honor your fathers and your mothers. Honor the names that you bear, because some day you will have the privilege and the obligation of reporting to them (and to your Father in heaven) what you have done with their name. ("Your Good Name," *Improvement Era*, March 1947, p. 139.)

Names of Daughters

My wife and I named our first daughter Marcianne. We did so for many reasons, not the least of which was the fact that we both loved and revered the name of my wife's grandmother. Our Marcianne was born as Grandmother Marci was dying. The one was introduced to the other in a brief moment of cradling on a deathbed. At the time it was wondered whether the one was conscious of the other in that brief exchange of love and whether a spiritual bonding had taken place.

Such bonding, however, did take place in some wonderful way. For as the years have passed, we have observed in Marci the younger's life a gradual acquisition of the priceless virtues shown in the life of Marci the elder. Yes, we have extolled to our daughter the goodnesses of her namesake time and time again. Yes, we have tried to keep alive the name of an elect lady who helped bring my wife and me together. But a miracle has happened to our daughter as she has acquired the personality, disposition, and inherent Christ-like qualities of one who lived years before. In some marvelous manner, a linkage between two people of different generations has occurred through a name and through a stream of blessed memories.

Our youngest daughter is named Carleen — half of *Car*los and half of Col*leen*. The name was given after long thought and consideration and at the end of a line of five consecutive

69

sons. We assigned the name because it represents the scripture, "Therefore shall a man leave his father and his mother, and shall cleave unto his wife, and they shall be one flesh" (Abraham 5:18). From the very beginning, our hopes have been that she would imitate and acquire the best from each of us and rise far above the stature we have carved out for ourselves. She is not disappointing us in the least degree. She is everything and more than we ever expected.

Names — Priesthood Ordinance

In The Church of Jesus Christ of Latter-day Saints, there is a priesthood ordinance referred to as the naming and blessing of children. This ordinance is performed by the power and authority of the Holy Melchizedek Priesthood and includes giving a child a name, adding words of blessings as the Spirit dictates, and closing in the name of Jesus Christ. It is written: "Every member of the church of Christ having children is to bring them unto the elders before the church, who are to lay their hands upon them in the name of Jesus Christ, and bless them in his name" (D&C 20:70).

This ordinance is sacred and should be performed properly. It must not be performed in a perfunctory manner with little thought to form or substance. It should be done with the child's best interests at heart and in the spirit of love and prophecy. Those who bring honor to this practice do the following: (1) select prayerfully and carefully the name to be given, (2) seek for inspiration and guidance in what to say, (3) retain in mind the blessing pronounced, and (4) help the child understand and gain appreciation for the name and blessing as he or she grows to maturity. By doing those things, the ordinance can become a sacred and happy experience for the family.

We should never forget that the ultimate pattern for the blessing of children was set by the Savior: "He took them [children] up in his arms, put his hands upon them, and blessed them" (Mark 10:16). "He took their little children, one by one, and blessed them, and prayed unto the Father for them" (3 Nephi 17:21).

First to Know

I like the spirit and humble intent shown in the following practice among some African people: "By ancient custom, for the next seven days, there was but a single task with which Omoro would seriously occupy himself: *the selection of a name for his firstborn son.* It would have to be a name rich with history and with promise, for the people of his tribe — the Mandinkas — believed that a child would develop seven of the characteristics of whomever or whatever he was named for.... Omoro then walked out before all the assembled people of the village. Moving to his wife's side, he lifted up the infant and, as all watched, whispered three times into his son's ears the name he had chosen for him. It was the first time the name had ever been spoken as this child's name, for Omoro's people felt that each human being should be the first to know who he was." (Alex Haley, *Roots* [Garden City, N.Y.: Doubleday & Co., 1976], pp. 2–3; italics added.)

Whenever I think of Omoro and the custom practiced by his people, I am reminded of some family folklore. It is said in family circles that only moments after my wife's birth, her father wrapped her in a towel and walked out of the house and onto the front porch. He then lifted his first-born child high into the air and declared, *"Colleen,* look at the world." According to the story reported in an old baby book, the infant stopped crying, opened her eyes, and looked about.

I don't suspect that anyone has ever been able to count or even estimate the number of times a person hears, reads, or says his or her name during a lifetime. The number is unquestionably high and in the millions. To most, I would guess, the sound or sight is pleasing and provokes good feelings. To others, however, the result is unfortunately the opposite. What makes the difference? It is in the choosing, the giving, and the guarding of the words that designate "you" and cause "you" to stand out from all the rest.

How very important it is that parents plant the "pecan tree" of names of significance in their family gardens and cause that tree to grow and to bear fruit! They must not pull names blindly from a hat and pin them upon their children. They must not bring disgrace upon the names shared with children, causing them to seek a change like the children of Amulon—children who were so displeased with the conduct of their fathers that they forsook the names of their fathers and took upon themselves another name (see Mosiah 25:1–12). Parents *must* help children retain good names in remembrance (see Jacob 1:10–11), cause good names to be written in their hearts (see Mosiah 5:12), and safeguard the names given by way of inspiration.

Keep Names Alive

Shakespeare wrote:

> But he that filches [steals] from me my good name,
> Robs me of that which not enriches him,
> And makes me poor indeed.
>
> (*Othello.*)

These words remind us that we should safeguard our names by living beyond reproach and by seeking to bring honor to namesakes and family members who have provided us with a rich inheritance.

Joseph Smith, Jr., must have been sobered somewhat when he learned of the prophecy made by Joseph, the son of Jacob, who was carried captive into Egypt. The prophecy was: "Behold, that seer will the Lord bless; and they that seek to destroy him shall be confounded; for this promise, which I have obtained of the Lord, of the fruit of my loins, shall be fulfilled. Behold, I am sure of the fulfilling of this promise; and his name shall be called after me; and it shall be after the name of his father.

And he shall be like unto me; for the thing, which the Lord shall bring forth by his hand, by the power of the Lord shall bring my people unto salvation" (2 Nephi 3:14–15).

Not only was Joseph Smith commissioned to keep alive an important name, but he was also commissioned to be "like unto" his namesakes — his father and Joseph of old. One can conjecture that the prophecy made and the name given did much to keep the prophet of the restoration in the path of duty. He had important promises to keep and high expectations to fulfill.

I ask three questions: If we don't keep alive the names of yesterday's heroes, who will? If we don't bestow names of significance, how will we weld one generation to another? If we don't help the rising generation bear nobly the names given them by parents, how shall they bear properly the name given them when they come unto Christ and take upon them his holy name? (see Moroni chapters 4 and 5).

Christians

We read of a great leader who rallied his followers in defense of their country by writing upon a piece of his coat and holding it before his people. The inscription read, "In memory of our God, our religion, and freedom, and our peace, our wives, and our children" (Alma 46:12).

This leader, whose name was Moroni, led the armies of a people "who were true believers in Christ" and who "took upon [themselves], gladly, the name of Christ, or Christians as they were called" (Alma 46:15). Chief Captain Moroni and his troops were willing to bear the name of Christ and were deeply honored to be members of his Church. They knew that if they were called by some other name, they would be found on the left hand of God. They also knew that the name could only be blotted out through transgression. Consequently, they retained the name written always in their hearts and heard and knew the voice by which they were called, and also the name by which God would call them (see Mosiah 5:10–12).

Those who take upon themselves the name of Christ are prepared to do so by bearing their family and given names nobly and honorably. True believers in Christ honor their fathers and their mothers; they possess a special love for family members; they fight zealously in defense of their God, religion, freedom, peace, wives, children, and *their good names;* and, they will not allow transgression or any influence to blemish the name that distinguishes them from all other members of Adam's family.

Some converts to the doctrine of Christ pleaded for a name that would distinguish themselves from all others. A name was given. Later, this same group of people "were also distinguished for their zeal towards God, and also towards men; for they were perfectly honest and upright in all things; and they were firm in the faith of Christ, even unto the end" (Alma 27:26–27). Just how much the name influenced the righteousness of the people of Ammon is not certain. But one is led to believe that the name helped to motivate the people in living as real Christians.

God Knows Our Names

In his personal history, Joseph Smith describes in detail his first vision or visit with the Father and the Son. Said Joseph: "One of them spake unto me, *calling me by name* and said, pointing to the other — 'This is My Beloved Son, Hear Him!' " (Joseph Smith–History 1:17; italics added).

Joseph must have thrilled at the sound of his name. God knew him! And, God acknowledged his presence by saying, "Joseph." It wasn't, "Hey, you," or "Fella," or some other impersonal and casual greeting. He was addressed by the name given him by his loving parents, even the name of his own father.

Later, the Angel Moroni also called Joseph by name. We

read from Joseph's account, "He called me *by name*, and said unto me that he was a messenger sent from the presence of God to me, and that *his name* was Moroni; that God had a work for me to do; and that *my name* should be had for good and evil among all nations, kindreds, and tongues, or that it should be both good and evil spoken of among all people" (Joseph Smith–History 1:33; italics added).

Two names were used in this conversation—the name of the messenger (Moroni) and the name of the person visited (Joseph). Both Moroni and Joseph were known to God, and both were worthy of the names given them. Remember always,

> *As the new heavens and the new earth, which I will make, shall remain before me, saith the Lord, so shall your seed and* your name remain *(Isaiah 66:22; emphasis added).*

CHAPTER SIX

PERSONAL PARENT INTERVIEWS

*Accordingly, as I had been commanded, I went at
the end of each year, and at each time I found the
same messenger there, and received instruction and
intelligence from him at each of* our interviews,
*respecting what the Lord was going to do, and how
and in what manner his kingdom was to be conducted in the last days (Joseph Smith–History
1:54; emphasis added).*

Few men and women are privileged to communicate face to
face with angels as did the Prophet Joseph Smith. Such spiritual
experiences are usually reserved for those who have special
missions to perform or special purposes to fulfill. Nevertheless,
all of God's children, including our sons and daughters, deserve
the opportunity of being interviewed from time to time by
loving parents who converse "like unto angels of God" and
who speak with the Holy Ghost or "tongue of angels" (D&C
42:6; 2 Nephi 32:2).

I am intrigued that Joseph referred to his interviews with
the Angel Moroni as "our interviews." One concludes that
Joseph, the interviewee, was fully involved as he received instructions and intelligence from his interviewer, else why
would he use the word "our"? Though the record doesn't
provide us with any details about Joseph's participation in the
interview, other than listening, one does wonder whether he
answered questions or expressed personal views.

A Model

When I think of the interviews conducted by the Angel Moroni with Joseph Smith, my mind turns to that inspiring exchange between the risen Christ and Peter: "When they had dined, Jesus saith to Simon Peter, Simon, son of Jonas, lovest thou me more than these? He saith unto him, Yea, Lord; thou knowest that I love thee. He saith unto him, Feed my lambs. He saith to him again the second time, Simon, son of Jonas, lovest thou me? He saith unto him, Yea, Lord; thou knowest that I love thee. He saith unto him, Feed my sheep. He saith unto him the third time, Simon, son of Jonas, lovest thou me? Peter was grieved because he said unto him the third time, Lovest thou me? And he said unto him, Lord, thou knowest all things; thou knowest that I love thee. Jesus saith unto him, Feed my sheep" (John 21:15–17).

Included in this sacred conversation between the Master and the chief apostle are all the elements of a successful interview. Questions were asked evoking personal feelings; answers were given revealing a depth of faith; a commission was given; and a commitment was received. No idle words were spoken, nor was there any obliqueness of purpose shown by either party.

Too many parents, I fear, ignore these examples and fail to hold parent-child interviews. Some may feel too busy to do so. Others may feel they can save all the children as a flock or as part of the herd. But whatever the excuse, those who allow this "pecan tree" practice to wilt and die are making a terrible mistake, forfeiting opportunities to give and receive instruction and intelligence.

Wet or Dry?

Several years ago, I approached one of my daughters and said, "My dear, it's time for an interview." Her response was less than enthusiastic, and I determined within my own mind that she might have found our past interviews somewhat boring. So instead of subjecting her to a formal conversation, I invited her into the car and drove to the Dairy Queen, where we both enjoyed a root beer float. All the way to and from the store, I asked questions, and she freely responded. She didn't even realize that she was being interviewed — or at least that is what I thought. A few weeks later, I announced once again that I wanted to interview her. This time she promptly asked, "Wet or dry?"

I wonder if our conduct of good practices — even the conducting of interviews with our children — is sometimes done in a dry and deadening manner. Is it possible that in our drive to perform or fulfill a Church expectancy, we collide with purpose? Can we not become so obsessed with form that we forget family? If so, perhaps we should ask ourselves whether within we are "full of dead men's bones" (Matthew 23:27).

When I think of dry performances, my mind turns to the ancients who altered the lesser law. They multiplied rituals, ceremonies, and symbols to the extent that the law itself was worshiped more than the Lord. In fact, the law was so abused that it pointed people away from, not forward to, the Messiah.

The acceptable performance, I feel, is made "wet" and given zest by the living waters that issue from Christ. It is a performance founded upon such inspired teachings as:

• "[You] must have no other object in view . . . but to glorify God, and must not be influenced by any other motive than that of building his kingdom" (Joseph Smith–History 1:46).

• "He that is greatest among you shall be your servant" (Matthew 23:11).

• "The letter killeth, but the spirit giveth life" (2 Corinthians 3:6).

• "When thou doest alms, let not thy left hand know what thy right hand doeth" (Matthew 6:3).

Living performances are void of vain repetition and stiffness and self-centered tendencies. They are made by Saints who speak and act according to the feelings of their hearts and the Spirit of the Lord, which is in them (see 2 Nephi 4:12).

A Classic Interview

Alma's interview with Helaman is a classic "wet" and refreshing performance. It is a short, three-question, forty-five second exchange between father and son. According to the record, Alma was approaching the end of his ministry. He knew that he must select someone to assume prophetic and record-keeping responsibilities. Helaman was his choice. Alma came to his son and asked: "Believest thou the words which I spake unto thee concerning those records which have been kept?"

Without hesitation, Helaman answered: "Yea, I believe." He might have said, "Yes, I believe in the scriptures; and yes, I believe all that you have taught me."

Alma's second question was simply, "Believest thou in Jesus Christ, who shall come?" Again, without delay, Helaman stated, "Yea, I believe all the words which thou hast spoken."

What a tribute to the father! He had talked of Christ, rejoiced in Christ, preached of Christ, and taught his son to know the source to which he might look for a remission of his sins (see 2 Nephi 25:26).

Up to this point in the interview, the father's questions were sampling the son's basic beliefs. Now it was essential that those beliefs be tested and determined as being more than idle lip service. Alma's capstone inquiry was, "Will ye keep my commandments?"

I am not certain what went through Helaman's mind as he prepared to give his final response. He knew the necessity of honoring his parents and respecting priesthood authority. His previous actions had verified this fact. I like to think that Helaman's reply was promoted by a heartfelt desire to be obedient rather than by a fear of authority. Deep love of God and father were reflected in his words: "Yea, I will keep thy commandments with all my heart."

It is a marvelous thing when a father is able to make his commandments square perfectly with God's expectations. Apparently, this condition was achieved by Alma, for Helaman was ready and willing to obey with all his heart.

This short, informative, and inspiring interview must have pleased Alma greatly. Not only had he communicated heart-to-heart and soul-to-soul with his son, but the son had openly declared his faith and pledged his devotion. To culminate the exchange, Alma, under the inspiration of the Spirit, prophesied and extended this blessing: "Blessed art thou; and the Lord shall prosper thee in this land" (see Alma 45:2–8).

I wonder if our interviews with our children are as inspirational and building as the one between Alma and Helaman. I find it significant that the father came to the son; the son was not summoned to stand inspection or to give a report. I find it refreshing that the conversation was direct and without any verbal sparring; it was not labored or rehearsed. I find it exemplary that commitment was drawn without prying, wringing, or pressuring. And I find it most beautiful that the father concluded with a tender blessing.

Is this not a performance, or a pattern of communicating, that we should follow? And I refer to the principles involved, not necessarily to the form.

Applying the Alma-Helaman Approach

On one occasion when I arrived home late from an assignment, my wife expressed concern about one of our sons. She was worried that his mind was not riveted upon serving a mission, and she said as much to me. Her concerns certainly captured my attention, and I asked where the son was. She told me that he was in his room getting ready for bed. Immediately I went to the room and sat on the edge of his bed. When I asked if I could speak with him a moment, he said, "Certainly."

The hour was late. He was tired, and so was I. I could see

that nothing would be gained by a long conversation. And following the direct Alma-and-Helaman approach, the conversation went something like this:

"Son, are you still planning on serving a mission?"

"Yes," he answered. "I've always planned on serving, and I haven't changed."

"Son, do you know what qualifies a young man to serve a mission? Do you know what worthiness means?"

"Yes, Dad," he said. "I understand the requirements and standards of worthiness that must be met."

I said, "Thank you. I have one last question: Are you clean and worthy to serve? Could you accept a call if one were issued you today?"

There was a moment of reflective silence; then he declared: "It isn't easy. Temptation is real and found everywhere. However, since you've asked, I am clean and I am worthy to serve."

This was a wonderful, beautiful, spontaneous, and sanctifying experience.

I thanked my son, kissed him, assured him of my love, and bid him goodnight. I returned to my bedroom and told my wife that all was well and that she could sleep peacefully.

Interviewing Skills

Textbooks have been written about interviewing skills and practices. Various experts have discussed the importance of creating the ideal setting, using the right body language, asking the right questions, and voicing the appropriate cues. But, however important these patterns and forms may be, no elements are more essential to a successful interview than purity of motive and a willingness to listen.

Children can discern quickly whether they are loved and appreciated. In conversations with adults, they can part the curtain of deceit and sort out the chaff very quickly. They can readily tell if your attention is divided or if your mind is running ahead to another appointment. Yes, they can perceive if the conversation is intended to fulfill your appointment or to fulfill their needs.

My wife is the world's best conversationalist. She can talk freely and easily with anyone, especially with our children. Her success is not attributed to her mouth, but rather to her ear and heart. She listens willingly and with empathy. Any conversation with her is face-to-face, ear-to-ear, and heart-to-heart.

Commitments

In my youth, I had a priesthood leader who believed in the worth of personal interviews. He was a marvelous speaker at the pulpit, and I enjoyed listening to his many sermons. However, as I think back over the years when I heard him instruct at stake conferences, I cannot identify one specific talk he gave. All of the messages he ever gave in my presence have melded into one general impression that rests in my mind.

What I do recall with great detail, however, are the three personal interviews he held with me — one on a bank corner, one on the welfare farm in a sugar-beet field, and one in his home. On each occasion, he centered all of his attention upon me and no one else. He didn't have to tell me he loved me and cared about my welfare. The effort he made to meet with me and the time allocated in my behalf was evidence enough. I was the focal point; my goals and aspirations were his concern; obtaining righteous commitments was his intent. I hold the man in cherished memory for what he did for me through personal interviews.

How wonderful it would be if parents followed the example of my former leader and did the same! Children and youth thrive upon the attention gained through one-on-one contacts and receive wonderful direction from those who care, who take the time to sit with one of the "little ones" and talk.

"Dad, May We Talk?"

While I was serving as a mission president, one of my sons taught me a valuable lesson. He returned home at the close of a school day with a burden on his mind—a burden too heavy for him to carry alone. He came immediately to my office but was turned away by an assistant who informed him that I had missionary interviews scheduled well into the evening. This information disappointed my son because he needed me *now*, not later. He sat in a corner brooding and wondering what he could do to change the situation. After a few minutes, he noticed that the assistant had placed a stack of interview sheets outside my office door on a chair and that I was working my way down the stack sheet-by-sheet, missionary-by-missionary. When the assistant's attention was distracted, my son took one of the interview sheets, scribbled on it, and placed it on top of the stack.

I opened the door and picked up a sheet. It read: "Dad, may we talk? I have a serious problem!" I did, of course, oblige my son, conducting one of the most important interviews I have ever held.

Children must have access to parents, especially when crises arise. The door must be kept ajar so that sons and daughters may enter and so that questions may be answered, instructions given, and assurance voiced at the moment children are ready to learn.

A Concluding Word

I do see great wisdom in the practices and performances we encourage parents to follow in the Church. There is virtue in sponsoring family home evenings, in conducting family prayers, in giving blessings, and in holding parent-child interviews. All of these are important and have their place. However, the participation in such performances and the reporting of such activity must not become the end. They are means of involving, teaching, and blessing people. All should be engaged in for the purpose of saving and exalting souls.

I thank God for my wife and my children; they make life so very meaningful. I thank God for the restored Church and for living prophets who have provided inspired programs that benefit me, my family, and others. And I'm grateful for the gospel, which comes from the fountain of living waters — even Jesus Christ.

It is imperative that we not confuse means and ends or become confused with performances at the expense of the spirit underlying all commandments. May our interviews, our prayers, our communications with our children, and other family practices be sanctifying to ourselves and our loved ones and free of dryness and "dead men's bones."

The fruit of the "pecan tree" practice of personal interviews is sweet and "desirable to make one happy" (1 Nephi 8:10). Those who plant and cultivate it carefully may rejoice as Lehi rejoiced:

I did go forth and partake of the fruit thereof; and I beheld that it was most sweet, above all that I ever before tasted. Yea, and I beheld that the fruit thereof was white, to exceed all the whiteness that I had ever seen. And as I partook of the fruit thereof it filled my soul with exceedingly great joy; wherefore, I began to be desirous that my family should partake of it also; for I knew that it was desirable above all other fruit (1 Nephi 8:11–12).

CHAPTER SEVEN

MEMORIES

In memory of our God, our religion, and freedom, and our peace, our wives, and our children (Alma 46:12).

A few years ago, I delivered a devotional address at Brigham Young University. I was introduced by President Jeffrey R. Holland, who gave a rather long and flowery biographical sketch of my life, including some flattering remarks about my basketball career at the University of Utah. My response began with these words: "President Holland's remarks about my former athletic accomplishments remind me that there is some virtue in growing older. That virtue is: (1) record books become covered with dust, and (2) memories of people tend to become fuzzy. Therefore, one can ride the bench with a team at the university, yet ten years later, in the minds of most, have been a regular performer. Twenty years after graduation, he is remembered as an all-conference player. Thirty years later, he is an all-American. In just two more years, if dust is not blown off the books and memories refreshed, I fully expect to be inducted into the Basketball Hall of Fame in Springfield, Massachusetts" (BYU Marriott Center, February 26, 1985).

Record books do collect dust if not used, and memories of people do fade with time unless something is done to preserve special experiences. That is why conscientious and caring parents not only strive to provide their children with pleasant

85

and unforgettable experiences, but they also try to retain these experiences with the use of photographs, diaries, tape recorders, and other means of storing memorable occurrences. All of this is done, I believe, because memories, especially those of parents and home, constitute a kind of "security blanket" for most people—a blanket that can be handled and cradled in times of emotional stress, imminent danger, or extreme challenge.

I have wondered about the circumstances of the one who wrote:

> I cannot go to rest, but linger still
> In meditation at my window sill,
> While, like the twinkling stars in heaven's dome,
> Come one by one *sweet memories of home.*
> And wouldst thou ask me where my fancy roves
> To reproduce the happy scenes it loves,
> Where *hope and memory* together dwell
> And paint the pictured beauties that I tell?
> . . . There is my home, the spot I love so well,
> Whose worth and beauty pen nor tongue can tell.
>
> (*Hymns,* no. 37; italics added.)

I wonder, too, what the Whitney family did to plant in the heart of Orson F. the feelings he expressed in these lines. His blanket of tender memories was surely not woven by chance or accident. It must have been sewn by those who knew that the "pecan tree" practice of preserving cherished memories was a matter of great importance.

The Mind

I find it incredible that the human brain has the storage capacity of one quadrillion bits of information, as some experts have said. If this is true, allowing for the possible error of ten or twelve bits, why do we have such difficulty memorizing the thirteen Articles of Faith, the six missionary discussions, the basics of a biology course? Or, why is it sometimes so hard to recall our home telephone number on the spur of the moment?

Nevertheless, the mind, where memories are stored, is a marvelous phenomenon. "The mind," said John Milton, "is its own place, and in itself can make a heaven of hell, and a hell of heaven." The difference would be in its contents and use. As stated in Proverbs: "The memory of the just is blessed: but the name of the wicked shall rot" (Proverbs 10:7).

I am not qualified to treat this topic as a professional psychologist would, nor as someone else would who understands the wonders of the human mind. I do, however, want to share some thoughts and feelings about memory and remembering, as related to the gospel of Jesus Christ and our spiritual welfare. I hope the thoughts I share will help you preserve cherished memories for yourself and your family.

Memory and Mood

Memory, according to the experts, often conditions our moods. Those who remember only the disappointing experiences of life tend to become bitter and cynical. Those who recall only their enemies and the forces mustered against them may lose their courage. Those who recall only past injuries may continue to feud with the world. But those who recall the positive and encouraging things remain bright and optimistic.

Dr. Ernest A. Fitzgerald observed: "The memory is a window through which life is viewed. The color of that window determines the color of our world." How awful it would be to walk through life with everything distorted by the red of anger, the blue of despair, the black of fear, or the green of envy.

I do not know the color of Enos's life when he went into the forests to hunt beasts and had his wrestle before God. I am led to think it was somewhat gray, for he had not received a remission of his sins. However, as he stimulated his memory by recalling the words of eternal life spoken by his father, and as he reflected upon the joy of the Saints, the cloud of gloom was dispelled. Through prayer and the exercise of faith, Enos emerged from the woods colored in the rays of heavenly light (see Enos 1:1–8).

I know the color of Alma's life as he and others sought to destroy the church of God. He states that when he remembered all of his sins, he was racked with eternal torment. Then, when he remembered all that his father had prophesied about Christ's atonement, something marvelous occurred. He said: "When I thought this, I could remember my pains no more; yea, I was harrowed up by the memory of my sins no more. And oh, what joy, and what marvelous light I did behold; yea, my soul was filled with joy as exceeding as was my pain! Yea, . . . there could be nothing so exquisite and so bitter as were my pains. Yea, and . . . on the other hand, there can be nothing so exquisite and sweet as was my joy" (Alma 36:19–21).

Elijah is another interesting case in point. Even though he had slain the prophets of Baal and witnessed heavenly powers, he lost his courage and the desire to live when hunted by wicked Queen Jezebel. The Lord sent an angel, the whisperings of "a still small voice," and other reassurances to change his mood (see 1 Kings 19).

At a critical time in Nephite history, Moroni rent his coat and wrote upon it, "In memory of our God, our religion, and freedom, and our peace, our wives, and our children" (Alma 46:12). This "Title of Liberty" was hoisted before the people to rally them to the colors of "true believers" or Christians. By stirring the memories of his people in this manner, their moods were changed, and a just cause was defended.

Do you allow your mind to wallow in memory of past hurts and injuries, thus becoming blind to everything else? Or do you recall the positive and encouraging things that cause your life to remain bright and optimistic? What is the color of your memories? Remember, the memories are yours, and the palette and brushes are in your hands. Be certain that you use the right colors as you paint the past and niche it in your mind.

Memory and Testimony

In our missionary service, we frequently invite our investigator friends to obtain a testimony by reading the Book of Mormon and praying about its contents. Our point of reference is chapter 10 of Moroni, verses 3–5. We usually say to our friends: "Read this book and ask God if it is not true." Then we promise, as the book states, that "he will manifest the truth of it unto you, by the power of the Holy Ghost."

I don't fault any who have used this process. I do, however, suggest a better and more successful approach. Let me read the verses and highlight four steps to a testimony, two of which are often neglected: "Behold, I would exhort you that when ye shall [1] *read* these things, . . . that ye would [2] *remember* how merciful the Lord hath been unto the children of men, from the creation of Adam even down until the time that ye shall receive these things, and [3] *ponder* it in your hearts. . . . I would exhort you that ye would [4] *ask* God . . . if these things are not true; and . . . he will manifest the truth of it unto you, by the power of the Holy Ghost" (Moroni 10:3–4; italics added).

I emphasize two words, *remember* and *ponder*. I do so because I feel strongly that reading the things of God without remembering and pondering how those things fit into the divine scheme tends to confuse, not enlighten. Enlightenment occurs and truth is revealed as things are fitted together in an understandable way. In the process, the mind is stimulated, the memory is stirred, and the heart is prepared to respond to the whisperings of the Spirit.

Ammon rehearsed many truths to King Lamoni before he was converted. Among other things, "he began at the creation of the world, and also the creation of Adam, and told him all the things concerning the fall of man, and . . . laid before him the records and the holy scriptures of the people, which had been spoken by the prophets" (Alma 18:36).

Similarly, Aaron did the same with the father of Lamoni. He, as did Ammon, preached of Adam, the Fall, the plan of redemption, and the atonement of Christ. All of this was done to place things in proper perspective and to build the foundations of a testimony.

When your testimony sags or appears to stumble along the way, why not remember the goodness of the Lord? In the process of positive recall, perhaps you can experience the spiritual healing that King Lamoni and his father expressed. How exhilarating it is to ponder the merciful nature of God, and how healing it is to remember the eternal gifts of Christ!

Memories and Models

Most of us have been deeply influenced by other men and women. I suspect that this is the way it should be. Elder James E. Talmage wrote that the Father's original purpose was "to use persuasive influences of wholesome precept and *sacrificing example* with the inhabitants of the earth, then to leave them free to choose for themselves" (*The Articles of Faith*, 12th ed. [Salt Lake City: The Church of Jesus Christ of Latter-day Saints, 1924], p. 55; italics added).

All of us, I would guess, have a model or hero tucked away in the recesses of our memory. You could have many. From time to time you may think of that model and from him or her draw needed inspiration. This is particularly true when the hill you are required to climb seems insurmountable or the decision to be made seems especially difficult.

Helaman knew the value of memories and models, for he instructed his sons: "I have given unto you the names of our first parents who came out of the land of Jerusalem; and this I have done that when you remember your names ye may remember them; and when ye remember them ye may remember their works; and when ye remember their works ye may know how that it is said, and also written, that they were good. Therefore, my sons, I would that ye should do that which is good, that it may be said of you, and also written, even as it has been said and written of them" (Helaman 5:6–7).

You should not clutter your memories with men or women of doubtful reputation. They will disappoint you and drag you downward. Rather, you should selectively place in your mind the giants of goodness and, each time you think of them, resolve that you will walk in their footprints and go beyond their mark.

Memory and Thoughts

"The mind," said Dr. Ernest A. Fitzgerald, "feeds on the food that is placed at its disposal." Therefore, "what we give to our minds will eventually determine what they contain." This certainly is no startling fact; everyone seems to know it. Yet, people continue to read pornographic materials, view smutty and suggestive films, and sing songs with filthy lyrics. Wittingly or not, those who do these things will store polluted memories and reap a bitter harvest.

I find it difficult to understand how some members of the Church can blatantly disregard this divine injunction: "Let virtue garnish thy thoughts unceasingly; then shall thy confidence wax strong in the presence of God; and the doctrine of the priesthood shall distil upon thy soul as the dews from heaven. The Holy Ghost shall be thy constant companion, and thy scepter an unchanging scepter of righteousness and truth" (D&C 121:45–46).

What a gold mine of promises is hidden in this scripture! Who in his or her right mind would place in jeopardy the promise of confidence, the doctrine of the priesthood, and the companionship of the Holy Ghost?

Christina Rossetti wrote:

> I have a room where into no one enters
> Save I myself alone.
> There sits a *blessed memory* on a throne
> There my life centers.
> (Italics added.)

If we counted or enthroned our blessings more, our memories would become pleasant, and our lives would be much happier. I like these thoughts:

> The sun was shining in my eyes
> And I could hardly see
> To do the necessary task
> That was allotted me.
> Resentment of the vivid glow
> I started to complain
> When all at once upon the air
> I heard the blindman's cane.
> (Earl Musselman.)

Over and beyond the counting of blessings and the garnishing of thoughts with virtue, let me share one more thing pertaining to memory and thoughts. A noted physician counseled: "Know the great souls that make up the moral radium of the world. You must be born of the spirit, initiated into their fraternity. . . . Life is a straight, plain business [game], and the way is clear, blazed for you by generations of strong men, into whose labours you enter and whose ideals must be your inspiration" (*A Way of Life,* pp. 37–38).

Do not become enslaved by destructive or degrading thoughts. They can become as strong and debilitating as Satan's iron chains. There is an old story about a man who was recalling the hardships of his early life. He exaggerated to such limits that his wife felt constrained to correct him. "Be quiet," he said to her. "Half of the fun of remembering the good old days is rearranging them." To rearrange one's memories may not be too bad, if we don't embellish to the point that we lose contact with truth.

I was in a meeting with one of my friends when he was requested to tell a story, one he had related on many occasions. Knowing his own tendency to embellish, he smiled and asked, "Do you want me to tell it as I told it last time or as it actually happened?"

Do not forget that memory and thoughts are inseparably

connected; one runs into the other. So garnish your thoughts with virtue, count your blessings, and have fellowship with the great minds of the race. Those actions will build you a sacred sanctuary of pleasant memories.

Memory and You

A number of years ago, I read these words: "It is said that God gave us memory so we could have roses in winter. But it is also true that without memory we could not have self in any season. The more memories you have, the more 'you' you have. That is why, as Swift said, no wise man ever wished to be younger" (George F. Will, "On Turning 40," *Newsweek*, April 27, 1981, p. 104).

I did not fully appreciate memories and self until I, with the help of others, compiled my oral history. I gave my wife a rough copy of my life story and asked her to edit it. My instructions were, "You know me better than I know myself, so please read it carefully and polish the manuscript."

A half hour later, when I returned to see how she was doing, she was crying. I said, "My goodness, is it that bad?"

"No," she answered, "it is that good!"

"Have you made any changes?" I asked.

"No," she replied, "it is you speaking, and I don't want to erase or edit you out of the record."

We later gave bound copies of my history to our children. Both of us thought that the book would probably be placed on a shelf and remain unread. A few weeks later, however, one of our daughters said to me, "Dad, I love you so very much."

I asked: "What brought this on?"

She explained, "It was your oral history; I have been reading about your life."

Do we not read that records kept by the ancients enlarged the memory of the people? Of course they did. Records do preserve language, safeguard truth, and inspire future readers if they are kept properly.

What a pity it would be if your children and grandchildren were denied that part of you that really should be recorded. Make certain that you are transmitting to your posterity, along with other graces of life, your innermost thoughts, your poignant feelings, and your sincere testimonies. You owe the rising generation this blessing and more.

Enlarge the memories of those who follow you with your records, leave for them a part of you, and extend to them an opportunity to hold you in cherished memory.

I could say so much more about memory and remembering as related to you and the gospel of Jesus Christ. For instance, I've said nothing about the need to remember our sacred covenants, our vows, our ordinances. I've said nothing about all of the "types and shadows" mentioned in the scriptures that have been given to direct our thoughts in the proper direction and keep us on the right path. Nor have I alluded to the role that memory will play on Judgment Day. I leave it up to you to research the subject further and to fill in all the blanks.

I stress the importance of memory. It does mold our moods. It is associated with testimony. It should include models of righteousness. Of a certainty, it is the product of thoughts. And, in the end, it is you.

The Formative Years

As you adopt the "pecan tree" practice of creating and preserving cherished memories, remember the critical nature of the "formative years" — those childhood years when the days of learning are saturated with new discoveries, when experiences are planted indelibly in the mind and heart. Of these formative years spent mostly at home, Robert Southey, a poet laureate of England, is reported to have said, "The first 20 years are the longest half of your life. They appear so while they are passing; they seem to have been so when we look back on them; and they take up more room in our *memory* than all the years that follow" (Bruce Schechter, "Why Time Flies," *Reader's Digest*, January 1992, p. 14; italics added).

If Southey's observation is correct or only partially correct, loving and caring parents will help their children obtain a room full of cherished and even sacred memories. How is this done? Here are a few suggestions:

• By doing things with them that *they love doing* and that are uplifting. Such activities might be as restful as reading a book together or as rugged as climbing a mountain.

• By involving them in *creative work*. Weeding a garden you have planted may be a dull chore for them, but weeding a garden they have planted themselves is a thrilling experience well worth remembering.

• By *accentuating successes attained*, however modest or simple the achievement may have been. Children have a way of blocking out the losses, especially when parents help them cover the past with wins.

• By providing children with *special experiences* that are well-planned and out of the ordinary. These experiences might be the result of a trip to some distant place, the observance of a birthday, a graduation party, or something else that allows performances to exceed expectations.

• By encouraging children to pause occasionally and *reflect upon things of import* that have happened to them. Keeping a journal may help young ones catalog memorable occurrences; preparing a report for a family gathering may have similar benefits. A blurred experience can become focused in the mind by reflecting about it and recording it for future reference.

• By teaching children *how to savor time*, which comes and goes on wings of lightning. Don't let them grow up too fast. Help them understand there is a time and season for all things — a time to be a child, a time to be a youth, and a time to be an adult. But, at the same time, don't allow them to stay longer than they should on any one stage of their lives. We need to take time to smell the roses, but not to watch them grow.

Ponder the "longest half of your life" and do whatever is necessary to place the "security blanket" of cherished memories into the hands of your family members. In doing so, keep in mind the words of Peter, who advised:

> *I stir up your pure minds by way of remembrance: that ye may be mindful of the words which were spoken before by the holy prophets, and of the commandment of us the apostles of the Lord and Saviour (2 Peter 3:1–2).*

GOOD HUMOR

*A merry heart maketh a cheerful countenance: but
by sorrow of the heart the spirit is broken. . . . All the
days of the afflicted are evil: but he that is of a merry
heart hath a continual feast. . . . A merry heart doeth
good like a medicine: but a broken spirit drieth the
bones (Proverbs 15:13, 15; 17:22).*

Several years ago, one of our sons asked permission to bring
a girl friend to one of our family home evenings. We had no
objections, providing the young lady's parents gave their con-
sent. It was not our desire to intrude upon someone else's
home night.

She came and had a delightful time. Though reluctant at
first, she participated as invited when the formal lesson was
given. Later, when we played games and ate refreshments, she
entered into the activities just as if she were a member of our
family. No one laughed harder; no one seemed happier; and
no one enjoyed the evening more than she.

As the evening drew to a close and she prepared to be
escorted home by our son, she thanked us profusely and asked
if she could come again. She said that there was no laughter
and no fun in her own home. Her father, she explained, was
very strict and staid in his ways and frowned upon any behavior
that seemed spontaneous and lighthearted.

She did come to other family home evenings in the months

that followed, and her personality seemed to become more and more sparkling as time went by and as we became better acquainted with her. Since moving from the community in which the young lady lived, I have wondered whether she was successful in changing the somber mood of her parents and whether she has been successful in establishing a happy home of her own. I pray that she has learned this truth: "Happy laughter and friendly voices in the home will keep more kids off the streets at night than the loudest curfew" (Burton Millis).

Moisture or Juice

Elizabeth Gray Vining wrote: "The word humor, according to the Oxford Dictionary, originally meant moisture or juice and only fairly recently, that is to say from the 17th century, came to mean that quality of action, speech or writing which excites amusement, or the faculty of perceiving what is ludicrous or amusing. *As anyone who has experienced the lubricating effect of even a small joke in a household well knows, humor still has an element of juice. It keeps life from drying up, gives it freshness and flavor"*(italics added).

Learning under the tutelage of a stoic and humorless teacher is much like eating an orange that has already been juiced. The instruction is dry, tasteless, and without flavor. Under such a condition the pulp of the subject is difficult to swallow, and the desire for more is quenched almost before the first mouthful. It is the same living with and learning under the direction of a humorless father or mother in the home. Without "spoons full of sugar" or spoons full of humor, parental teachings do not go down very well.

"The sense of humor," states C. S. Merriam, "is the oil of life's engine. Without it, the machinery creaks and groans. No lot is so hard, no aspect of things is so grim, but it relaxes before a hearty laugh."

Humor Heals

In his delightful book *Anatomy of an Illness*, Norman Cousins includes some interesting thoughts on humor. Some of the thoughts are his own and others are statements made by noted persons. Included in his writing are the following, along with some personal comments of my own:

• Sir William Osler regarded laughter as the "music of life" (Norman Cousins, *Anatomy of an Illness* [New York: Bantam Books, 1979], p. 85). This is particularly true when the melodious laughter of children is allowed to blend with the laughter of parents. Such mirth is a sure indicator of harmony in the home.

• Robert Burton observed that "humor purges the blood, making the body young, lively, and fit for any manner of employment" (p. 84). I am not familiar with the chemical changes within the human body resulting from good humor and laughter. I do know, however, that good humor can alleviate feelings of stress, change one's outlook on life, and rid the body of many negative influences.

• Immanuel Kant stated that "he never knew a man who possessed the gift of hearty laughter to be burdened by constipation" (p. 84). I don't know of any medical evidence that would support this claim, but the older I grow the more plausible this statement seems.

• Norman Cousins said, "It has always seemed to me that hearty laughter is a good way to jog internally without having to go outdoors" (p. 84). Have you ever laughed to the extent that you felt physically spent and emotionally drained? If you have, the words of Cousins make sense. Hearty and appropriate laughter is stretching to the spirit, just as jogging is stimulating to the physical body.

• Cousins also said that laughter is "as specific and tangible as any other form of physical exercise" (p. 85). He added: "It provides internal exercise for a person flat on his or her back — a form of jogging for the innards. . . . It creates a mood in which the other positive emotions can be put to work, too. In short, it helps make it possible for good things to happen" (pp. 145–46).

• It is said of Albert Schweitzer that "his use of humor . . . was so artistic that one had the feeling he almost regarded it as a musical instrument" (p. 82). Schweitzer was an "artist" of religion and music. He knew the importance of timing and the use of appropriate selections. And his renditions of humor were allowed to complement his organ and piano renditions.

Cousins claimed that humor was a major factor in curing his life-threatening illness. It was his feeling that humor had an anesthetic effect upon him when he needed some pain-free sleep. He also regarded humor as therapy and became an expert on slapstick comedy.

I, too, have experienced the healing influence of good humor. At a critical time during a recent illness, my bishop delivered a box full of cards, drawings, and messages prepared by the Primary children of my home ward. Some had tried their hand at verse; others expressed themselves in sketches and cut-outs. All were sweet remembrances that touched my heart.

A number of the greetings, however, were very funny. For example, one young lad drew a picture of me stretched out on a coffin. Protruding out of my chest was a single rose. Off to the side of the sketch were these words: "Please get well, but if not, have fun!" I laughed so loud and hard that the nurses came rushing into the room, wondering what was wrong. Those moments of humor were lifting to my spirits and, I believe, healing to my body.

Good and Bad Humor

Like almost everything else in life, humor has both a good and a bad side. It can heal, or it can hurt; it has the power to lift and the power to pull down; it can exalt, or it can demean.

Those who use it in or out of the home must be prudent and wise so that it blesses rather than curses others.

The various types of humor are described plainly in the following words: "There is a humor that heals, a humor that helps, and a humor that harms and hurts. And one kind of humor that hurts is the humor that brings embarrassing attention to adverse personal attributes and physical features; the humor, for example, that ridicules what people can't help: The 'baldy,' 'fatty,' 'skinny,' 'stand-up-shorty' kind of humor that is, at best, unkind, and is, at worst, cruel and crude and cutting" (Richard L. Evans).

"The manner of jesting ought not to be extravagant or immoderate, but refined and witty. . . . There are, generally speaking, two sorts of jests: The one, coarse, rude, vicious, indecent; the other polite, refined, clever, witty [which], if well timed, is becoming to the most dignified person. The other is unfit for any gentleman" (Cicero).

In my youth, I shared a questionable story with a friend as my parents listened in. I thought the account was most humorous despite its light-mindedness. My friend felt the same as I did and laughed heartily. Mother and Father, however, didn't even smile. After some awkward moments, my mother said to me in a soft voice, "Carlos, I never thought that I would ever hear you speak such degrading words."

Elder Richard L. Evans taught:

> Humor is essential to a full and happy life. It is a reliever and relaxer of pressure and tension, and the saving element in many situations. But there are different kinds of humor, prompted by different spirits, some sincere, some unacceptable. There is a delightful, wholesome humor that heals and helps the spirit and gives a lift to life. There is giddy, trivial humor that produces light-minded laughter — the all-but-vacant and inconsequential kind that comes with little content, little cause. There is evil humor, grim humor, humor that embarrasses, and humor that is cruel, unkind.

There is humor that is unclean, and that has no place among considerate people or in decent society. There is an account of a man who cautioned a speaker against telling off-color stories, because, said he, "There are ladies present" — to which someone added the observation that there were also gentlemen present. The assumption that something suggestive, low-minded, or unclean is all right in one kind of audience but not in another is a questionable assumption. Anything filthy or basically unclean is wrong in any audience (*Improvement Era*, February 1968, p. 71).

Though I still enjoy a *good* story and have sought to maintain a sense of humor, I have never forgotten my mother's disappointment in me. To this day, my rule-of-thumb in telling stories or in using humor is to share only those accounts that I feel might appropriately be told in the presence of my mother.

Guidelines

Here are some added guidelines for the use of humor that may prove helpful. Such guidelines apply to the use of humor in any situation, particularly in the home:

• *Look for the humor in tense situations.* Don't allow circumstances to control your moods. An out-of-humor person is not pleasant to be around.

• *Laugh more at yourself than at others.* Fun at the expense of others is too expensive. If anyone is to be the brunt of a joke, let it be yourself. "You grow up the day you have your first real laugh — at yourself" (Ethel Barrymore).

• *Be conscious of the feelings of others.* There is no place for sick humor — the humor that demeans others and injures feelings. "The best humor," said William Makepeace Thackeray, "is that which contains the most humanity, that which is flavored throughout with tenderness and kindness." The worst humor, if it may be called humor, is sarcasm or cutting remarks that dampen the spirit of others.

• *Keep it clean.* Don't permit the use of smutty or suggestive stories. Said Goethe, "By nothing do men show their character more than by the things they laugh at."

• *Use humor as the means, not the end, of conversation.* I was told of a man who performed brilliantly before an audience, cracking one joke after another. Later, he asked a colleague to evaluate his talk. The response: "Some of the listeners will remember some of your stories and jokes, but I question whether any of the people will remember any of the truths you 'danced' around."

• *Shun the "cute syndrome."* Those who try to be "cute" in the presence of others often value entertainment and social reassurances more than propriety, honesty, and accuracy. Their humor is short-lived, if lived at all.

• *Watch the timing.* Ill-timed humor is worse than no humor at all. It is capable of injuring when healing was the intent. But if the timing is right, humor can serve as a safety valve and release pent-up emotions. President Hugh B. Brown commented: "A wholesome sense of humor will be a safety valve that will enable you to apply the lighter touch to heavy problems and to learn some lessons in problem solving that 'sweat and tears' often fail to dissolve. A line from Proverbs advises us that 'a merry heart doeth good like a medicine: but a broken spirit drieth the bones' (Proverbs 17:22)." (*Conference Report,* April 1968, p. 100.)

• *Avoid excesses.* Don't let the laughter get out of hand. A quiet story or joke that provokes a simple chuckle can easily grow into an exchange of crude guffaws unless some restraint is exercised. In one scripture, we read, "Do these things with thanksgiving, with cheerful hearts and countenances, not with much laughter, for this is sin, but with a glad heart and a cheerful countenance" (D&C 59:15).

Happiness

Reference to a "glad heart" and a "cheerful countenance" 6reminds us of a statement made by the Prophet Joseph Smith.

Said he, "Happiness is the object and design of our existence; and will be the end thereof, if we pursue the path that leads to it; and this path is virtue, uprightness, faithfulness, holiness, and keeping all the commandments of God" (*Teachings of the Prophet Joseph Smith*, sel. Joseph Fielding Smith [Salt Lake City: Deseret Book Co., 1938], pp. 255–56).

Much has been written about the purpose of our existence. It is significant that the plan of salvation or the gospel of Jesus Christ is referred to as "the great plan of happiness" (Alma 42:8, 16). It is interesting to note that Lehi "beheld a tree, whose fruit was desirable to make one happy" (1 Nephi 8:10). It is noteworthy that Alma warned his son that "wickedness never was happiness" (Alma 41:10). All of these scriptures and many more instruct us that life can and should be a time of happiness, and that we can live happily if we keep the commandments and labor for the happiness of others.

No, life was not meant to be a frivolous experience or a quest for worldly pleasure. Happiness — true happiness — is the goal. That type of happiness is described beautifully by Elder James E. Talmage:

> Happiness includes all that is really desirable and of true worth in pleasure, and much beside. Happiness is genuine gold, pleasure but gilded brass, which corrodes in the hand, and is soon converted into poisonous verdigris. Happiness is as the genuine diamond, which, rough or polished, shines with its own inimitable luster; pleasure is as the paste imitation that glows only when artificially embellished. Happiness is as the ruby, red as the heart's blood, hard and enduring; pleasure, as stained glass, soft, brittle, and of but transitory beauty.
>
> Happiness is true food, wholesome, nutritious and sweet; it builds up the body and generates energy for action, physical, mental and spiritual. . . .
>
> Happiness leaves no bad after-taste, it is followed by no depressing reaction; it calls for no repentance, brings no regret, entails no remorse. . . .

True happiness is lived over and over again in memory, always with a renewal of the original good. . . .
Happiness is not akin with levity, nor is it one with light-minded mirth. It springs from the deeper fountains of the soul, and is not infrequently accompanied by tears. Have you never been so happy that you have had to weep? I have ("A Greeting to the Missionaries," *Improvement Era*, December 1913, p. 173).

In the minds of many, religion is a supremely solemn proposition, something almost devoid of happiness. Suffering, deprivation, seclusion, extreme seriousness, limited funeral-parlor conversation, and other aspects of a weary life are seen as appropriate observances of religion. This fallacious notion is refuted by latter-day prophets. Note their words:

I do not believe the Lord intends and desires that we should pull a long face and look sanctimonious and hypocritical. I think he expects us to be happy and of a cheerful countenance (Joseph F. Smith, Jr., *Conference Report*, October 1916, p. 70).

I have never believed that in order to be righteous one must be sad-faced and solemn. People approved of the Lord have always been those who have laughed and danced and sung as well as worshipped, but at all times within the proper bounds and not to excess (Harold B. Lee).

Good humor expressed in the home must become a contributor to happiness. It should be free of "light-mindedness," of a "bad after-taste," and of similar negative effects. It should be full of nutrition, renewing to the spirit, and building in every respect. In the end, it must be allowed to gladden the heart and give rise to the cheerful countenance.

Joy

A discussion of good humor and happiness would be incomplete without some reference to the gospel concept of joy.

Good humor, I believe, contributes towards one's happiness; happiness can grow into joy.

Joy is one of the fruits of the Spirit (see Galatians 5:22). It is a fruit of missionary service (see Alma 29:9). It was a part of the message given to herald the birth of Jesus: "I bring you good tidings of great joy" (Luke 2:10). In a modern declaration, the Lord states, "In me your joy is full" (D&C 101:36). These and a string of other scriptures help us to understand something about the inspired couplet, "Adam fell that men might be; and men are, that they might have joy" (2 Nephi 2:25).

How is this joy obtained? I believe that President Marion G. Romney said it best: "The key to happiness (or joy) is to get the Spirit and keep it" (*Conference Report*, October 1961, p. 61). The Spirit will not abide with us unless we watch our thoughts, our words, and our deeds, and "observe the commandments of God" (see Mosiah 4:29–30).

If joy is the fruit of one's living, happiness is the plant, and good humor, as mentioned previously, is the juice that gives the fruit its flavor.

A Model

The Prophet Joseph Smith, by his own admission, sought "jovial company" and possessed a "cheery temperament" (Joseph Smith–History 1:28). There is no question that he was a seeker of joy and happiness, and he had a place for humor in his life. It is written of him:

> *The Prophet recognized as unhealthy the mind that lacked balance, perspective, and humor.* In the society of his day there were many earnest people who habitually looked on the serious side of things that had no serious side, who regarded humor as incompatible with religion. It was common for these descendants of the Puritans to see displays of humor as a mark of insincerity. For humor suggested that nothing really mattered and that life was basically comic. To be overly humorous, they thought, was to be cynical toward life.

But Joseph Smith saw humor and religion as quite reconcilable. As he saw it, once one acknowledges that there is something beyond laughter—a core of life that is solemn, serious, and tender—there is still plenty of room for jesting. At least, that is the way he was—"a jolly good fellow" as one contemporary described him (Leonard J. Arrington, "Joseph Smith and the Lighter View," *New Era*, August 1976, p. 10; italics added).

Happy Homes

We are warned against the evils of loud laughter, evil-speaking, light-mindedness, and other forms of shallow living that make a mockery of sacred things. Yet we are expected to keep our homes warm and inviting to all who cross the threshold. We must, therefore, find the proper balance between the "core of life" or pure religion and the "spice of life" in planting the "pecan tree" practice of good humor in our families.

President Ezra Taft Benson declared: "One great thing the Lord requires of each of us is to provide a home where a happy, positive influence for good exists. In future years the costliness of home furnishings or the number of bathrooms will not matter much, but what will matter significantly is whether our children felt love and acceptance in the home. *It will greatly matter whether there was happiness and laughter,* or bickering and contention" (Ezra Taft Benson, *Ensign*, April 1981, p. 34; italics added).

Without humor, the home can become cold and uninviting. Parents are seen as ogres, and children are regarded as things to be seen and not heard. The atmosphere can become tense, and the relationships between family members can become strained. With appropriate and good humor, however, the "inner man or woman" is provided quiet refreshment through jovial company and lively conversation.

Remember always:

If thou art merry, praise the Lord with singing, with music, with dancing, and with a prayer of praise and thanksgiving. If thou art sorrowful, call on the Lord thy God with supplication, that your souls may be joyful (D&C 136:28–29).

CHAPTER NINE

PERSONAL AND FAMILY HISTORIES

*Whatsoever things we write upon anything save it
be upon plates must perish and vanish away; but
we can write a few words upon plates, which will
give our children, and also our beloved brethren,
a small degree of knowledge concerning us, or concerning their fathers (Jacob 4:2).*

There are two general approaches to personal and family histories. One approach is taken by genealogists who *dig* or research into the past looking for facts and artifacts that tie one
generation to another. The second approach is taken by record-
keepers who *plant* or preserve information for the good of
children, grandchildren, and unborn posterity. Both historical
efforts are essential, for they produce information that serves
as a "welding link" between generations and turn "the heart
of the fathers to the children, and the heart of the children to
their fathers" (D&C 128:18; Malachi 4:6).

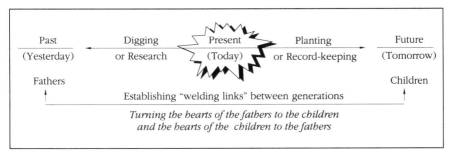

Since all of us are expected to invest ourselves in *digging* and *planting* personal and family histories, I shall discuss each approach in turn. My intent is not to make historiographers of all readers; I have neither the expertise nor space to accomplish this task. Rather, my intent is to help readers understand what records are important, why histories must be written, and how we may become involved in history-making and soul-saving activities.

"Digging" History (Research)

The Lord said to Moses, "This is my work and my glory—to bring to pass the immortality and eternal life of man" (Moses 1:39). This is a short and powerful declaration of God's avowed purpose; however, what does it really mean? Such meaning emerges from an understanding of the two pivotal words contained in the statement: *immortality* and *eternal life.* When we compare these words, we can see some interesting distinctions or comparisons:

IMMORTALITY		ETERNAL LIFE
• is to live forever in the resurrected state with body and spirit inseparably connected.	Focal Point: Christ's Atonement	• is the kind of life that our Eternal Father lives–God's life is eternal life.
• is victory over physical death (Alma 11:42, 45).		• is victory over spiritual death (Alma 11:40-41; 12:16-18).
• is a free gift that comes by grace alone without works on our part.		• results from obedience to the laws and ordinances of the gospel.
• is a gift for all people.		• is a synergistic product of God's grace and our good works.
• comes through Christ's resurrection.		
• is universal salvation.		• is promised only to the righteous (repentant) and obedient.
• is unconditional salvation.		• is individual salvation.
		• is unconditional salvation.

Three general conclusions may be drawn from this chart. They are:

1. There is "no other name given nor any other way nor means whereby salvation can come unto the children of men, only in and through the name of Christ, the Lord Omnipotent" (Mosiah 3:17).

2. Immortality is an accomplished fact; it is guaranteed to all members of Adam's family.

3. Eternal life is the burning issue of the moment; it is God's greatest gift to all people and will be claimed by those who exercise the faith to repent, obey divine laws, receive gospel ordinances, engage in good works, and endure to the end (see D&C 14:7).

Obviously, living men and women may fulfill the conditions of eternal life by accepting the truth as it is preached to them, submitting themselves to saving ordinances (such as baptism, celestial marriage, and so on) and by living righteously. But what about those millions of people who have lived upon the earth and never heard the name of Christ? Are they loved any less by God — the same God who gave them life? Are their souls less precious to God than the souls of those who are privileged to live in the Dispensation of the Fulness of Times? (see Alma 39:17–19).

Our minds are set at rest about these questions when we read and ponder the scriptures and the words of modern prophets, for it is through revealed truths that we learn of doctrines pertaining to salvation for the dead. We learn that the gospel is preached to those who are dead and who have not had the opportunity to hear of Jesus Christ. The Savior himself was involved in this missionary effort (see 1 Peter 3:19–20; 4:6; D&C 138:30–34). We learn that baptism for the dead was performed in New Testament times and reinstituted during the nineteenth century, after the holy priesthood was restored to the earth (see 1 Corinthians 15:29; D&C 128:15–18). Yes, we learn that "God is no respecter of persons: but in every nation [and in every age, I might add] he that feareth him, and worketh righteousness, is accepted with him" (Acts 10:34–35).

With these truths planted in our minds and hearts, the "true believers in Jesus Christ" (Alma 46:14) immerse themselves in the work for their kindred dead; that is, they *dig* history as genealogists and strive to identify individuals and family members who have not had the saving ordinances performed in their behalf. Names are found, family lines traced, dates established, and past generations tied to the living generation. Said Elder Dallin H. Oaks: "The process by which we identify our place in our eternal family is called genealogy. Genealogy is family history" (Regional Representatives Seminar, April 3, 1987).

The purpose of digging or researching family history is explained succinctly by David H. Pratt: "LDS interest in family history is based on the fundamental doctrines of salvation, agency, and exaltation. It is the plan of God that all persons shall have the opportunity to hear the gospel of Jesus Christ and receive the saving ordinances, regardless of when they lived on earth. If they do not hear the gospel preached through the Lord's authorized servants in this life, they will hear it in the spirit world after death. Latter-day Saints identify their ancestors and arrange for baptism and other ordinances to be performed by proxy—that is, with a living person standing in for the deceased person—in a temple. This is not an optional function of LDS belief: it is, rather, a commandment of God. As Elder Oaks further explained, 'We are not hobbyists in genealogy work. We do family history work in order to provide the ordinances of salvation for the living *and the dead*' (*Ensign*, 19 [June 1989]:6)" ("Family History, Genealogy," *Encyclopedia of Mormonism* [New York: Macmillan Publishing Co., 1991], p. 492; italics added).

Some bystanders observe the Latter-day Saints digging the records and moving in and out of the temple in rapid succession and ask: Why are you so intent in getting this work done?

Why do you store the volumes of records and labor with the computers? We respond with the words of Joseph Smith, the Prophet. He wrote: "Let me assure you that these are principles in relation to the dead and the living that cannot be lightly passed over, as pertaining to our salvation. For their salvation is necessary and essential to our salvation, as Paul says concerning the fathers — that they without us cannot be made perfect — neither can we without our dead be made perfect" (D&C 128:15).

We add the words of Brigham Young: "We have a work to do just as important in its sphere as the Savior's work was in its sphere. . . . We are now called upon to do ours; which is to be the greatest work man ever performed on the earth. . . . All the angels in heaven are looking at this little handful of people, and stimulating them to the salvation of the human family" (*Journal of Discourses,* 18:213, 304).

If the work for the dead is something that "cannot be lightly passed over" and something that "all the angels of heaven are looking at," little wonder that President Wilford Woodruff declared: "We want the Latter day Saints from this time to trace their genealogies as far as they can, and to be sealed to their fathers and mothers. Have children sealed to their parents, and run this chain through as far as you can get it. . . . This is the will of the Lord to this people . . . we have got to enter into those temples and redeem our dead — not only the dead of our own family, but the dead of the whole spirit world" (*Messages of the First Presidency* 3:256–57).

"Digging" or researching personal and family history must not be regarded as just a hobby or another way of idling away one's free time. Actually, it is a matter of life or death! Unless we seek out our dead and perform vicarious ordinances in their behalf, their progress is stopped and their possibilities of obtaining eternal life are placed in abeyance. We must, therefore, look to the past as genealogists and link ourselves to our fathers. Moreover, we must become partners with the

Savior — even saviors on Mount Zion (Obadiah 1:21) — by doing for dead ancestors things that they cannot do for themselves.

"Greater love hath no man than this," said Jesus, "that a man lay down his life for his friends" (John 15:13). No one is asked to give up his or her life in fulfilling family history responsibilities. Intense suffering in Gethsemane or a walk to Calvary is not a requirement for any of us. All that is expected of us is that we think of others and sacrifice some time and effort. In the process, we demonstrate our love of God and of forebears who have left us blessings without number.

President Joseph Fielding Smith had this to say about love for humankind and family history and temple work: "It is a work that enlarges the soul of man, broadens his views regarding the welfare of his fellowman, and *plants in his heart* a love for all the children of our Heavenly Father. There is no work equal to that in the temple for the dead in teaching a man to love his neighbor as himself" (*Doctrines of Salvation,* vol. 2 [Salt Lake City: Bookcraft, 1793], p. 144; italics added).

"Planting" History (Recording)

Let us now turn our attention to the second approach to personal and family history — the approach I call "planting" or recording history.

A noted scholar wrote: "If nothing were to remain of present-day American culture a thousand years hence but a single one-cent piece, any historian of that day would nevertheless be able to make some shrewd guesses about the man who designed the coin, and still more about the civilization in which he lived, merely from a careful analysis of the coin itself. Even a casual glance at the Lincoln penny will suffice to prove that statement" (Louis Gottschalk, *Understanding History* [New York: Alfred A. Knopf, 1965], pp. 87–88).

Take out a penny and look at it. You will note that it reveals a culture that had some knowledge of metallurgy and agriculture; of dies and engravings; of barbering; of cloth and tailoring; of English and Latin; of Arabic numerals; of chronology and geography; of God ("In God We Trust"), liberty, and political confederation ("E Pluribus Unum" — out of many, one); of arithmetic and the decimal system; and perhaps of other cultural features.

Gottschalk's provocative statement about culture and a coin causes me to wonder about the legacy we will leave our posterity. I wonder whether you and I will leave behind us, when we complete our mortal experiences, evidences of our faith, love, belief in God, devotion to family, and other "pennies" of worth. I wonder what our grandchildren, great-grandchildren, and others in some future generation will guess about us after examining our remnants, such as memories, traditions, family folklore, records, histories, artifacts, pictures, and other traces of our existence.

Journals and Records

During the three years I served abroad in an Area Presidency for the Church, I kept a record I referred to as my "Narrative Report." I was not required to write this account, nor was I asked to submit it to Church Headquarters. Nonetheless, I maintained this monthly history because I wanted to preserve memories and evidences of my stay in Europe. I wanted proof beyond doubt that I was actually there, that my ministry was sprinkled generously with spiritual experiences, and that the Lord blessed me in the calling.

The report contained a log of my travels in Africa, the British Isles, Europe, the Middle East, and beyond. In it are the names of people I met and the experiences we shared. Highlighted, of course, are many, many spiritual and faith-promoting experiences.

Who knows? Perhaps someday my narrative report (now bound professionally and placed in the family library) will be the means of lifting a sagging soul or inspiring a progenitor to serve a mission. It will certainly enable readers to know me better, for much of "me" is preserved in it. Most important of all, those who read my report, whether tomorrow or a hundred years hence, will have no cause to question my love of God or speculate about the depth of my faith.

One of President Spencer W. Kimball's own journal entries of July 1951 reads: "I might hope that my children will take from my many journals and write a simple story or biography for me. I would like for my posterity to remember me and to know that I have tried so hard to measure up and to live worthy."

My European report was not my first attempt at record-keeping. I maintained religiously a missionary journal (day-by-day) while serving in the Holy Land years ago. That record was priceless when written and gains added value with each passing year. In it are two types of entries — the day-to-day happenings and the collection of spiritual and unusual experiences. I relive the mission each time I peruse the journal, and so will my children and grandchildren live my mission vicariously when they read what I have written. In the end, perhaps the journal will help to turn the hearts of my children to their father (see D&C 2:2).

Records — Language — Faith

One need not probe very deeply into the scriptures to learn that record-keeping is a well-established expectancy in the eyes of the Lord. Father Adam, earth's first man, was commanded to keep a book of remembrance. It is written: "And a book of remembrance was kept, in the which was recorded, in the language of Adam, for it was given unto as many as called upon God to write by the spirit of inspiration; and by them their children were taught to read and write, having a language which was pure and undefiled" (Moses 6:5–6).

This scripture turns our minds to another scripture about records and language. You will recall that Lehi sent his sons back to Jerusalem at the peril of losing their lives to obtain the plates of brass in the custody of Laban. Such action was justified in these terms: "It is wisdom in God that we should obtain these records, that *we may preserve unto our children the language of our fathers;* and also that *we may preserve unto them the words which have been spoken by the mouth of all the holy prophets,* which have been delivered unto them by the Spirit and power of God, since the world began, even down unto this present time" (1 Nephi 3:19–20; italics added).

Who can doubt the "wisdom in God" concerning records, language, and the words of prophets? In the Book of Mormon, we read of a people who left Jerusalem at the time of King Zedekiah. This group, however, brought no records, as did Lehi and his family. Hence, "their language had become corrupted; and . . . they denied the being of their Creator" (Omni 1:17).

Three Lessons in Record-Keeping

Over and above the corruption of language and the loss of faith, other problems may develop in the absence of conscientious record-keeping and reporting, such as:

Loss of the priesthood. The children of an ancient people were "put from the priesthood" because some records were neglected, as recorded in the book of Ezra: "Of the children of the priests: the children of Habaiah, the children of Koz, the children of Barzillai; which took a wife of the daughters of Barzillai the Gileadite, and was called after their name: These sought their register among those that were reckoned by genealogy, but they were not found: therefore were they, as polluted, put from the priesthood" (Ezra 2:61–62).

Loss of faith-promoting experiences. After his resurrection, the Savior taught the Nephites a direct and very important lesson. He insisted that something which had been overlooked by the record-keepers be added to the books. Said Jesus: "How be it that ye have not written this thing, that many saints did arise and appear unto many and did minister unto them?"

117

Then, "Nephi remembered that this thing had not been written. And it came to pass that Jesus commanded that it should be written; therefore it was written according as he commanded" (3 Nephi 23:11–13).

Loss of Church members. In conformity with what the Lord had counseled earlier about the need to know, number, and minister to the Saints (see 3 Nephi 18:31–32), the early inhabitants of the Americas followed this procedure: "After they had been received unto baptism, and were wrought upon and cleansed by the power of the Holy Ghost, they were numbered among the people of the church of Christ; and their names were taken, that they might be remembered and nourished by the good word of God, to keep them in the right way, to keep them continually watchful unto prayer, relying alone upon the merits of Christ, who was the author and the finisher of their faith" (Moroni 6:4).

Records – Thoughts

I have always been impressed by the wisdom of King Mosiah. When some records were delivered to him, he "read, and caused to be read" to his people the two accounts (Mosiah 25:15). He did this, I believe, to teach his subjects some valuable lessons and to evoke some poignant thoughts. I quote three verses:

• "When they thought of their brethren who had been slain . . . they were filled with sorrow, and even shed many *tears of sorrow."*

• "When they thought of the immediate goodness of God, and his power in delivering Alma and his brethren . . . they did raise their voices and *give thanks to God."*

• "When they thought upon the Lamanites, who were their brethren, of their sinful and polluted state, they were *filled with pain and anguish for the welfare of their souls"* (Mosiah 25:9–11; italics added).

Mosiah's intent was not to entertain his listeners. His pur-

118

pose in reading the histories of Zeniff and Alma was to humble his own followers and to help them profit from the mistakes of others. Thus, by use of the recorded materials, he took his people from the depths of sorrow to the peak of concern for the welfare of their enemies. And, whether he intended to do so or not, he surely must have reinforced in the minds of his listeners many of the reasons for record-keeping, including those already cited, which are:

• The preservation of language.
• The preservation of the words of the prophets.
• The preservation of lineage and priesthood rights.
• The preservation of faith-promoting experiences.
• The retention of Church members.
• The preservation of personal memories.
• The welding of the readers (children) to the writers (parents).

These reasons and others that could be listed should convince us of the need to plant the "pecan tree" practice of personal and family histories. It should be our desire to "keep a proper and faithful record" of our lives (see D&C 128:9). In the end, we will have preserved for ourselves and for future generations a handful of "pennies" of worth.

President Spencer W. Kimball promised: "Those who keep a book of remembrance [or other historical records] are more likely to keep the Lord in remembrance in their daily lives. Journals [and similar books] are a way of counting our blessings and of leaving an inventory of these blessings for our posterity" (*The Teachings of Spencer W. Kimball*, ed. Edward L. Kimball [Salt Lake City: Bookcraft, 1982], pp. 349–50).

Types of Records

Many types of records are used to compile personal and family histories. Each has its place, each serves its purpose, and each tells its story. But when many records are passed to the rising generation the story becomes more complete and more enticing to the "children."

Here are but a few of the records that deserve our attention:

1. Photo albums. Years ago, whenever our family visited Grandpa and Grandma Asay's home, the children would rush to the shelf where they stored the family photo albums. They would sit in rapt attention for several minutes as their grandparents turned the pages and spoke about the "olden times." The children loved to note the differences in hair, dress, and other styles between their generation's and that of a bygone era.

One author described the fascination of a family album and the talk about progenitors that it provokes. In reference to his aging sister, he wrote: "And as a sort of dessert she tells us about the Danas, the Aikens and the Carnahans, who are, in various relationships, her progenitors. We gravitate into the other room, and presently she shows us, in the plush album, the portraits of various cousins, aunts, and uncles. And by-and-by Harriet warms up and begins to tell about the Scribrers, the MacIntoshes, and the Strayers, who are *our* progenitors" (David Grayson, *Adventures in Friendship* [Frederick, Colorado: Renaissance House Publishers], pp. 125–26).

2. Vital records. President Joseph Fielding Smith instructed: *"It is necessary for us to keep an accurate record of our families and record accurately the dates of births, marriages and deaths, and ordinances and everything that is vital. Every important event in our lives should be placed in a record, by us individually....* What do we mean by *vital* records? We mean those records containing the dates of *births, marriages,* and *deaths,* the three great events in the life of the individual. Other vital things in the life of members of the Church are to know the dates of *blessing, baptism, ordinations* and other matters that pertain to our welfare and may be of benefit to our posterity (*Doctrines of Salvation,* comp. Bruce R. McConkie, 3 vols. [Salt Lake City: Bookcraft, 1954–56], 2:204, 205).

Sometimes records are kept in Bibles or other books containing pages designed specifically for the recording of vital information. Family group records and pedigree charts published by the Church may also be used for this purpose. Whatever the tool or instrument used, the important thing is to preserve data that is accurate and capable of binding families together.

3. Books of remembrance. Books of remembrance have become rather popular in our day. Many families keep such records and regard them as precious heirlooms, which they are. This means of preserving family information, however, dates back to the days of Adam and his seed. In the book of Moses we read: "A genealogy was kept of the children of God. And this was the book of the generations of Adam. . . . For a *book of remembrance* we have written among us, according to the pattern given by the finger of God; and it is given in our own language" (Moses 6:8, 46; italics added).

Since the pattern for writing a book of remembrance was given by God, it stands to reason that such books would be kept by those who feared or loved the Lord. Note the words of Malachi: "Then they that feared the Lord spake often one to another; and the Lord hearkened, and heard it, and a book of remembrance was written before him for them that feared the Lord, and that thought upon his name" (Malachi 3:16).

4. Personal journals and diaries. One of the greatest advocates of personal journals was President Spencer W. Kimball. Not only was he a model record-keeper himself, but he also shared many practical suggestions on the subject. Listen to his counsel: "Get a notebook. . . . Begin today and write in it your goings and comings, your deepest thoughts, your achievements and your failures, your associations and your triumphs, your impressions and your testimonies" ("The Angels May Quote from It," *New Era,* October 1975, p. 5).

In a later article, President Kimball added:

You should continue on in this important work of

recording the things you do, the things you say, the things you think, to be in accordance with the instructions of the Lord. Your story should be written now while it is fresh and while the true details are available. . . .

Your journal should contain your true self rather than a picture of you when you are "made up" for a public performance. There is a temptation to paint one's virtues in rich color and whitewash the vices, but there is also the opposite pitfall of accentuating the negative. . . .

I promise you that if you will keep your journals and records, they will indeed be a source of great inspiration to your families, to your children, your grandchildren, and others, on through the generations" ("President Kimball Speaks Out on Personal Journals," *Ensign*, December 1980, p. 61).

I don't suppose that President Kimball would care whether you used a notebook or a professionally printed book in which to record your personal story. He would, in all likelihood, say something like this: "Choose your book, and do it!" By listening to a Prophet's voice and taking appropriate action, you, too, will leave a record that will indeed be a source of great inspiration to your family.

5. Autobiographies and biographies. If a person were to compile a detailed account of his or her life, including thoughts, words, and actions, he or she would end up with an autobiography. But few people maintain such complete journals or diaries. Most commonly, the personal journals, books of remembrances, vital records, letters, and so on, are used as resource materials by a writer who tells his or someone else's life story. Such efforts result in the writing of an autobiography or a biography.

Carolyn Gates wrote her life story. She claimed that the project was a catharsis for herself and a blessing to her children: "People now have such a sense of rootlessness and non-belonging. Give children and grandchildren something to live up to and attach to. They can say this is where I came from and where I'm going" (Barbara Bradley, "Writing Your Life Story Will Capture Memories Often Unknown to Younger Kin," *Deseret News,* April 17–18, 1991, p. 2C).

How sad it is when people fail to maintain records and write stories of themselves and loved ones. They allow great men and women to become known to their progenitors as just a name on a headstone, part of a vague memory recounted occasionally in family circles, or something less. Such negligence is an affront to heros and heroines of the past, and such negligence denies blessings to the children of the present.

6. *Oral histories.* A method of preparing a personal or family history that is growing in popularity is the oral history approach. This approach requires an interrogator and a respondent. The one asks carefully worded questions; the other answers, recalling information from memory. Both questions and answers are recorded and later transcribed, reviewed, corrected, and printed. The final product is an oral history.

Since I have been personally involved in the compilation of an oral history, I would offer four suggestions:

• The interrogator must research the subject's life thoroughly and prepare an outline of each phase: ancestry, childhood, education, mission, and so on.

• Recording sessions must be scheduled so that adequate time is allowed for reflection and recall.

• In reviewing and polishing the transcription, the subject must not erase himself or herself from the account (this can happen if language is changed radically and style of presentation altered).

• A professionally printed and bound copy of the history will add dignity to the project and entice broader readership (see chapter 7).

7. *Memorabilia chests.* Most families collect and store in files or boxes heirlooms of one sort or another. These heirlooms may include pieces of clothing, jewelry, letters, silver-

ware, and many other collector's items. Each item tells its own story and testifies of the reality of a person or an event. When preserved and accompanied by a written explanation of its significance, the articles make the children of the present feel closer to the fathers and mothers of the past.

Years ago, Elder Boyd K. Packer offered an approach to personal histories that involves collection boxes, the phasing of one's life, vital records, and other things already discussed. It is worth repeating. Said he:

> There is a place to begin. You don't need to begin with the pedigree charts or the stacks of forms, or the blank spaces, or the numbers, the procedures, or the regulations. You can begin with *you*. . . .
>
> There are two very simple instructions. Here's what you are to do:
>
> Get a cardboard box. Any kind of box will do. Put it some place where it is in the way . . . anywhere where it cannot go unnoticed. Then, over a period of a few weeks, collect and put into the box every record of your life . . . everything that you can find pertaining to your life — anything that is written or registered or recorded that testifies that you are alive and what you have done.
>
> Don't try to do this in a day. Take your time with it. Most of us have these things scattered around here and there. . . .
>
> Gather all of these together; put them in the box. Keep it there until you have collected everything you think you have. Then . . . sort out all that you have collected. Divide your life into three periods . . . [child], youth, and adult.
>
> Start with the childhood section and begin with your birth certificate. Put together every record in chronological order. . . .
>
> Once you have that accomplished you have what is necessary to complete your life story. Simply take your birth certificate and begin writing. . . .
>
> It really won't take you long to write, or dictate into

a tape recorder, the account of your life, and it will have an accuracy because you have collected those records.

Now don't say that you can't collect them. All you are asked to do is to collect what information you have and what you know. It is your obligation" ("Someone Up There Loves You," *Ensign*, January 1977, pp. 10–11).

8. *Pedigree charts, family group sheets, and other family history forms used in the Church.* There are carefully designed and printed forms used in the Church for the submission of names to the temples for processing. Such forms include Individual Entry, Personal Record, Marriage Entry, Family Group Record, Pedigree Chart, and others.

In fulfillment of a divine expectation, we should use these forms so that individuals may be properly identified and so that saving ordinances may be performed in behalf of the dead in holy temples.

I have mentioned eight types of records used in developing personal and family histories. By way of review, they are: photo albums, vital records, books of remembrance, journals and diaries, autobiographies and biographies, oral histories, memorabilia chests, and Church family history forms. I have said nothing about scrapbooks, tape recordings, filmstrips, videos, and other means of preserving the treasures of the ever-changing generations.

It is left to you to choose the means most suitable to you and to your circumstances for the creation of histories. You may elect to start with one type of record and branch off into others as your time permits and as your interests expand.

As Elder Dallin H. Oaks counseled, "Our effort is not to compel everyone to do everything, but to encourage everyone to do something" (*Ensign,* June 1989, p. 6).

Conclusion

I have written about God's purposes, eternal life, genealogical research, saving ordinances, and temple activities. All of these subjects relate to the "digging" aspect of personal and family history. And all of these subjects remind us of the need to become "saviors on Mount Zion" (see Obadiah 1:21).

I have also written about pictures, memorabilia, biographies, and other traces of our existence. These traces, much like the Lincoln penny, will verify that we actually walked the earth and occupied a space in history. But whether those who pick up our remnants choose to follow in our footsteps will depend largely upon *what* we leave, *where* we leave it, and *how* we leave it. Such remnants will indicate the extent of our involvement in "planting" personal and family histories and our success in becoming "saviors of men" (see D&C 103:9–10).

The process of being "saviors on Mount Zion" and "saviors of men" is indeed humbling, particularly when one contemplates this statement of George Q. Cannon: "When you think that you are chosen to be saviors to the children of men, to stand as a medium through whom salvation shall flow unto unnumbered thousands, what manner of people ought we to be? They pray for you today in the spirit world, as they have been no doubt from the beginning praying for their descendants, that they may be faithful to the truth" (*Journal of Discourses*, 22:131).

In summary, I share the illustration on the following page:

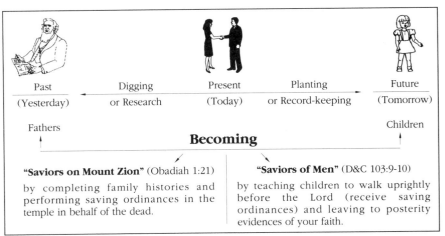

Past	Digging	Present	Planting	Future
(Yesterday)	or Research	(Today)	or Record-keeping	(Tomorrow)

Fathers ╵   **Becoming**   Children ╵

"Saviors on Mount Zion" (Obadiah 1:21)	**"Saviors of Men"** (D&C 103:9-10)
by completing family histories and performing saving ordinances in the temple in behalf of the dead.	by teaching children to walk uprightly before the Lord (receive saving ordinances) and leaving to posterity evidences of your faith.

I can promise you that a special spirit surrounds this work—the spirit of Elijah. So, I admonish us all to place the "pecan tree" practice of personal and family histories in our lives and to retain in mind these words:

In our pre-existent state, in the day of the great council, we made a certain agreement with the Almighty. The Lord proposed a plan, conceived by him. We accepted it. Since the plan is intended for all men, we become parties to the salvation of every person under the plan. We agreed, right then and there, to be not only saviors for ourselves, but measurably saviors for the whole human family. We went into a partnership with the Lord. The working out of the plan became then not merely the Father's work, and the Savior's work, but also our work. The least of us, the humblest, is in partnership with the Almighty in achieving the purpose of the eternal plan of salvation (John A. Widtsoe, "The Worth of Souls," Utah Genealogical and Historical Magazine, *October 1934, p. 189).*

CHAPTER TEN

FAMILY ORGANIZATIONS

Organize yourselves; prepare every needful thing, and establish a house, even a house of prayer, a house of fasting, a house of faith, a house of learning, a house of glory, a house of order, a house of God (D&C 109:8).

In the January 1977 issue of the *Ensign*, an article entitled "Six Families Tell How (and Why) They Organized" contained this account:

> My father died when I was a boy and left my mother with ten children to raise. I remember hearing my mother express her feeling that he would come back and visit us and let us know that he was thinking of us. That impressed me. I remember wondering when he would come, if he did at all. I went to a solemn assembly in the St. George Temple, almost expecting to see him, but he didn't come.
>
> Then a few years ago, my brothers and sisters got together and organized our family. We went to a priesthood genealogy seminar in the day and talked in the evening and, under the inspiration of the Spirit, drew up the constitution and bylaws for our family. Then we called a meeting of all our father's children and grandchildren over eight years of age. We had a great meeting. The Spirit was there; and after the meeting, one of the little granddaughters said to her mother, "Mama, who was that man standing by Grandma all

during the meeting?" Our hearts burned within us as we realized that our father had been there at *his* meeting. That solemn assembly was not for him, but how could he think of missing his own family meeting, organizing in his name? I testify that the veil is very thin when families meet, and often family members from both sides attend (J Ballard Washburn, *Ensign,* January 1977, p. 38).

Those who believe in the eternal nature of the family unit appreciate the sacredness of the experience related by Elder Washburn. Such true believers know that the veil between the living and the dead is indeed thin—only a heartbeat separates the one from the other. They also know that couples, like Grandma and Grandpa Washburn, can be sealed for time and for all eternity, and that family ties are not broken by that temporary separation we call death. So, why wouldn't the deceased attend a family gathering held on earth? Why wouldn't the deceased show interest in a family organization that works in behalf of both mortals and immortals?

Binding—Turning

An ancient prophet declared: "The day cometh that shall burn as an oven, and all the proud, yea, and all that do wickedly shall burn as stubble; for they that come shall burn them, saith the Lord of Hosts, that it shall leave them neither root nor branch. . . . Behold I will reveal unto you the Priesthood, by the hand of Elijah the prophet, before the coming of the great and dreadful day of the Lord. . . . And he shall plant in the hearts of the children the promises made to the fathers, and the hearts of the children shall turn to their fathers. If it were not so, the whole earth would be utterly wasted at his coming" (Joseph Smith–History 1:37–39; see also Malachi 4:1, 5–6).

A modern prophet taught: "I would have you consider seriously whether or not that binding with your family will be secure if you have waited until you have passed beyond the veil before your hearts then yearn for your children whom

130

you have neglected to help along the way. It is time for us to think of turning the hearts of parents to children now while living, that there might be a bond between parents and children that will last beyond death. It is a very real principle, and we should consider it" (Harold B. Lee, quoted by Boyd K. Packer, "The Family and Eternity," *Ensign,* February 1971, p. 11).

These statements (made by two men who lived centuries apart) remind us of three vital eternal truths: (1) there is a revealed power (the priesthood) that enables us to bind on earth that which shall be bound in heaven (see Matthew 16:19); (2) there is a need to plant in the hearts of the children the promises made to the fathers; and (3) if the hearts of the children do not turn to their fathers and if a binding between parents and children does not occur, certain actions of serious consequence will be neglected.

What are these actions of serious consequence? They pertain to the saving ordinances performed in holy temples — ordinances including baptisms for the dead, endowments, and proxy marriages for time and for all eternity. All of these blessings were promised our ancestors by a kind, loving, and impartial God, one who does not esteem one person above another. These blessings, however, are related to earthly rites and are obtained by mortals in behalf of those who have died without an opportunity to know and to participate in such ordinances. It is, therefore, our duty and privilege to demonstrate our love for our ancestors by completing family histories, exercising the powers of the holy priesthood, and performing work vicariously for loved ones who have gone before.

Three Levels of Organization

The "binding" and "turning" that ought to take place between the generations should be done in an orderly manner, for it is God's work, and he is a God of law and order. He expects us to organize ourselves and to establish our houses so that things will be done according to his mind and will.

As early as 1978, Church leaders asked all families to organize themselves at three levels: immediate families, grandparent families, and ancestral families. Through these levels of organization, many benefits will come, including the following:

• *A sense of continuity and belonging.* President Spencer W. Kimball said: "Analysts of our modern time point out that in a fast-changing world, people suffer a kind of shock from losing a sense of continuity. The very mobility of our society means that our children are often moved from place to place and lose close contact with the extended family of grandparents, uncles, aunts, cousins, and long-time neighbors. It is important for us also to cultivate in our own family a sense that we belong together eternally, that whatever changes outside our home, there are fundamental aspects of our relationship which will never change. We ought to encourage our children to know their relatives. We need to talk of them, make effort to correspond with them, visit them, join family organizations, etc." (*Ensign*, November 1974, p. 112).

• *Greater efficiency and effectiveness in "binding."* A proper family organization will expedite the binding of hearts between the living and the dead. Greater efficiency is achieved through sharing resources, and greater effectiveness results from pooling time and energies.

• *Added strength through intimacy and numbers.* On the one level (the immediate family organization), intimacy is fostered. Everyone knows everyone else, and there is no nameless person enrolled. At the grandparent or ancestral family organization levels, however, intimacy may be lessened somewhat, but strength of numbers increases noticeably. Who is not impressed by a large crowd gathered in one spot, all descendants of a common ancestor?

• *Increased respect for one's heritage.* All organizations that concern themselves with ancestral names, origins, and histories build within their members added respect for their heritage. A knowledge of parents from the past helps us know and appreciate more fully the parents of the present.

Since we have been given specific instructions to organize, perhaps it would be well to review the purposes and responsibilities of the three levels already mentioned.

1. *The immediate family organization.* President Ezra Taft Benson said, "Our responsibility to organize our families at the immediate family level begins when a couple is married" (*Ensign*, November 1978, p. 30). President Joseph F. Smith wrote: "There is no higher authority in matters relating to the family organization, and especially when that organization is presided over by one holding the higher Priesthood, than that of the father. The authority is time honored, and among the people of God in all dispensations it has been highly respected and often emphasized by the teachings of the prophets who were inspired of God" (*Gospel Doctrine* [Salt Lake City: Deseret Book Co., 1973], pp. 286–87).

"Immediate families, with the father as president or natural patriarch and the mother as partner and counselor to her husband, meet in weekly family home evenings and frequent family councils, creating an organization to meet the family's particular needs. (The mother is head of the family if the father is not present.)" (*Ensign*, October 1978, p. 11).

What are the responsibilities of the immediate family organization?

Many leaders have indicated that members of immediate family organizations should help accomplish the three-fold mission of the Church; that is, they should *proclaim* the gospel, *perfect* the Saints, and *redeem* the dead. Of such responsibilities, President Benson summarized: "Every family in the Church should become actively involved in missionary work, family preparedness, genealogy [family history] and temple work, teaching the gospel, and cultural and social activities" (*Ensign*, November 1978, p. 30).

We should not forget that in doing all these things, we help

133

the Lord to accomplish his avowed purposes — to bring to pass the immortality and eternal life of man — and we earn the distinction of being called saviors of men and saviors on Mount Zion (see President Spencer W. Kimball, Regional Representatives Seminar, April 3, 1981; Moses 1:39; D&C 103:9–10; and Obadiah 1:21).

The forum or setting through which the immediate family organization operates is the family home evening or family council. In this weekly gathering, assignments are made, reports received, progress noted, instruction given, and encouragement offered.

2. *The grandparent organization.* The following questions and answers pertaining to this organization were provided by the Church's Family History Department:

> *What constitutes a grandparent organization?* "The grandparent family organization develops as children from the immediate family marry and have children" (Ezra Taft Benson, *Ensign,* Nov. 1978, p. 30).
>
> *What are the responsibilities of a grandparent organization?* The grandparent family organization has essentially the same responsibilities with respect to the mission of the Church as the immediate family organization. To be effective, however, it is important for a grandparent family to be properly organized.
>
> *What positions need to be filled in a grandparent organization?* Most grandparent family organizations today function through elected officers in a manner similar to civic organizations. In a grandparent family organization, however, some offices are received by right. The most common offices in grandparent family organizations today are: president, one or more vice-presidents, secretary, treasurer, family history specialist, and historian. Besides these, other officers are needed to fill the goals of a family organization, such as missionary chairman, welfare chairman, publications chairman, etc. Small family organizations may choose to combine the functions of officers. Large fam-

134

ily organizations may increase the number of officers to handle their more complex needs.

What is the value of a grandparent family organization? Speaking of the Ezra Taft Benson Organization, President Benson said: "Under my direction we are in the process of verifying our pedigree charts and supporting family group record forms.

"I have further commissioned the preparation of family histories by my immediate family members. My wife and I have tried to set the examples by preparing and distributing a brief summary of our own personal histories to our posterity. Further histories have been prepared, or are in the process of preparation, on each of our ancestors on my lines and my wife's lines as they appear on our first pedigree chart for four generations back. To our children this represents five generations of family histories; to the grandchildren, six; and the great-grandchildren, seven.... We have encouraged members of our family organization to use these histories as a basis for family home evenings, held in their immediate families, to teach their children appreciation, love, and respect for their ancestors" (*Ensign*, Nov. 1978, pp. 31–32).

What is the primary forum for the grandparent organization? Periodic family reunions are to this organization what family home evenings are to the immediate family organization. Nevertheless, other meetings or gatherings are scheduled as needed for this organization to accomplish its goals and objectives.

3. *The ancestral family organization.* Again, I refer to some information provided by the Church's Family History Department and containing statements of President Benson:

> *What comprises an Ancestral Family Organization?* "Now may I say a word about ancestral-type family organizations. Ancestral family organizations are comprised of descendants of a common ancestral couple" (Ezra Taft Benson, *Ensign*, Nov. 1978, p. 31).
> *What are the purposes of an Ancestral Family Organization?* "The major purpose for organizing or per-

petuating an ancestral family organization is to coordinate genealogical [family history] activity on common ancestral lines. When ancestral family organizations deviate from this major objective and seek primarily to provide social, cultural, or other types of activities, they take over the legitimate domain of the immediate and grandparent organizations. . . .

"Another legitimate function of the ancestral organization is to provide resource material from which the immediate and grandparent family organizations can draw to complete family histories—especially on their first four generations. Thus the ancestral organizations may accumulate, properly file, catalog and preserve histories, photographs, letters, manuscripts, diaries, journals, and published books. . . .

"Ancestral organizations exist only for the coordination of genealogical [family history] activity" (Ezra Taft Benson, *Ensign*, Nov. 1978, p. 31).

Phillip R. Kunz has written:

The purpose of the ancestral organization is to coordinate genealogical activity on common lines. Such an organization frequently raises money for family history research, publishes family histories, and generally directs the activities of the larger family.

Many families use the ancestral organization to house materials such as photographs, journals, family histories, and other materials that might be used by family members or by general researchers as they prepare their own histories. Some families have an ancestral family reunion occasionally, but more usually they have representatives who meet to coordinate family history and genealogical activities. Some may be organized as nonprofit corporations or trusts that may be recognized as charitable organizations if their purposes are limited to religious activities ("Family Organizations," *Encyclopedia of Mormonism*, Daniel H. Ludlow, ed. [New York: Macmillan Publishing Co., 1991], p. 498).

The Church's Family History Department maintains files to

assist family organizations. Family organizations are invited not only to use these files but also to contribute appropriate research data. Such files make use of the latest computer technology and consist of large amounts of information about people past and present.

Getting Started

Following are some practical suggestions about starting an organization, as reported by Janice Smith:

1. "Organize as an individual family. Decide in family council how you will carry out your responsibilities in welfare, missionary work, and temple/genealogy work. Make these efforts part of some family home evenings. Set goals and work to reach them."

2. "All family organizations should be led by the father, as patriarch, but he needs support from all members. In extended family organizations, contact all you know and have them contact others. One family put ads in newspapers. Another contacted all the persons who had submitted information to the genealogical library for the family line."

3. "At the first meeting of your extended family, decide what you want to accomplish and how. Discuss your constitution and bylaws, your purpose, officers, responsibilities, channels of communication, and sources of funding. Spread the work out and give specific assignments to members. As soon as this is done, send the names and addresses of officers to the [Family History] Department, 50 East North Temple Street, Salt Lake City, Utah 84150, for their family files."

4. "If many activities or parts of all of them are informal, interest will be higher. Total solemnity can kill an organization with boredom."

5. "Involve all members of the family. An older, single person can organize according to the same principles as an individual family to do welfare, missionary work, and temple/genealogy work. A single person needs food storage just as an

137

individual family does. In one family, the home of the sister who never married is the rallying point for the families of her brothers and sisters.

"Inactive members or nonmembers certainly belong in family organizations too. In one family, a brother-in-law was so motivated by the success of his wife's family organization that he got the members of his own family together. They are moving forward even though their father is not particularly active in the Church. In another case, one man was the only member of the Church in his family, but he asked one of his sisters if she would work with their father to write his history. The whole family became excited about it. He later reported that their most spiritual gathering was the evening they read their father's personal history. He also asked one of his farmer brothers to raise enough potatoes each year for the whole family. The fall meeting to pick up their winter supply of potatoes became an enjoyable reunion.

"Multitudes of blessings await families and individuals, regardless of Church standing. The family, by the Lord's commandment, is the most important organization you can belong to" (*Ensign*, January 1977, p. 39).

A Return to Family

I have always been intrigued by the concept of a jubilee year mentioned in the Old Testament. It was held every fifty years and was distinguished from other years by a hallowing process, the proclamation of liberty, a returning of borrowed possessions, and a *"return [of] every man unto his family"* (Leviticus 25:10; italics added).

I view family organizations as jubilee organizations. When allowed to function in harmony with the teachings of living prophets, they do enable people to return unto families (immediate, grandparent, and ancestral). They also cause children and parents to pause and to assess their possessions of greatest worth. And, after records are completed and verified, saving

138

services may be performed under the direction of the holy priesthood in the house of the Lord. Such services turn the hearts of the children to the fathers, bind families together forever, and proclaim liberty to the dead — even prisoners — whose progress depends upon the completion of essential ordinances by the living (see Isaiah 42:7).

Let us not forget:

Every good [family] tree bringeth forth good fruit. . . . A good tree cannot bring forth evil fruit, neither a corrupt tree bring forth good fruit. . . . Wherefore, by their fruits ye shall know them (3 Nephi 14:17–18, 20).

CHAPTER ELEVEN

FAMILY TRADITIONS

Therefore, [let us] stand fast, and hold the [righteous] traditions which [we] have been taught, whether by word, or our epistle (2 Thessalonians 2:15).

When our children were young, New Year's Eve was sometimes a nightmare! If we permitted them to stay up late and to usher in the New Year with the adults, they were grouchy and miserable the next day. If we insisted that they go to bed at the regular time and forego any celebration, they complained bitterly like martyrs to a cause and reacted as if Mother and I were Scrooge, the Grinch, and the Wicked Witch of the West all wrapped up in one. So, we prayed for a solution to our family crisis.

The solution came — clear and simple. We turned the clock ahead six hours on New Year's Eve and celebrated early as a family. After all, few of the children could tell time and didn't know the difference. Those who could read the dial and who could see through our well-intended charade were assured that it was midnight someplace in the world and that we had merely elected to celebrate with the people of Germany.

It is true that the neighbors thought that we were a little strange. Not many people are accustomed to hearing whistles, drum beats, congratulatory shouts, or other such noises at 1800 hours. Nonetheless, our children loved the unique practice, for all were included in the celebration, all obtained a good night's sleep, and all enjoyed the next day.

This distinct method of ringing out the old and ringing in the new was repeated many times and became traditional in the Asay family. Some of our children have since adopted the practice and are keeping it alive. Who knows how long the tradition will continue as one generation succeeds another?

Cultural Transmissions

Most families hand down from father to son or mother to daughter (orally and otherwise) stories, behaviors, customs, and teachings. Such cultural transmissions are wholesome and binding to the group, if they are based upon correct principles. Said George F. Will, "The great task of life is transmission: the task of transmitting the *essential tools* and *graces of life* from our parents to our children" ("On Turning 40," *Newsweek*, April 27, 1981; italics added).

Mr. Will believed that "the two most important things to be transmitted are a mastery of logic and a capacity for sympathy." No one will dispute that the ability to think through a problem is an essential tool to be mastered or that the capacity to be empathetic is an essential grace of life to be acquired. Both should be passed along to the young. But are there other tools and graces of life of equal or greater significance?

Let us consider the words of the Apostle Paul. His counsel to the Saints in Philippi was: "Whatsoever things are *true*, whatsoever things are *honest*, whatsoever things are *just*, whatsoever things are *pure*, whatsoever things are *lovely*, whatsoever things are of *good report*; if there be any *virtue*, and if there be any *praise*, think on these things" (Philippians 4:8; italics added).

Paul, I believe, provides us with a standard that may be used in measuring the value of a tool or grace or tradition. If the tradition is true, honest, just, pure, lovely, of good report, virtuous, or praiseworthy, it should be transmitted. If, however, the tradition is lacking in the virtues listed by Paul, that "thing" should be buried and forgotten; otherwise, the transmission

141

will prove to be a curse rather than a blessing to those who receive it.

I would add one more thought relative to the goodness of traditions. In answer to the question "Which is the great commandment in the law?" Jesus answered: "Thou shalt love the Lord thy God with all thy heart, and with all thy soul, and with all thy mind. This is the first and great commandment. And the second is like unto it, Thou shalt love thy neighbour as thyself. On these two commandments hang all the law and the prophets" (Matthew 22:36– 40).

Love should be added to the standard of measurement for traditions. Anything that fosters love of God, love of mankind, love of parents, or love of family is certainly worthy of continuance down to the second and third generations and beyond. On the divine attribute of love hang the future well-being and togetherness of all families.

The Burning of the Calendar

Years ago, I was introduced to a wonderful Armenian tradition called "the burning of the calendar." This occurred in Alexandria, Egypt, while I was serving as a full-time missionary in the old Palestine-Syrian Mission with headquarters in Beirut, Lebanon. The setting was the palatial home of a wealthy merchant where approximately one hundred people had gathered to end the year and to begin another.

The party began early as the host family and guests enjoyed a sumptuous dinner consisting of exotic foods and a wide variety of drinks, including milk for me. People ate and talked and listened to entertainers for several hours. No one, however, became boisterous or misbehaved during the evening; all showed tremendous respect for the gracious merchant and his home.

As midnight approached, the dining ceased, and the mood of the group changed noticeably. I wondered what was going to happen. Quietly and even reverently, the host and his family

142

led the group into a nearby drawing room. No verbal commands were given. Everyone moved as if drawn by a strong, unseen power. I held back and tagged along behind the others, not understanding what was taking place.

Once inside the drawing room, I raised on tiptoe to see over the crowd. I saw our host's mother, the family matriarch, seated in a soft chair surrounded by her children, grandchildren, and invited guests. She was a beautiful old woman with snow-white hair and an angelic countenance. No one spoke; I hardly breathed. I have rarely been in a place or among people outside of the temple where the atmosphere was more solemn or sacred.

Then, just before the stroke of twelve, the butler entered with a large silver tray in his hands. On the tray was a colorful Armenian calendar of the year coming to a close. The old woman slowly struck a match and lighted the paper. In perfect silence, we all watched as the burning calendar symbolized the end of the year.

I expected bedlam to break out and for the usual New Year's shouts to fill the room. But there were no shouts or wild demonstrations. Another servant entered from the other side of the room. He carried another tray with another colorful calendar on full display. The old woman took from the tray the calendar of the new year and showed it to the group at the stroke of midnight. The timing was perfect.

I thought to myself, now comes the explosion! It didn't. I saw the old woman whisper something to her son, who stood nearby. He, in turn, whispered to another and still another until the wave of whispers reached me. "The lady," said my companion, "knows that you are a minister of the Lord Jesus Christ and she wonders if you would be willing to lead the group in a New Year's prayer." Though somewhat stunned by the invitation, I said that I would be honored to give the prayer, providing I could give it in my own language. (I feared that my command of the Armenian language was too limited for me to do the occasion justice.)

My response was conveyed by the wave of whispers back to the old woman. To my further surprise, another message was sent to me. My companion explained: "The old lady said that you should pray in your native language. She said that God understands all languages and that we will know what comes from your heart. She also said that you should thank God for the blessings received this past year and ask for his continued blessings in the year ahead."

I prayed in behalf of the group and felt the presence of the Holy Spirit. And I vowed that this tradition would be planted and cultivated in my family garden. However long I live, I shall be eternally indebted to my Armenian friends for sharing with me a correct family tradition — one that transmitted pure love of God and pure love of humanity — one that was true, honest, just, pure, lovely, of good report, virtuous, and praiseworthy in every respect.

Truth and Tradition

I like what Herbert Hoover said near the end of his life: "A nation [or family] is strong or weak, it thrives or perishes upon what it believes to be *true*. If our youth is rightly instructed in the faith of our fathers; in the *traditions* of our country [and our religion]; in the dignity of each individual man, then our power will be stronger than any weapon of destruction that man can devise" (*Braude's Handbook of Stories for Toastmasters and Speakers*, Jacob M. Braude, ed. [Englewood Cliffs, N.J.: Prentice-Hall, 1957], p. 403; italics added).

Hoover spoke of truth and tradition. This combination is vital in our discussion of family performances that sanctify participants and cement groups together in accord with divine will.

Traditions are mentioned many times in the holy scriptures. References to false or incorrect traditions include words like

144

"inherited lies" (D&C 123:7–8), "vain customs" (Jeremiah 10:3), incorrect" traditions of their fathers" (Mosiah 1:5), "vain deceit" (Colossians 2:8), "vain conversation" (1 Peter 1:18), and similar expressions. These expressions remind us that great damage may be inflicted upon children if fathers and mothers teach less than the truth or model less than the good. Note this latter-day warning: "That wicked one cometh and taketh away light and truth, through disobedience, from the children of men, and because of the *tradition of their fathers*" (D&C 93:39; italics added).

We generally associate false traditions with the people in the Book of Mormon called Lamanites. We do this because they failed to preserve records and revealed truths. Hence, they were led by their fathers to hate others, live in ignorance, and wallow in the belief that they had been wronged by their brethren, the Nephites (see Alma 9:16; 60:32; Mosiah 10:12).

Nor was it the nature of the Pharisees to wed truth with tradition. The Savior reproved these "blind guides" for their false traditions and idle ceremonies in these words: "Howbeit in vain do they worship me, teaching for doctrines the commandments of men. For laying aside the commandments of God, ye hold the tradition of men.... Full well ye reject the commandment of God, that ye may keep your own tradition" (Mark 7:7–9; Matthew 23:24).

Correct or true traditions are based upon "laws, regulations, beliefs, doctrines, and practices" inspired by God. They constitute an untarnished baton of truth and goodness that must be passed to the rising generation with clean hands and purity of motive (Bruce R. McConkie, *Mormon Doctrine*, 2nd ed. [Salt Lake City: Bookcraft, 1966], p. 801).

Examples of Correct Traditions

The number of righteous, correct, and noteworthy traditions or customs is almost endless. It is limited only by our devotion to our families, our imaginations, and our will to do.

145

One who really cares will carry out; one who thinks ahead will think of something; and one who has the will, will find the way to bless his family through approved traditions.

For example:

• I know of families who traditionally gather together on Christmas Day and read Luke's account of the birth of Jesus Christ. (The story never grows old.)

• I know of a family that traditionally meets during the Christmas holiday and acts out the "Little Match Girl" story. (The drama always brings tears to the eyes of the viewers.)

• I know of many families who traditionally engage in a sub-for-Santa project. (Such traditions foster the true spirit of Christmas.)

• I know of families who meet together at the close of each General Conference of the Church and review the talks given. (Some even voice new resolves prompted by the speakers and the Spirit.)

• I know of families who traditionally sponsor a summer outing where feelings of oneness are strengthened. (Respect for nature, real togetherness, and a dependency upon each other are fostered on such occasions.)

• I know of families who traditionally meet together on Sunday afternoons and discuss truths taught in Sunday School, Priesthood meeting, Relief Society, Primary, and sacrament meeting. (Through this practice questions are answered and teachings are reinforced by loving parents.)

• I know of families who traditionally meet together and read aloud Charles Dickens's "A Christmas Carol." (A love for good literature and the simple pleasures of life often bloom from this tradition.)

• I know of families who have built a strong tradition of missionary service — all of the young men and many of the young women keep themselves clean and worthy of a call. (High and achievable expectations can be established if this is done in the right way.)

• I know of a family that shouts "Hip-hip hurrah!" in the car as they pull out of their driveway at the start of each summer vacation. (A simple thing to do, but one that sets the tone for a positive family get-away.)

• I have read of a family that says "Home again, Finnigin," upon returning home from a trip.

• I know of a couple that sings their favorite love song in family gatherings, demonstrating their ever-growing love for each other. (Neither one has an operatic voice; however, each rendition elicits tears and applause from all listeners, including sons, daughters, and grandchildren.)

All of these traditions and many, many more are both instructive and edifying to all members of the family, young and old alike. Each activity, if handled honestly and properly, deposits gold in each person's memory bank, and each activity represents a wise investment in the future of children.

Traditions Teach and Bind

William F. Russell wrote: "Traditions not only provide that common glue that helps bind a family together and identify its individual members as a family, but some traditions also carry great potential for learning, or can be made to do so. Traditions are, after all, just activities that have a momentum of their own; their force pulls everyone along in spite of anyone's feigned or fervent will to resist. Parents today need that extra force behind them because it is so easy to be swayed by those small voices of reluctance or resistance" ("Traditions Can Teach — and Bind Family Together," *Deseret News,* December 17–18, 1990, p. C3).

Russell made reference in his article to an immigrant father who used the tradition of the family dinner to promote learning among his children. Of that experience, a son wrote, "Without being aware of it, our family was growing together, sharing experiences, and participating in one another's education."

147

Such can be the case if traditions are virtuous and founded upon truth.

Speaking of binding traditions and children, Brigham Young declared: "Whether surrounded with error or truth, the web woven around them in childhood's days lasts, and seldom wears threadbare. . . . The traditions of my earliest recollection are so forcible upon me that it seems impossible for me to get rid of them. And so it is with others; hence the necessity of correct training in childhood" (*Journal of Discourses,* 13:243, 252).

Traditions Bridge Past and Present

Said one who made history and who eventually became a part of a nation's tradition: "It is no good living in the past. But in facing the future we are fortified by tradition. Tradition does not mean that the living are dead — it means that the dead are alive" (Prime Minister Harold McMillan, in *Braude's Handbook of Stories for Toastmasters and Speakers,* p. 822).

Tradition has two faces, much like Janus, the mythical Roman god. One face looks forward, while the other face looks backward. The backward look proves edifying, if it registers things worth remembering, things that give meaning and guidance to the future. The forward look provides vision and purpose so long as it is not encumbered by myopic views and reflections of the past. Truth and tradition from the past must always be allowed to light the way into the future. Otherwise, progress is impeded and a fullness of living is never enjoyed.

Follow Christ

We read or hear of children who are blinded by tradition. Such blindness is caused by teachings or practices that have a negative impact upon their minds and conduct. For instance, some parents encourage their offspring to hate certain families or to carry on grudges that have plagued the family for generations. The hate or grudge causes the minds and hearts of the children to be closed to any good that may come from those who have been judged by others to be of little value. In the process, the hate and grudge is allowed to canker the souls of the innocent.

Parents must understand and comprehend the power of traditions. They must also make certain that the traditions they transmit to future generations are correct ones! It is such a waste of time and energies when children are required to uproot and overcome false traditions. Life is too short for this type of unnecessary labor. It behooves parents to follow the counsel of Brigham Young, who said to parents: "Teach them [children] correct principles, and by imbibing them they will be enabled to lead lives of purity, joy, peace and tranquility that surpasses all understanding. So let our traditions be, and never do or say a wrong thing. . . . *Let our traditions and practices be such that we can say, to the whole world, in the words of the Apostle, 'Follow us, as we follow Christ'* " (*Journal of Discourses*, 13:252; italics added).

As the Lord said:

> *Lift up your eyes, and look on the fields; for they are white already to harvest. And he that reapeth receiveth wages, and gathereth fruit unto life eternal: that both he that soweth and he that reapeth may rejoice together (John 4:35–36).*

CHAPTER TWELVE

COMMUNICATION LIFELINES

If the trumpet give an uncertain sound, who shall prepare himself to the battle? So likewise ye, except ye utter by the tongue words easy to be understood, how shall it be known what is spoken? for ye shall speak into the air. There are, it may be, so many kinds of voices in the world, and none of them is without signification. Therefore if I know not the meaning of the voice, I shall be unto him that speaketh a barbarian, and he that speaketh shall be a barbarian unto me (1 Corinthians 14:8–11).

A family, like any other organization, becomes splintered and loses its effectiveness when communication lifelines are severed. If the dialogue between mother and father becomes clogged with selfish feelings or grudges, uncertain signals are sent to the children, causing great confusion. If the talk between parents and children becomes filled with static, voices of the world will take on added significance and drown out the counsel given in the home. And if the conversation between siblings is quarrelsome and loud, hopes for peace and harmony among the group are lost. How terrible it is when we engage in barbaric behavior and alienate ourselves from other members of the family by speaking unkind words or by breaking off communication lifelines.

The "many kinds of voices in the world" spoken of by the Apostle Paul bombard the ears of young and old each day.

150

They come via the streets, the radio, the television set, the newspaper, the magazines, the movies, and other sources. A few of these voices give a certain and pleasing sound; such sounds generally come from parents, Church leaders, loyal friends, and people who genuinely care. More than a few voices, however, issue uncertain and confusing sounds. Many of these uncertain sounds are sleazy, seductive, and sinful, spoken by those who do not care in the least about the eternal welfare of people. They flaunt the good, the true, and the beautiful; and, they invite people to "eat, drink, and be merry" all the way down to hell (2 Nephi 28:7–8).

It is, therefore, imperative that "life-giving sounds" issue from the home. I speak of sounds easy to be understood, with signification, full of meaning, and spoken as benefactors, not barbarians, speak. Parents must help the children make the distinction in the sounds; whether piped or harped or blared over a loudspeaker. In return, the children must block out the barbaric influences and attune themselves to the proper wavelength so that edifying and building voices may be heard, understood, and followed (see 1 Corinthians 14:7).

Lifelines

A lifeline is a line to which people may cling to preserve life. It can be a wire, a rope, a railing, or some other tangible object. For example, a lifeline is attached to a diver's helmet to raise him or her from the water. Another type of lifeline is used to lift people from burning buildings. Other illustrations of lifelines made of various materials could be cited. In every instance, however, the line preserves life only when it is anchored securely to a safe source and the threatened person maintains a firm grip.

There are also intangible lifelines. To an alcoholic, the Alcoholics Anonymous association and its program are a lifeline. To a military general and troops, the army's supply system is a lifeline. To a business organization, interoffice communication becomes a lifeline. Such programs and systems often determine the success or failure, victory or defeat, and even life or death of the individuals and groups involved.

So it is with families. Communication lifelines must be continually extended to all family members. Otherwise, relationships will become strained; activities will become segmented; and the welfare and well-being of parents and children will be placed in jeopardy.

A Supportive Word

On one occasion, a regional representative and I had conducted a number of interviews with priesthood leaders in conjunction with the reorganization of a stake. When a decision had been made and confirmed by the Spirit, a certain man was issued the call to preside as stake president. He was humbled and shocked by the invitation extended him. In response, he said something like this: "I am flattered that you would consider me worthy to serve in this capacity. Please know that I am anxious to serve the Lord in whatever way possible. But, before you proceed further, you need to know that I have failed as a father."

The man explained that he had an eighteen-year-old son who had rebelled against heaven and home. In fact, the young man had dropped out of school, out of Church activity, and almost out of the family. With great emotion and in a choking voice, the man acknowledged that communications with his son had been sparse and mostly negative over the past several months. At the close of his explanation, he added: "Many of the stake members know of the problems with my son, and they probably have no respect for me as a leader. So, knowing of my problem at home, if you want to withdraw the call, I'll understand."

I was impressed by the man's candor and honesty. But I did not cancel the call. Instead, I reaffirmed that his selection had been inspired, and I indicated that his first task as stake president was to recover the boy and make proper reconciliations.

The next morning, prior to the start of the Sunday general session of the conference, I sat next to the newly called stake president, listening to the prelude music, when a young man walked down the aisle of the chapel, approached the man, and said: "Dad, I know what is occurring this morning. I know that you have been called as the new stake president. I do love you, and I will sustain you."

This was the prodigal son whom the man felt that he had lost. Thank God, however, the boy stepped forward at a crucial moment and threw his father a lifeline. Later in the meeting, when the man stood at the pulpit to give his first address as stake president, he spoke with confidence and spirit—a confidence and spirit instilled by the reassuring words of a loving son.

A Telephone Call

While serving as a mission president, I received a telephone call early one morning from a bishop in a distant city. The bishop informed me of the death of a woman in his ward who had a son serving under my direction. The bishop asked me to break the news to the missionary and warned me that the news would be jolting to the boy because his father had died only a few days before his entrance into the mission field.

I sought out the missionary and delivered the message of his mother's death as gently as I could. He wept uncontrollably for several minutes. Then, through the tears, he told me that his mother had called him on the telephone late the night before. In receiving the call, he had asked his mother's reason for calling. It wasn't his birthday, a holiday, or any other special day meriting a telephone call from home. The mother answered that she knew her call was spontaneous and irregular. But she said she had been prompted to call and tell her son one more time that she loved him and wanted him to be a good missionary.

That spontaneous telephone call was a lifeline to the son. It caused him to live and serve on a much higher level than he would have. And it provided him a spiritual motivation that prevailed throughout his mission. I hope that one day I can meet this special woman who was living close to the Lord and who cast a communication lifeline to her son as a final testament of her love and faith.

A Look

Some years ago I was seated in the Tabernacle waiting for one of the sessions of general conference to begin. Seated next to me was my good friend and regional representative, Mark Benson, son of President Ezra Taft Benson. As we conversed quietly, he looked anxiously toward the general authority seats and asked, "Can you see my Father?"

"Yes," I answered, "I can see him off to the right of the pulpit." And, I continued, "It appears that he is concerned and looking for someone."

"I may be that person," said Mark. "Father is speaking in this session, and each time he speaks we have a practice of exchanging sustaining smiles and nods of the head before the conference begins."

I then observed some of the most eloquent muted language ever expressed. The son's face communicated, "I love you, father. I'm praying for you, and I know that you will do well." In return, the father's countenance seemed to answer, "Thanks, son. I do feel of your sustaining power and influence."

A look, a smile, a touch, a positive gesture, or other muted language can sometimes convey powerful messages between loved ones. Each is a communication lifeline with saving virtue when expressed at an appropriate time and in the proper manner.

154

A Note

I once sat in a meeting with butterflies in my stomach, waiting my turn to speak. A large and important audience was in the hall, and several auspicious guests were seated on both sides of me. My mind was full of doubts as to whether I could say anything that would be meaningful to the assembled group.

Only moments before I was introduced as the next speaker, an usher handed me a note. It read: "I love you and am praying for you. What a blessing to be your wife and be involved with you in the Lord's work."

This note was a lifeline to me. It brought me a resurgence of confidence and power.

A Letter

Soon after his son began his training at the Missionary Training Center in Provo, Utah, a father penned this message:

Dear Phil:

We received your letter of October 11, and it was wonderful hearing from you. Guess what — your father quit smoking the day you reported to the MTC. . . . I haven't had a cigarette since then, and I don't intend to ever have one again. And that's not all. I went to church last Sunday and stayed for the whole three sessions. I expect to go each and every Sunday from now on. I feel so close to you when I am in church, especially in priesthood meeting. I paid my tithing last Sunday, and I expect to be a full tithe-payer from here on. I also expect to have my temple recommend renewed very shortly. . . .

You said in your letter that you were so thankful to be our son. Well, I want you to know that I am very thankful to be your father. . . . I want you to know that I am doing everything in my power to be a good church-going Mormon, one that you can be proud of. In one way, it's like we both are going on a mission. I want to be in a position to give you strength when you have had a long, hard, and discouraging day, and you will have those kind of days. . . .

155

All my love, Dad
(In Joe J. Christensen, *To Grow in Spirit* [Salt Lake City: Deseret Book Co., 1983], p. 43).

Perhaps no one will ever know what caused the father to write this tender letter. But we may conclude that the father had been influenced by the spirit of repentance. Perhaps his recommitment to righteous living had been sparked by the son's mission call and departure from home. Whatever caused his change of heart, it is obvious that the father loved his son and wanted to share with him a memorable mission experience. It is certain that the son received strength from his father through this beautiful and timely communications lifeline.

A Final Testament

One of the most poignant letters ever written was the second epistle of Mormon to his son Moroni. It was written in perilous times, when both were threatened with extinction at the hands of a fierce enemy. Little hope was held by the father or the son that their lives would be spared much longer. Still, the father wrote these tender and instructive lines:

> And now, my beloved son, notwithstanding their hardness, let us labor diligently; for if we should cease to labor, we should be brought under condemnation; for we have a labor to perform whilst in this tabernacle of clay, that we may conquer the enemy of all righteousness, and rest our souls in the kingdom of God.
>
> Behold, my son, I cannot recommend them unto God lest he should smite me.
>
> But behold, my son, I recommend thee unto God, and I trust in Christ that thou wilt be saved; and I pray unto God that he will spare thy life, to witness the return of his people unto him, or their utter destruction; for I know that they must perish except they repent and return unto him.
>
> My son, be faithful in Christ; and may not the things which I have written grieve thee, to weigh thee down unto death; but may Christ lift thee up, and may his

sufferings and death, and the showing his body unto our fathers, and his mercy and long-suffering, and the hope of his glory and of eternal life, rest in your mind forever (Moroni 9:6, 21–22, 25).

We can only speculate about how Moroni must have felt when he read this communication lifeline from his father. We do know, however, that Moroni remained faithful to the end and completed his record-keeping responsibilities. He, like many others before and after his time, gained strength from a father who cared enough to write and share the innermost feelings of his heart.

Other Lifelines

Other communication lifelines are used by families who have planted this "pecan tree" practice. Some use bulletin boards. Others tape notices on refrigerator doors. Still others circulate family newsletters to keep in touch with married children who have established homes of their own. Whatever the means used, the intent is always to give a certain sound and to build understanding in the family.

Parental Example

I have a strong feeling that open and edifying communication within the family depends upon the parents. They are the ones who must set the example and create the environment wherein constructive dialogue may occur. If parents become contentious in their speech, the children will likely mimic their talk or refuse to communicate altogether. When a parent sulks or delights in giving a companion the silent treatment, the little ones may pick up the same bad habit. Therefore, parents must encourage honest expression and open communication between family members by providing the proper example.

My wife and I may not be the greatest communicators in the world, nor are we always the parents we should be. However, our children have paid us two noteworthy compliments.

All attest that they have never heard their mother and father quarrel or exchange ugly words. This is a fact, something we promised each other even before our first child was born. The second compliment was given by a son who said to his mother: "Whenever you expressed your opinion on a subject and told us to go speak with Dad, we didn't need to because we knew that Dad would say the same thing." It pleased us to know that we were united in thought and consistent in the direction we gave our children. Our trumpets were in tune and gave a certain sound.

Perhaps we should sing more often in our family home evenings the following hymn:

Let us oft speak kind words to each other;
At home or where'er we may be;
Like the warblings of birds on the heather,
The tones will be welcome and free.
They'll gladden the heart that's repining,
Give courage and hope from above.
And where the dark clouds hide the shining,
Let in the bright sunlight of love.

Like the sunbeams of morn on the mountains,
The soul they awake to good cheer;
Like the murmur of cool, pleasant fountains,
They fall in sweet cadences near.
Let's oft, then, in kindly toned voices,
Our mutual friendship renew,
Till heart meets with heart and rejoices
In friendship that ever is true.

Oh, the kind words we give shall in memory live
And sunshine forever impart.
Let us oft speak kind words to each other.
Kind words are sweet tones of the heart.
(*Hymns*, no. 232).

Points to Remember

Many suggestions for effective communication have been printed by experts in psychology and family relations. One such list published in a Boy Scout publication is worthy of our consideration. It includes six points for parents to remember and practice:

• Never be too tired or too busy to listen to one another.

• Avoid judgmental attitudes. Do not say, for example, "I did not think you were that kind of a person."

• Disapprove of the undesirable act without condemning the child. (Reject the behavior, not the child.)

• Try to understand why your child behaved as he or she did.

• Listen more than you talk, and try to help family members get feelings into the open.

• Try to understand how family members feel and reflect these feelings back to them.

(*BSA Family Book* [Boy Scouts of America, 1990], p. 39).

This publication includes a reference to an instructive conversation between a father and a daughter printed in a popular novel. After a father learned that his daughter was having trouble getting along with others at school, he counseled: "First of all . . . if you can learn a simple trick, . . . you'll get along a lot better with all kinds of folks. You never really understand a person until you consider things from his point of view — until you climb into his skin and walk around in it."

Toward the end of the story, the daughter acknowledged: "Atticus was right. One time he said you never really know a man until you stand in his shoes and walk around in them" (Harper Lee, *To Kill a Mockingbird* [Philadelphia and New York: J.B. Lippincott Co., 1960], pp. 36, 294).

In a literal sense, parents cannot climb into the skins of their children nor walk around in their shoes. Still, they must make an honest attempt to remember former days when their own skin was more taut and shoe sizes were much smaller. Through such remembering, harsh words will likely be replaced by kindly counsel and rash judgments by conciliatory conversations.

Practical Advice

In one of his broadcasts, Elder Richard L. Evans gave parents the following practical advice about communicating:

"Lately I have thought a lot about 'listening,' " said Hannie Struve. "How often you hear a little child complain . . . 'you're not *listening!*' And how easily the mother replies, 'What do you *want?*' And mostly the child does not really 'want' anything, only to communicate."

Take time to listen — to children, young people, others! Sometimes they are reluctant to seek counsel because they receive impatient replies.

"Why do we parents so often say, 'I'm busy now,' " asked Robert M. Neal. "Why do we . . . not realize that a child is like a sunbeam, here for a moment and then gone somewhere else."

Talking — listening — patience, willingness to learn enough before jumping to quick conclusions: Sometimes in just letting them talk and using us for listening, they will come soberly, safely to their own conclusions. But when two people both talk at once, when they cut each other short, or when they don't talk at all, there aren't likely to be any satisfactory solutions.

Yes, it takes time to listen, but it takes more time to correct mistakes once they have been made. With too many misjudging, too many making mistakes, and too few taking time to listen, counsel cannot seem as satisfactory as it should.

"The key is communication," reported a *Time* essay. " 'Can't you see I'm busy?' . . . ought to be banned. 'Listen' ought to be [implanted] over every parent's heart."

If only we could feel we have been heard! If only we would listen when we should! (*Richard Evans' Quote Book* [Salt Lake City: Publisher's Press, 1989], p. 26).

Those who apply this counsel will be found planting the "pecan tree" practice of communication lifelines in their family gardens. They will know the meaning of this prayer: "Dear

Lord, make me a better parent. Teach me to understand my children, to listen patiently to what they have to say and to answer all their questions kindly. Keep me from interrupting them, talking back to them, and contradicting them. Make me as courteous to them as I would have them to be to me" (Gary Cleveland Myers as quoted in *Richard Evans' Quote Book*, p. 26).

Scriptural Guidance

"Fathers," wrote the Apostle Paul, "provoke not your children to anger, lest they be discouraged" (Colossians 3:21). Paul understood the damning effect of harsh words spoken by parents in fits of hot anger. Like a sharp sword, such words sever relationships and cut deeply into the soul, sometimes causing irreparable damage.

In another writing, Paul counseled: "But bring them up in the nurture and admonition of the Lord" (Ephesians 6:4). The word "nurture" suggests kindness, and the word "admonition" suggests gentle persuasion. Such a Christian approach brings to mind the words included in a revelation given to the Prophet Joseph Smith: "He that speaketh, whose spirit is contrite, *whose language is meek and edifieth*, the same is of God" (D&C 52:16; italics added).

The capstone advice about communication provided below never becomes out-of-date:

> Let no corrupt communication proceed out of your mouth, but that which is good to the use of edifying, that it may minister grace unto the hearers.
>
> And grieve not the holy Spirit of God, whereby ye are sealed unto the day of redemption.
>
> Let all bitterness, and wrath, and anger, and clamour, and evil speaking, be put away from you, with all malice:
>
> And be ye kind one to another, tenderhearted, forgiving one another, even as God for Christ's sake hath forgiven you (Ephesians 4:29–32).

Parents who shout at children and who speak unkind words are parties to a serious form of abuse—verbal abuse. Every harangue is not only an admission of weakness on the part of the adult but also a contradiction to any expression of love before or after the act. Each ugly word spoken is insulting and demeaning to the person who mouths them. And each tirade seems to lead the uncontrolled parent closer and closer to the fist or belt or stick or some other instrument of added abuse.

God, our Father, introduced his son to a people in a small, piercing voice: "While they were thus conversing one with another, they heard a voice as if it came out of heaven; and they cast their eyes round about, for they understood not the voice which they heard; and it was not a harsh voice, neither was it a loud voice; nevertheless, and notwithstanding it being a small voice it did pierce them that did hear to the center, insomuch that there was no part of their frame that it did not cause to quake; yea, it did pierce them to the very soul, and did cause their hearts to burn" (3 Nephi 11:3).

A Plea

Parents who truly love the Lord and themselves will plant the "pecan tree" practice of communication lifelines in their family units. They will model before the children wholesome and loving speech, and they will use edifying language in teaching the young ones to walk uprightly before God. They will give a certain sound, utter words easy to be understood, give significant counsel, and allow life-giving sounds to echo quietly in all parts of the home.

In the end, they will merit this lifeline communication from on high:

Then, my [sons and daughters], ye shall reap the rewards of your faith, and your diligence, and patience, and long-suffering, waiting for the tree to bring forth fruit unto you *(Alma 32:43; emphasis added).*

CHAPTER THIRTEEN

LOVE AND SERVICE AT HOME

*Ye will teach them [children] to walk in the ways of
truth and soberness; ye will teach them to love one
another, and to serve one another (Mosiah 4:15).*

A few years after our marriage, my wife and I purchased our
first house. It was a modest brick building located in a new
subdivision where land was relatively inexpensive. Though the
number of square feet in the structure was limited and the
construction very simple, we were thrilled with the prospects
of moving in because we had been involved in the planning,
and the place was to be "ours"!

Once the papers had been signed and the closure procedures completed, the contractor handed us the keys and
gave us this charge: "I have constructed the house; now you
must make it a home."

The contractor was a wise and experienced man. He knew
that houses consist of wood, cement, bricks, mortar, and other
perishable materials. He also knew that homes are built out
of the nonperishable materials such as love, service, faith, and
Christian living. His commission to us was not to drive more
nails or to lay more bricks — the construction workers had
already completed their assigned jobs. Rather, his commission
to us was to do what the carpenters, painters, plumbers, and
other workers could not do for us — to add the spirit and love
that would transform our modest dwelling into a wonderful
home.

164

Hearts Build Homes

I have learned over the years that hands build a house but hearts build a home. That is why I regard acts of service as the material out of which the bricks of an eternal family unit are molded, and love as the mortar that holds the bricks together. Both love and service are essential and inseparable. Love is that inner feeling that sparks the desire to do someone good; service — selfless service — is that outward expression of love that blesses the receiver and the giver. So, each heartbeat in behalf of others adds mass to the mansion, strength to the structure, and beauty to the building we call home.

King Benjamin knew all of this and more, much more, about love and service in the home. His ageless counsel to parents was: "Ye will not suffer your children that they go hungry, or naked; neither will ye suffer that they transgress the laws of God, and fight and quarrel one with another, and serve the devil, who is the master of sin, or who is the evil spirit which hath been spoken of by our fathers, he being an enemy to all righteousness. But ye will *teach them* to walk in the ways of truth and soberness; ye will *teach them to love one another,* and *to serve one another* (Mosiah 4:14–15; italics added).

This scripture reminds us that each home should be a school and every parent a teacher. Moreover, the words of King Benjamin suggest that the "core" of the home curriculum should be love and service. Such virtues provide the foundation upon which other teachings are added as students of righteousness are taught and as homes "arise and put on [their] beautiful garments" (see D&C 82:14).

Gifts of Love and Service

I once visited a home clad in beautiful garments. It was the home of a stake president whose unit I was visiting on assignment. The place was not ostentatious. Yet it was clean and comfortable and big enough to accommodate a large family. Every courtesy was extended me, including a lovely room and delicious meals.

Early on Sunday morning, the president and his wife invited me to participate in a daily family devotional. They, their children, and I gathered in the living room. Eight sons and one daughter surrounded the parents. When all were in place, Bibles were distributed, a prayer was given, and scripture reading took place. One by one around the circle the children read verses. Even the youngest son, a nonreader, recited a verse or two as prompted by an older and very patient brother.

When the reading period ended, the father announced to the children that he and their mother were celebrating a wedding anniversary that very day. The children exchanged knowing glances and smiles but said nothing. Three of the children rose to their feet, walked out of the room, and soon reappeared with packages in hand. A look of happiness and excitement was on every face.

A package was presented by one of the children to the mother. She unwrapped the gift, revealing a colorful hair dryer. As she thanked the giver, the father explained to me off to the side that the dryer was an old machine that had broken down months before. Some of the boys had repaired and polished the hair dryer and were now presenting it to their mother as a token of their love.

The second gift, much bigger than the first, was handed to the father. He opened it and found inside the long box a weed-eater. With a smile and an emotion-filled voice, he said to me that the tool had broken a year or so ago and that the boys, on their own, had purchased new parts and repaired the machine so that it now worked like a new one.

Finally, a third and even larger package was given to the parents. It proved to be an old, reconditioned, and operable vacuum cleaner. Like the other two gifts, the vacuum cleaner had been restored and made serviceable by the boys with purchased parts and clever labor.

What followed was an indescribable exchange of love and gratitude for each other. The children had given of themselves from the very depths of their hearts. The parents had received the gifts in a spirit of sincere gratitude and with a deep sense of joy felt by all mothers and fathers who know that their "children walk in truth" (3 John 1:4).

"I don't have a present to offer your mother," said the father to the children, "other than this: I love her with all my heart." Tears appeared in his eyes and in the eyes of all who were in the room. None seemed embarrassed or ill at ease by the open display of affection, for love and service had been taught in this home from the very beginning.

As I observed this exchange of love and service within the stake president's home, I recalled these words of Elder Richard L. Evans: "The gift without the giver is a very empty and hollow thing. Service must be an experience in the giving of oneself as well as of material things. It is a sharing experience, or it misses much of what it might hold for all of us, and much of the result that is hoped for it" (*Richard L. Evans: The Man and the Message,* comp. Richard L. Evans, Jr. [Salt Lake City: Bookcraft, 1973], p. 239).

Scriptural Rootings — Love

Those who seek diligently to plant the family "pecan tree" practice of love and service in their home gardens are acting in full compliance with instructions received from the Lord through holy prophets living and dead.

John wrote: "If a man say, I love God, and hateth his brother, he is a liar: for he that loveth not his brother whom he hath seen, how can he love God whom he hath not seen? And this commandment have we from him, that he who loveth God love his brother also" (1 John 4:20–21).

The Savior himself spoke often of love and the need to share it with others. He identified love as something possessed by all of his true followers. Said Jesus: "A new commandment

167

I give unto you, That ye love one another; as I have loved you, that ye also love one another. By this shall all men know that ye are *my disciples, if ye have love one to another*" (John 13:34–35; italics added).

Alma preached against contention and taught his people that "they should look forward with one eye, having one faith and one baptism, having their hearts knit together in unity and in love one towards another" (Mosiah 18:21).

Every family should seek to achieve the enviable condition described by Jacob. In reference to a loving people, he said: "Their husbands love their wives, and their wives love their husbands; and their husbands and their wives love their children" (Jacob 3:7). We might assume that the children responded favorably to this outpouring of love by loving and honoring their parents in return.

These and a groundswell of other scriptures that could be cited teach us that love of God, love of brother and sister, and love of all people are expected of all who have taken upon themselves the name of Christ. After all, "God is love" (1 John 4:8). "The pure love of Christ" is charity (Moroni 7:47). And love is the keystone of family unity (see Colossians 3:18–21).

Who is not inspired by the lyrics of the hymn "Love at Home"?

There is beauty all around
When there's love at home;
There is joy in ev'ry sound
When there's love at home.
Peace and plenty here abide,
Smiling sweet on ev'ry side.
Time doth softly, sweetly glide
When there's love at home.

In the cottage there is joy
When there's love at home;
Hate and envy ne'er annoy
When there's love at home.
Roses bloom beneath our feet;

All the earth's a garden sweet,
Making life a bliss complete
When there's love at home.

Kindly heaven smiles above
When there's love at home;
All the world is filled with love
When there's love at home.
Sweeter sings the brooklet by;
Brighter beams the azure sky.
Oh, there's One who smiles on high
When there's love at home.
(*Hymns,* no. 294.)

Scriptural Rootings — Service

It is significant, I believe, that the Lord distinguished the righteous from the wicked in terms of "him that serveth God and him that serveth him not" (3 Nephi 24:18; Malachi 3:18). I interpret this statement to mean that declaration of belief is not enough. As they say, talk is cheap and idle lip-service comes easy. However, those who have faith not only profess their love of God but also demonstrate their love by serving the Master and his followers (see Matthew 25:31–46).

Perhaps no one spoke more eloquently about service than did King Benjamin. Among other things, he declared: "When ye are in the service of your fellow beings ye are only in the service of your God. . . . I say unto you that if ye should serve him who has created you from the beginning, and is preserving you from day to day, by lending you breath, that ye may live and move and do according to your own will, and even supporting you from one moment to another — I say, if ye should serve him with all your whole souls yet ye would be unprofitable servants" (Mosiah 2:17, 21).

Commenting upon the Savior's teachings about love and service, President Gordon B. Hinckley said: "It seems to me that he [the Savior] is saying to each of us that unless we lose ourselves in the service of others our lives are largely lived to no real purpose.... He who lives only unto himself withers and dies, while he who forgets himself in the service of others grows and blossoms in this life and in eternity" ("Forget Yourself," in *Speeches of the Year, 1977* [Provo: Brigham Young University Press, 1978], p. 43).

The tap-root statement pertaining to love and service was provided by the Apostle Paul, who wrote, "By love serve one another" (Galatians 5:13). Need more be said? We fulfill both the letter and the spirit of the law when we love each other and serve each other, beginning within the family circle and reaching beyond to all people.

Guidelines for Service

Library shelves are laden with books written to help families love and serve one another. As prompted by the Spirit, we should use the best of such books to guide all in planting the "pecan tree" practice of love and service. In the process, however, we must not neglect the teachings from the holy scriptures and the guidelines provided below.

Selection of Seed

Just as farmers carefully select their seed before planting, so must we determine with our spouses the type of marriage we want to create. We must take the time to create that marriage spiritually, in our minds, before the marriage is consummated. Such creation involves the setting of goals, reaching an understanding about children, resolving to create a real home founded upon love and service, and committing fully to the adventure that lies ahead. Those who fail to invest themselves in such a process will reach blindly into the bag of marriage possibilities and run the risk of selecting a blighted seed.

Plant the Seed

Seeds of love and service must be placed in the soil immediately and without delay. This is done by cultivating the right habits and practicing the right procedures well before children come. I refer to such habits and procedures as speaking kindly to one another, working together in the home, praying together, and doing other things of a helpful nature. If these good things do not become second nature to the couple before the children are born, new habits will need to be formed overnight, thus exposing the seed to the elements and jeopardizing its opportunity to sprout.

Water the Plant

An unknown author wrote, "The most important thing a father can do for his children is to love their mother." If she, in return, loves the father and both serve one another, they provide a model for the children that waters freely the "love and service" plant.

How awful it is when innocent children are exposed to contentious argument and physical abuse by their parents! Not only does this behavior mock sacred marriage vows, but it also raises questions in the minds of the impressionable young, such as: "Do mother and father love each other?" "Will they stay together?" God must weep over such actions. Surely he takes note of such offenses to his little ones (see Matthew 18:3–10).

It is a wonderful thing when grown men and women can reflect back upon their childhood experiences and attest that they never heard an ugly word pass between their parents. And it is equally wonderful when children can say of parents, "They conducted a lifetime courtship and lived for each other."

I know of a couple who loved and served in the right way. He was a small man; she was a large woman. In the evening after a day's work, he would sit in his soft easy chair to read the paper. She would come and sit gently on his lap and almost sink him out of sight. This open display of love and affection was observed and appreciated by the children. They had no

171

reason to question the depth of love between mother and father or to wonder about their staying together.

Cultivate and Nourish the Plant

Cultivate and nourish the "love and service" plant:

• *By expressing love to one another openly and sincerely.* Some people have a difficult time expressing their love because they haven't been taught to do so. For one reason or another they have grown up with the notion that verbalizing love cheapens the relationship. Or they are taught that too frequent use of the word love betrays its meaning.

I concur that expressions of love can be misused or overused. However, we shouldn't become so guarded in these expressions that we virtually erase them from our vocabulary. The Savior used the word *love* freely and with deep feeling. Should we not do the same?

• *By making mealtime or dinner time a special occasion when peace abides and love is communicated by word and deed.* A proverb reads, "Better is a dinner of herbs where love is, than a stalled [fattened] ox and hatred therewith" (Proverbs 15:17). Teach the children to set the table, position the chairs, serve the meal, clear away the dishes, and do other helpful tasks. Engage the family in enlightening discussions governed by quiet talk and thoughtful listening.

• *By catching the children doing and saying good things.* Too much of our time and energy is spent trying to catch children doing bad things. In doing so, we become more policeman than parent and teach the wrong lessons about love and trust. We must be positive in our approach, looking for good without countenancing evil, and allowing positive reinforcement to foster acts of love and service.

• *By engaging the children in family service opportunities, not chores.* The word *chore* is frequently associated with dull and difficult duties imposed by others. This negative connotation does little to motivate children to respond in a congenial manner. Why not drop the term and appeal to the good nature of children by extending them "service opportunities?" And why not teach them that service opportunities are a special privilege extended to them?

We can help children understand that each act of kindness is an expression of love for someone else. It doesn't matter whether it is a shoe shined, a room cleaned, or an errand run — all declare the message "I care about you" and "I love you."

Moreover, we can teach the children that acts of love and service shared with another are acts of love and service shared with God. Over the long haul, the children will internalize this truth: "Inasmuch as ye have done it unto one of the least of these my brethren, ye have done it unto me" (Matthew 25:40). Little by little, the foundation of family and church service will be established, and missionary, temple, and other service will follow naturally.

Laman and Lemuel accepted reluctantly some tasks received through their father. They never could make the connection between the chores and God. Nephi, however, possessed a deep faith and a sincere love for God, family, and father. He accepted the assignments given as service opportunities and completed them in a spirit of love and concern (see 1 Nephi chapters 3, 4, and 7).

• *By praying for each other.* Love for family members is often expressed or implied in prayers. The seeds of service may also be planted in prayer. By personalizing our prayers and being more specific in our requests, the possibilities of evoking positive responses in the form of acts of love and service from those present and not present are increased.

• *By teaching the children that the home is a sacred place and that its occupants are special people.* It has been said that the home is the most sacred and holy place outside of a dedicated temple. If this is a true statement, all parents should be devoted to the work of maintaining the quiet dignity of the home and making it a place of refuge for all family members.

173

This can be accomplished only in an atmosphere of love and an environment of helpful service.

• *To parents—by modeling love and service in all you do.* Said David Bly: "Tell a child which way to go and perhaps he'll go that way, but walk the path with him and he'll not stray from it."

• *To all—by remembering the tests of love, even true love,* which are: (1) It is always founded in truth; (2) it does not offend or hurt or injure another; (3) it is a positive, active force (one that finds expression through service); and (4) it involves sacrifices in behalf of others (see John A. Widtsoe, *An Understandable Religion* [Salt Lake City: Deseret Book Co., 1944], pp. 72–73).

I have often asked parents this searching question: If a stranger were to visit your home unannounced and spent only a few minutes with your family, what would he conclude about your faith? Exposure to chaos, rough language, furniture and furnishings in disarray, and so on might cause the stranger to go away wondering if you believed in anything of worth. If, however, he or she experienced cleanliness, congenial talk, and dignified behavior and surroundings, the stranger would know of your love for that which is good and of God.

I am not suggesting that a home should be void of play, laughter, or similar things. But I am suggesting that love and service will flourish best in an organized home of prayer, faith, learning, glory, order, and happiness (see D&C 109:8).

Models of Love and Service

Love and service come naturally to those who are reared in a home where both virtues are modeled by parents. In the little country community where I grew up, one of the great social occasions of the year was the annual fathers and sons' banquet. This gala event was held in the high-school gymnasium and featured a dinner and a special program. Most of the men and boys in the town looked forward to the affair with great anticipation. In fact, it was said by one enthusiast, "If you don't attend the banquet, you have lived a whole year for nothing."

Since there were four boys in our family, my father would take two sons with him on alternate years. He could not afford more than three tickets. So it was a bonus opportunity for me to attend the banquet on an "off year" when an uncle invited me to be his companion. I accepted his offer with joy and excitement for I loved being with him, and I savored the prospects of the evening's food and fun.

By prior arrangement, I was to meet my uncle at 7:30 on the appointed night in the school across the street from our home. My mother dressed me in my hand-me-down suit, opened the door, pointed me in the right direction, and instructed me to run quickly so that I wouldn't get wet in the rain and so that I wouldn't keep my uncle waiting.

I made my break out the door and leaped off the porch. But my feet slipped in the soft dirt, and I landed on my back in a large pool of water. I was drenched and covered with mud. Slowly, I rose to my feet and returned to the house crying and knowing that my evening had been spoiled.

Without wasting a moment, my mother took off my clothes, dried me, and placed several flatirons on our coal stove. At the same time, she soothed my injured feelings and assured me that all would be well. In a matter of just a few minutes, she cleaned me up, dried and pressed my suit, and had me poised at the door for one more try at the dash to the school.

The second dash was successful, and I had an enjoyable time at the community's big social function. As I reflect back upon that experience, I am reminded of my mother's deep love for me. A woman of less love and determination might have given in to the mud and water and written it off as just a bad break for her son. Mother knew, however, how much the banquet meant to me, and her quick service and demonstrated love will always be an inspiration to me.

My father was a farmer and schoolteacher. He taught school during the day, but in the evenings and on weekends he raised animals, cultivated a large vegetable garden, and cared for a fruit orchard. The animals, garden, and orchard served two purposes: they helped feed his large family, and they helped keep his boys engaged in meaningful work.

Dad had one cardinal rule for his young sons: Work in the morning; play in the afternoon. He also had the disposition to make the work as enjoyable as possible for my brothers and me. He could turn any chore into a game or add zest to any labor by placing a cold watermelon or cold root beer on the ditch bank as a reward for honest labor.

On one occasion, when we grumbled at the prospects of picking up apples and feeding the pigs, my father placed boards in the form of a man at the back of the pigpen. He then stepped off the distance from the board to form a pitcher's mound. Once the preparations were in place, we filled our buckets with apples that had fallen off the trees and rushed to the mound to strike out pretended batters. We threw the gathered apples at the wooden silhouette, just as a baseball pitcher would in a game. What could have been dull work and drudgery was transformed into something exciting and enjoyable by a loving father who cared more for his sons than for apples and pigs.

A Concluding Word

One day, all parents will stand before the judgment bar of God and give an accounting of their stewardships. Those who have taught their children to love and serve one another will stand before that bar with clear consciences. Those who have neglected to teach such virtues will shrink from the presence of God with scorched feelings and wish that they had been faithful to the commission given them. So, it should be the desire of each mother and father to become a wise and faithful steward, keeping in mind the words of John Ruskin: "This is the true nature of home, it is a place of peace, the shelter not only from all injury, but from terror, doubt, and division."

It would be well for all of us in preparation for that day of accounting to understand that the failure to teach children love and service is almost tantamount to teaching them to hate and to be selfish. The results of inaction and misguided action are often the same. We read of a people who taught their children to carry "an eternal hatred towards the children of Nephi" (Mosiah 10:17). However, we also know of many parents who simply omit from their schedules time to teach the crucial virtues of love and service on the pretext that they are too busy or that it isn't that important. Consequently, the rising generation is made to suffer in ignorance and unbelief (see Mosiah 26:1). We might wonder whether the sin of omission is greater than the sin of commission in this instance.

If any hatred is to be taught, it must be "an everlasting hatred against sin and iniquity" (Alma 37:32). If any teaching is to be omitted, it must be teachings that matter the least, not the weightier matters of the law or the core instructions of love and service.

Luther Burbank, one of the world's foremost naturalists said, "If we paid no more attention to our plants than we have to our children, we would now be living in a jungle of weeds." We may not be living in the weeds referred to by Burbank, but we are certainly living in a world overrun by selfishness and hate. Wars, rumors of wars, crime, abuse, divorce, and all the other problems of modern society are evidences that better gardening must occur among us, beginning within our own homes. A jungle of weeds is a Garden of Eden compared with the jungle of a serviceless and loveless people.

A modern song includes the line, "What the world needs most is love." I concur with these words as long as the love yearned for is founded in faith, centered in service, and grounded in goodness.

President Thomas S. Monson provides us with this pro-

177

vocative summary about love and service: "Time passes. Circumstances change. Conditions vary. Unaltered is the divine command to succor the weak and lift up the hands which hang down and strengthen the feeble knees. Each of us has the charge to be not a doubter, but a doer; not a leaner, but a lifter. But our complacency tree has many branches, and each spring more buds come into bloom. Often we live side by side but do not communicate heart to heart. There are those within the sphere of our own influence who, with outstretched hands, cry out: 'Is there no balm in Gilead . . . ?' (Jeremiah 8:22). Each of us must answer." (*Ensign*, December 1971, p. 132.)

God bless all parents everywhere to plant the "pecan tree" practice of love and service in their family gardens. My prayer is:

• *That Christ may dwell in your hearts by faith; that ye [be]* rooted and grounded in love *(Ephesians 3:17; emphasis added).*

• *That all of us will serve God and our families and others "with a perfect heart and with a willing mind" (1 Chronicles 28:9).*

CHAPTER FOURTEEN

CHURCH SERVICE

I tell you these things that ye may learn wisdom;
that ye may learn that when ye are in the service of
your fellow beings ye are only in the service of your
God (Mosiah 2:17).

On a Sunday afternoon a family gathered for dinner following a ward sacrament service. After the blessing was spoken and as the food was being served, one of the teenage boys announced, "I'm never going to church again!"

A hush fell over the group. All were shocked by the announcement, and all eyes turned toward the father, who continued to fill his plate, almost as if he hadn't heard the rash statement.

An anxious mother broke the awkward silence by asking, "Why? Why do you say such a thing? Don't you enjoy church?"

The son blurted out, "I don't like church because every time I go they ask me to speak or pray or bless the sacrament or usher or run errands or to do something else. And," he continued, "I'm tired — I'm all participated out!"

"Son," said the wise father, eager to take advantage of a precious teaching moment, "I appreciate your feelings, but there is something you don't understand fully. God, Our Heavenly Father, loves us. He placed us on earth so that we might acquire knowledge, be tested, and gain experience. He established a Church organization with a lay leadership so that all

179

might become involved and so that all might be edified — not just a select group of ministers."

Then, to clinch his point, the father added, "If God loved only one person in a ward or congregation and wanted only one person to grow toward perfection, only that one would be invited to pray, preach, sing, usher, and handle other necessary assignments. However, such is not the case. God cares about you and me and all of his children; he wants everyone to develop talents and to grow through Church service. Because he loves us and trusts us and wants us to become more like him, he extends us callings through his authorized representatives."

Service and Salvation

More than a few, both young and old, shy away from Church callings because they do not understand the relationship between Christian service and personal salvation. Hence, they show the empty hand to the beggar, turn their backs upon those who have been stripped and wounded, say no to priesthood leaders when invited to get involved, and live their own selfish lives as if they were alone on some remote island. Such people fail to remember that full salvation is the product of Christ's atonement (grace) and the *good works* of our faith. Consequently, they miss the joys of service and opportunities for personal growth, and they estrange themselves from the family of God.

Those parents who do understand the plan of life and salvation plant the "pecan tree" practice of Church service in the hearts of their children by teaching the following truths:

1. *Service to God distinguishes the righteous from the wicked.* Speaking of the time when the "Son of Righteousness" will judge all nations and "make up [his] jewels," the Lord said, "Then shall ye return and discern between the righteous and the wicked, between him that serveth God and him that serveth him not" (3 Nephi 24:17–18; see also Malachi 3:14–18).

2. Service to a brother or sister is an expression of our love for God. It is recorded: "If a man say, I love God, and hateth his brother, he is a liar: for he that loveth not his brother whom he hath seen, how can he love God whom he hath not seen? And this commandment have we from him, That he who loveth God love his brother also" (1 John 4:20–21).

How very contradictory it is to profess love of Deity and then refuse an invitation to serve as a home teacher or in some other helpful position!

3. Service is a means of knowing and becoming closer to the Savior. King Benjamin asked, "For how knoweth a man the master whom he has not served, and who is a stranger unto him, and is far from the thoughts and intents of his heart?" (Mosiah 5:13).

My answer to this question is, "He can't." We can never begin to appreciate Christ's infinite atonement until we place our own infinitesimal offering upon the altar by lifting another fellow being. No one can catch the slightest intimation of Jesus' profound love for humanity without becoming involved in service to others — service rendered without hint of recognition or recompense.

4. Service to a friend, neighbor, stranger, or others is service to God and has eternal implications. Those who balk at service opportunities should sensitize themselves by reading these words of the Savior, as related to the judgment day: "Inasmuch as ye have done it unto one of the least of these my brethren, ye have done it unto me. . . . And these [who turned away the stranger in need] shall go away into everlasting punishment: but the righteous [those who fed, clothed, and administered to the needs of the stranger] into life eternal" (Matthew 25:40, 46; see verses 31–46).

Fathers and mothers appreciate these truths more than most people do. They do so because they have experienced the special feeling that accompanies news that someone has extended saving and sanctifying service to a son or daughter living away from home. Whenever I hear that someone has blessed the life of a son or daughter serving in a faraway mission, I feel as though that someone has blessed me directly. The same applies to God and the whole human family.

5. *Service to others enriches our lives in many ways and results in a clear conscience.* We may diminish the purity of our service by thinking too much of the promised blessings. On the other hand, is it really wrong to serve, knowing that it will bring peace of conscience, remission of sins, personal growth and other serendipitous benefits? (see Mosiah 2:15–21; 4:24–26).

6. *Service to others can strengthen both the Church and the family.* In a revelation to Hyrum Smith, the Lord said: "Thy calling is to exhortation, and to strengthen the church continually. Wherefore thy duty is unto the church forever, and this *because of thy family*" (D&C 23:3; italics added). Some have concluded that this direction had "reference to the office of Patriarch and in this office, it was his duty and that of his family forever" (Smith and Sjodahl, *Doctrine and Covenants Commentary*, rev. ed. [Salt Lake City: Deseret Book Co., 1978], p. 120). Whether this is true or not, the fact remains that church service by an individual can and does bless members of his or her family. Such has proven to be the case with full-time missionaries, bishops, and others who have been quickened spiritually and made more sensitive to family responsibilities through church service.

It seems to me that growth grace-by-grace is related to growth service-by-service. The one refers to the merits of the Master and the other to our merits. And all of these merits blended together have bearing upon our salvation—our eternal destiny.

Dos and Don'ts

In addition to the truths discussed above, there are some dos and don'ts that all, particularly new converts and young ones, need to understand as the "pecan tree" of Church service is planted. Study the chart below, reading across the page or going from one "do" to a related "don't." Such reading, with some pondering, will help you appreciate service in the Lord's Church where "every man stand[s] in his own office, and labor[s] in his own calling . . . [so] that all may be *edified* together, that the system may be kept *perfect*" (D&C 84:109–110; italics added).

Church Service Do's and Don'ts

• We do *prepare ourselves* to serve when called upon.

• We do *respond humbly* and gratefully to all service opportunities.

• We do *learn our duties* and serve diligently in our specific assignments (see D&C 107:99–100).

• We do *magnify our offices and callings* unto the Lord, and we do take upon ourselves the attendant responsibilities (see Jacob 1:19).

• We do *sustain our leaders* in righteousness, and we do seek to be faithful in our assigned stewardships.

• We do *help others* around us to develop talents, abilities, and gifts of the Spirit in preparation for added Church service.

• We do not seek or "politic" for offices or callings.

• We do not turn down or refuse callings extended us.

• We do not wait to be commanded or compelled to perform our work (see D&C 58:26–29).

• We do not serve half-heartedly, as caretakers only; nor do we forfeit or circumvent our obligations (see D&C 4:2).

• We do not ignore scriptural commissions, instructions of leaders, or approved policies and procedures, nor do we hesitate to give an accounting of our services.

• We do not attempt to monopolize the work or to deny others opportunities for growth and development.

• We do *accept release* graciously when the time comes, and we do support wholeheartedly those who succeed us in a calling.

• We do not resist release or change of assignment when it is extended us, nor do we resent those who carry on after us.

Becoming Saints

The Church of Jesus Christ of Latter-day Saints is an organization of people who are striving to become Saints (see D&C 125:2). We do not automatically become Saints by entering the waters of baptism. We become Saints by repenting, by being baptized, by receiving the Holy Ghost, by putting off the natural man, and by acquiring saintly virtues through Christian living and *Christian service* (see Mosiah 3:19).

Each commandment we live has a refining influence upon us. Each act of service or goodness shown others polishes us in some respect. So, we should serve one another willingly and gladly, knowing that in the process we shall grow grace by grace and become more like Christ.

All members of the Church should understand that (1) service distinguishes the righteous, (2) service is an expression of our love for God, (3) service enables us to know and draw closer to Christ, (4) service to others is service to God, (5) service enriches our lives, and (6) service to others can strengthen both the Church and the family. Would that all would regard Church callings and other personal services as *blessings*, not burdens; as *sacred trusts*, not social stations; and as *opportunities for growth*, not onerous tasks strapped upon our backs.

Blessings

Upon my return from the mission field as a young man, my father embraced me and said: "Welcome home, son! Please turn around and go back." He explained, "The Lord has showered us with many blessings during your absence." My father, like thousands of others, testified that service and a little sacrifice does bring forth the blessings of heaven.

Many families do prosper financially while supporting a missionary son or daughter. A few do not for reasons known only by the Lord. However, all acknowledge an increase of love and respect for home, parents, and other dear ones. Such spiritual blessings do not line the pocketbook, but they do pile up eternal riches that cannot be stolen by another nor destroyed by moth or rust.

Things to Do

Parents can do many things to make their children service-conscious. Here are a few ideas:

1. *Serve in Church positions as called upon by leaders.* Extend your service willfully and happily so that the children will sense the joy related to good works. Never express negative thoughts about your assignment in the presence of the family members. Such negativism or criticism may seem harmless at the time, but it will take its toll later on with the young.

2. *Sustain one another in Church service callings.* A mother who sends her husband off to a bishopric meeting with a smile on her face and a blessing on her lips does two things: (a) She strengthens her companion and gives him confidence, and (b) she preaches a powerful lesson to her children about serving and sustaining another.

3. *Engage your family in neighborhood, Church, or civic service projects.* The service may be as simple and spontaneous as cleaning a neighbor's yard or removing snow from a widow's driveway. It may be as large and organized as a city's sub-for-Santa project or even the feeding of the homeless in a com-

munity kitchen. Whatever the service, if it is given in the right way and with the right attitude, the family receives the joy related to "pure religion" (see James 1:27) and experience a knitting of their souls.

4. *Speak openly in family settings about people who serve as the Savior served.* It doesn't matter whether those people mentioned helped you or someone else. What does matter is that the children understand your feelings about others who go about doing good.

5. *Refer to scriptural giants like King Benjamin, Ammon, Alma, and others who were models of Christian service as you conduct family home evening programs.* Highlight the motives of these people and discuss their selfless service.

6. *Encourage your children to save and to plan for full-time missionary service.* Help them to understand that home teaching and other invitations to serve before their mission are a part of the preparation program.

7. *Review with family members the scripture-based truths reported earlier in this chapter.* Any child who is not taught the truth about Christ and the working out of one's own salvation suffers the severest type of deprivation.

8. *Love and serve each other at home.* If seeds of service are not planted at home, how can we expect the fruits of service to appear away from home?

A Serving Family

I know of a family of sixteen who at last count had rendered more than thirty-two years of full-time missionary service. They have also served in almost every Church position on the ward and stake level during the past generation. In addition to all of this, they have made significant service contributions to community and professional causes. Service to God and others has forever been their watchword. One daughter commented, "We have a great heritage and so much to live up to because of the blessings we've been given" (Letter from Martha B. Checketts dated December 12, 1991).

Father Boone and his wife, James and Ruth, the parents of Martha Checketts and thirteen other children, planted the "pecan tree" practice of Church service in their family garden years ago. Such practice has been watered and cultivated by word and precept. Now they and the children are harvesting the fruits and joys of their Christ-like living and service. So, as with the Boones:

> *Give, and it shall be given unto you; good measure, pressed down, and shaken together, and running over, shall men give into your bosom. For with the same measure that ye mete withal it shall be measured to you again (Luke 6:38).*

CHAPTER FIFTEEN

HOME AND CHURCH WORSHIP

I desire that ye should remember these things, and that ye should work out your salvation with fear before God, and that ye should no more deny the coming of Christ; that ye contend no more against the Holy Ghost, but that ye receive it, and take upon you the name of Christ; that ye humble yourselves even to the dust, and worship God, in whatsoever place ye may be in, in spirit and in truth; *and that ye live in thanksgiving daily, for the many mercies and blessings which he doth bestow upon you (Alma 34:37–38; emphasis added).*

I have seen many beautiful sights in my lifetime, especially during the years that I have traveled about the earth on the Lord's business. For example, the view of Iguassu Falls, Brazil, was breathtaking; the view from the Eagle's Nest in Austria was spectacular; the view of the Holy Land from the crest of Mount Nebo was inspirational; the view of the Southern Lights from a jungle in Africa was heavenly. I could mention other marvelous views of nature and the handiwork of God that I have experienced. But none of these sights can compare in beauty with the scenes of home and church worship that I have been privileged to observe. I refer specifically to five scenarios: (1) a mother reading the scriptures with an impressionable child on her lap; (2) a husband and wife kneeling together at the bedside toward the close of a day; (3) a group gathered together near the fireside singing a hymn to begin a family home evening; (4) a father, mother, and children sitting and worshiping together in a sacrament service; and (5) a young couple exchanging vows in the house of the Lord with family members present. These five sights, and similar glimpses of godliness, please the eye, gladden the heart, and remind us that there is beauty all around when love of God and family is expressed at home, in church, and in other sacred places.

Worship is an act of religious devotion, wherein a person shows reverence, love, and adoration for Deity. It usually involves offerings of prayer, attendance at church services, the singing of beautiful hymns, and listening to inspirational sermons. It is not an act restricted to a specific place or bridled by a certain ritual. Love of God may be expressed in many ways, by many people, in many places, and under many circumstances. However, worship in its truest form seems to find its best expression in three sacred places: holy temples, happy homes, and dedicated chapels.

In the process of planting the "pecan tree" practice of home and church worship, we need to address these questions: *Whom* should I worship? *Why* should I worship? and *How* should I worship. Unless suitable answers to these questions are found, we may be led to engage in false worship—a type of worship that brings disappointment, damnation, and an emptiness of soul (see 2 Nephi 27:3).

Whom to Worship

Modern revelation warns us that people in these last days would walk in their own ways and after the images of their own gods, "whose image is in the likeness of the world, and whose substance is that of an idol" (D&C 1:16). This reminds us of what the Apostle Paul said about the last days: "Men shall be lovers of their own selves, covetous, boasters, proud, blasphemers, disobedient to parents, unthankful, unholy, without natural affection, trucebreakers, false accusers, incontinent, fierce, despisers of those that are good, traitors, heady, high-minded, lovers of pleasures more than lovers of God; having a form of godliness, but denying the power thereof: from such turn away. . . . Ever learning, and never able to come to the knowledge of the truth" (2 Timothy 3:2–5, 7).

Know God

Perhaps there have been times when God winked at ignorance and false worship, as intimated by Paul. You will recall that he observed the superstitious practices of the Athenians wherein they paid devotions "to the unknown God." His instructions to the Greeks are worthy of mention:

> As I passed by, and beheld your devotions, I found an altar with this inscription, TO THE UNKNOWN GOD. Whom therefore ye ignorantly worship, him declare I unto you.
>
> God that made the world and all things therein, seeing that he is Lord of heaven and earth, dwelleth not in temples made with hands; neither is worshipped with men's hands, as though he needed any thing, seeing he giveth to all life, and breath, and all things; and hath made of one blood all nations of men for to dwell on all the face of the earth, and hath determined the times before appointed, and the bounds of their habitation; that they should seek the Lord, if haply they might feel after him, and find him, though he be not far from every one of us: for in him we live, and move, and have our being; as certain also of your own poets have said, for we are also his offspring.
>
> Forasmuch then as we are the offspring of God, we ought not to think that the Godhead is like unto gold, or silver, or stone, graven by art and man's device.
>
> And the times of this ignorance God winked at; but now commandeth all men every where to repent: because he hath appointed a day, in the which he will judge the world in righteousness by that man whom he hath ordained; whereof he hath given assurance unto all men, in that he hath raised him from the dead (Acts 17:23–31).

If the time of winking at ignorance had passed in Paul's day, after the death and resurrection of Christ, it has surely passed in our day. For God has revealed himself in our day and dispelled the numerous and misguiding myths about his nature and purpose that had accumulated through centuries of spiritual darkness. Those who lived during the dark ages may have deserved the wink from Deity; however, we who live in the fullness of times and bask in the light of a restitution of all things have no excuse. Our worship should be conducted "in spirit and in truth" (Alma 34:38).

In Spirit and Truth

Worship in spirit indicates the need for thoughts and feelings to take precedence over form, pattern, or set words. Worship in truth requires a knowledge of the true nature and concept of God. Nephi explained: "The *right way* is to believe in Christ and deny him not . . . wherefore ye must bow down before him, and worship him with all your *might, mind,* and *strength,* and your *whole soul*" (2 Nephi 25:29; italics added). All of this is summarized by Christ himself, who stated: "True worshipers shall worship the Father in spirit and in truth; for the Father seeketh such to worship him. For unto such hath God promised his Spirit. And they who worship him, must worship in spirit and in truth" (JST John 4:25–26).

Who is this Father or God to whom we pay our devotions? He is God, the Father of all spirits, the Father of mankind (see Hebrews 12:9). He is the "God of our fathers," the God of Abraham, Isaac, and Jacob (1 Nephi 19:10). He is the only true and living God, and his name is Elohim. It was he who "so loved the world, that he gave his only begotten Son [Jesus Christ], that whosoever believeth in him should not perish, but have everlasting life" (John 3:16).

This Only Begotten Son instructed, "I give unto you these sayings that you may understand and know how to worship, and know *what you worship,* that you may come unto the Father

191

in my name, and in due time receive of his fulness" (D&C 93:19; italics added). We do, therefore, pray to the Father in the name of Jesus; we look to the Son as our advocate, redeemer, and savior, for it was he who wrought the holy atonement and broke the bands of death. He marked the path; he led the way; and he has provided us an escape from death and hell (see 2 Nephi 9:1–41). We do, therefore, come unto God the Father through Christ, for there is "no other name given nor any other way nor means whereby salvation can come unto the children of men, only in and through the name of Christ, the Lord Omnipotent" (Mosiah 3:17).

The veil of ignorance about the true nature of God was lifted in the spring of 1820 when two Personages appeared to the boy prophet, Joseph Smith. One of them called Joseph by name and said, pointing to the other, "This is My Beloved Son, Hear Him!" (JS–H 1:17). In one glorious moment, all myth and mystery concerning a living and personal God was dispelled. God was not dead or even mute. He was not some indescribable power or substance of the past who had nothing more to say to a modern world. He revealed himself as a glorified being. He introduced himself as the Father. He invited Joseph and all others to seek him, to feel after him, to find him, and to worship him.

Why Worship?

I offer six reasons for worship at home and at church. Many other justifications could be given. In reality, however, if our love of God is real and not pretended, there is no need to offer numerous reasons for our worship. The adoration and devotions we extend our Father in Heaven and his Only Begotten Son, the Savior of mankind, should flow freely and liberally from the love for Deity that wells up within us. Nevertheless, we worship them for other reasons as well.

1. *To keep the Lord's commandment.* An angel of the Lord asked Father Adam, "Why dost thou offer sacrifices unto the

192

Lord?" Adam responded, "I know not, save the Lord commanded me" (Moses 5:6). I like the directness and simplicity of Adam's reply. He did not grope for justifications nor did he lose himself in wordy explanations. He did what he did because God told him to do it, and that was the end of the matter.

A similar answer could be given to the question, Why worship? We respond, because God has commanded us to do so. Jesus taught, "Thou shalt worship the Lord thy God, and him only shalt thou serve" (Matthew 4:10). Through Moses, God declared: "Thou shalt have none other gods before me. . . . Thou shalt not bow down thyself unto them [graven images]. . . . Keep the sabbath day to sanctify it. . . . The seventh day is the sabbath of the Lord thy God" (Deuteronomy 5:7, 9, 12, 14). Many other scriptures remind us that worship is a divine expectation and that it should be done in obedience to divine command.

2. *To remember.* Said Brigham Young: "We are under the necessity of assembling here from Sabbath to Sabbath, and in Ward meetings, and besides, have to call our solemn assemblies, to teach, talk, pray, sing, and exhort. What for? *To keep us in remembrance of our God and our holy religion.* Is this custom necessary? Yes; because we are so liable to forget—so prone to wander, that we need to have the Gospel sounded in our ears as much as once, twice, or thrice a week, or, behold, we will turn again to our idols" (*Discourses of Brigham Young,* sel. John A. Widtsoe [Salt Lake City: Deseret Book Co., 1941], p. 165; italics added).

Most of us seem to have the "Nephite cycle" as part of our character. There is a point when we are teachable; our humility enables us to grow and to ride the crest of spirituality. Then there are other times when we begin to feel self-sufficient and puffed up with pride. These times cause us to fall of our own weight and ill-doing into pits of spiritual darkness. How much better it would be if we kept in remembrance our God and our religion and broke the cycle by consistent worship and righteous living. How much better it would be if we were humbled by the word of the Lord and strong enough in spirit to remember our God in whatsoever circumstances we find ourselves (see Alma 32:12–25).

3. *To renew our covenants.* When the Savior instituted the sacrament among the Nephite people, he broke the bread, blessed it, and gave it to those who believed and were baptized in his name. He instructed: "This shall ye always observe to do. . . . And this shall ye do in remembrance of my body, which I have shown unto you. And it shall be a *testimony* unto the Father that ye do always remember me. And if ye do always remember me ye shall have my Spirit to be with you" (3 Nephi 18:6–7; italics added).

Afterward, he blessed the wine and gave it to the others to drink. Jesus said: "Blessed are ye for this thing which ye have done, for this is fulfilling my commandments, and this doth *witness* unto the Father that ye are willing to do that which I have commanded you. And this shall ye always do to those who repent and are baptized in my name; and ye shall do it in remembrance of my blood, which I have shed for you, that ye may *witness* unto the Father that ye do always remember me. And if ye do always remember me ye shall have my Spirit to be with you" (3 Nephi 18:10–11; italics added).

We therefore have the opportunity to attend Church service each week and partake of the sacrament. As we do so, we renew our covenants and pledge afresh to stand as witnesses of God.

4. *To keep ourselves unspotted from the sins of the world.* "That thou mayest more fully keep thyself unspotted from the world, thou shalt go to the house of prayer and offer up thy sacraments upon my holy day," said the Lord through Joseph Smith (D&C 59:9). These words bring to mind one aspect of "pure religion" included in James's definition. Said he, "Pure religion and undefiled before God and the Father is this, To

visit the fatherless and widows in their affliction, and *to keep himself unspotted from the world"* (James 1:27; italics added). Those who worship regularly in spirit and truth at home and at church build up an immunity against the worldly influences that stain or spoil their happiness. This process of spiritual immunization occurs as hymns are sung, prayers are uttered, covenants are renewed, new truths are learned, and resolve is strengthened. Each portion of this process is related to true worship.

5. *To mingle with the Saints.* Many years ago, President Joseph F. Smith counseled Church members:

> It is imperatively necessary, at all times, and especially so when our associations do not afford us the moral and spiritual support which we require for our advancement, that *we go to the house of the Lord to worship and mingle with the Saints,* that their moral and spiritual influence may help to correct our false impressions and restore us to that life which the duties and obligations or our conscience and true religion impose upon us.
>
> "Good times" are often dangerous times, and social fraternity, if not of the right character, will prove more harmful than helpful. Let us, therefore, in the midst of our worldly callings and associations, not forget that paramount duty which we owe to ourselves and to our God *(Gospel Doctrine,* 5th ed. [Salt Lake City: Deseret Book Co., 1939], p. 243; italics added).

Beyond the family, no affiliation is more important or sanctifying than that found within The Church of Jesus Christ of Latter-day Saints. It was the Apostle Paul who said of those who took upon them the name of Christ, "Now therefore ye are no more strangers and foreigners, but fellowcitizens with the saints, and of the household of God" (Ephesians 2:19). It was Moroni who wrote about Church members and meetings, "The church did meet together oft, to fast and to pray, and to speak one with another concerning the welfare of their souls"

(Moroni 6:5). Both Paul and Moroni knew the importance of mingling with good people.

There is truth in the saying that a family who prays together stays together. The same can be said of worshiping together, for it is through worship that family members are drawn closer, the family receives the support of friends and neighbors, and the family allows God to become a vital part of their lives.

6. *To instruct and edify one another.* Few scriptures have intrigued me over the years more than the following: "I give unto you a commandment, that when ye are assembled together ye shall instruct and edify each other, that ye may know how to act and direct my church, how to act upon the points of my law and commandments, which I have given. And thus ye shall become instructed in the law of my church, and be sanctified by that which ye have received, and ye shall bind yourselves to act in all holiness before me—that inasmuch as ye do this, glory shall be added to the kingdom which ye have received. Inasmuch as ye do it not, it shall be taken, even that which ye have received. Purge ye out the iniquity which is among you; sanctify yourselves before me" (D&C 43:8–11).

I glean from these inspired words various thoughts about how we should worship:

• We are *commanded* to meet together regularly.

• A *perfecting process* is alluded to in verses 8 and 9. This process has two parts: (1) "Ye shall *instruct* [inform] and *edify* [build morally] each other . . . " Instruction may be given with or without the Spirit. Edification occurs only through the Spirit. Therefore, those who instruct must be prepared to disseminate information; they must also be prepared to do so under the direction of the Holy Ghost. (2) "Ye shall *bind* [obligate by duty or love] yourselves *to act* [covenant] . . . " Instruction and edification are short-lived if the participants fail to bind themselves to act upon those things taught. The listeners must resolve to improve their lives and to perfect their service at home or in the Church. Otherwise, they go their way and forget what manner of people they should be (see James 1:22–25).

• Two *promises* are extended to those who perform the two parts of the process. One is hidden in the scripture cited above, and the other is clearly stated. They are: "[Ye shall] be sanctified by that which ye have received" — a personal blessing; and "glory shall be added to the kingdom" — a collective blessing.

In planting the "pecan tree" practice of home and church worship in your family garden, you will want to help your children find personal answers to the question, Why worship? Perhaps the six reasons discussed above will prove helpful to you as you encourage and teach the young ones. You may also choose to speak about:

• The continuing need for spiritual nourishment.

• The need to find refreshing escape from worldly influences.

• The need for quiet reverence and a change of pace.

• The need to make covenants and perform saving ordinances.

• The need for Church service and the development of faith and spiritual gifts.

• The need to be kept in "the right way."

• The need to learn our duties and to stand as witnesses of Christ.

How to Worship

The Prophet Joseph Smith received this instruction from the Lord: "I give unto you these sayings that you may understand and know *how to worship*, and *know what you worship*, that you may come unto the Father in my name, and in due time receive of his fulness" (D&C 93:19; italics added).

This instruction was accompanied by an appeal to keep the commandments so that all might receive "grace for grace" the full blessings of God. Such "grace for grace" growth occurs as we seek to sanctify or cleanse our lives through righteous living and true worship.

True worship is more a matter of attitude and spirit than it is a matter of time and place. Let me illustrate this conclusion by sharing a personal experience.

A few years ago, a group of us stood in the celestial room of the Frankfurt Germany Temple. The building was under construction, and materials and tools were scattered over the floor. Workers were busily engaged in placing finishing touches on the walls and ceiling. Though the room was untidy and a beehive of activity, we were subdued by the emerging beauty of the place.

I asked Brother Henry Haurand, the construction supervisor, "Do the workers appreciate the significance of this project?"

"No," he answered. "They are not members of the Church, and they don't understand the sacred nature of temples. To them," he added, "this is just another job."

My wife inquired, "Do you always feel the Spirit of the Lord when you come here?"

"No, I do not," he responded. "When I enter the temple during the working day, I do so as a building supervisor, and I look with a critical eye for flaws in the construction. In this inspective mood, I feel nothing special about the place. But," Brother Haurand continued, "when I come here in the quiet of the evening and the place is free of noise and confusion, I am able to reflect upon the holy purposes of the temple. Then I am overwhelmed by the Spirit of the Lord."

I have pondered Brother Henry's words many, many times. I've concluded that he taught us two profound truths: (1) Sacred things are seen and appreciated only through "the eye of faith," and (2) things of the Spirit can only be discerned by "purer eyes" (Alma 5:15; D&C 131:7).

Eyes of Faith

I do not fault the workers who regarded the building of the temple as "just another job." They did their work, and they did it well, even though their eyes were blinded to the eternal worth of the building. Without knowledge of the restored gospel, without testimony of priesthood powers, and without faith in the living God, how could they have known that they were building something that would bridge heaven and earth?

People without faith and understanding of God's purposes "have eyes, and see not" (Jeremiah 5:21). Their vision is limited to immediate surroundings and the events of here and now. However, those who believe in the divine and who possess a hope in Christ have a more expanded view because they see through the *eyes of faith.*

A farmer who plants corn sees more than the warm earth and a small kernel in his hand. He exercises faith and envisions the ripened ear and the nourishment it will bring. We may look into the starry sky and marvel at the planets moving in their regular orbits. But when we scan the heavens through eyes of faith, the awesome wonders of the universe are magnified many times over, causing us to witness that there is a Supreme Creator (see Alma 30:44).

Sir Arthur Conan Doyle wrote, "God hath written Himself and His laws very broadly on all that is around us, if our *dull eyes* and *duller souls* could but read what He hath set before us" ("The White Company," in *The Works of Doyle,* p. 313; italics added).

Purer Eyes

Brother Haurand did not feel the Spirit of the Lord when he came into the temple looking for flaws in the construction. He was, however, overwhelmed by the Spirit when he entered in a reverent and charitable mood.

His experience reminds us that we see what we want to see; we feel what we want to feel. One with "purer eyes" will see and sense goodness in someone or something. But one with jaundiced eyes will never experience things of the Spirit.

"The light of the body," said Jesus, "is the eye: if therefore thine eye be single, thy whole body shall be full of light. But if thine eye be evil, thy whole body shall be full of darkness" (Matthew 6:22–23).

Moroni worried that readers would mock his record because of his weakness in writing. He was assured that fools would mock but weak things would become strong unto those who are meek, humble, and full of grace (see Ether 12:27).

We will never feel the Spirit of the Lord:

• If we attend worship services and count the grammatical errors made by speakers.

• If we look for flaws in the lives of Church leaders.

• If we fix our gaze upon spurious doctrine or "look beyond the mark" (Jacob 4:14).

We will, however, feel a closeness to the Lord:

• If we show charity toward all our brothers and sisters.

• If we try to catch others doing something good.

• If we look to living prophets and give heed to their inspired words (see D&C 1:14–38).

President Joseph F. Smith counseled: "Change the focus of your view, and of your eyes, from watching for evil to watching for that which is good, *that which is pure*. . . . Look for good in men, and where they fail to possess it try to build it up in them" (*Conference Report*, April 1913, p. 8; italics added).

Those who call themselves Saints have the continuing responsibility to sanctify their minds and bodies so that they might discern the finer or purer things of the Spirit (see D&C 131:7–8). Such a process begins when they discipline themselves to look for light rather than darkness. It grows as they become less inspective of others and more introspective of themselves. It matures as they learn to measure their words and throw light upon subjects discussed rather than spreading darkness. And it is fully achieved when they have cast out the beam from their own eyes and when they have actively sought "to be a light unto the world . . . and saviors of men" (see Matthew 7:1–5; D&C 103:9–10).

The Apostle Paul stated, "The natural man receiveth not the things of the Spirit of God: for they are foolishness unto him: neither can he know them, because they are spiritually discerned" (1 Corinthians 2:14). We must, therefore, put off the natural man and become Saints through the atonement of Christ. Then, as we acquire meekness, humility, patience, submissiveness, and love, we shall see through "purer eyes" and obtain a clearer vision of spiritual things (see Mosiah 3:19).

Other thoughts about how to worship are provided below. Each is worthy of prayerful consideration as the "pecan tree" practice of home and church worship is established in your home.

Meditation

President David O. McKay spoke these words in a General Conference of the Church:

> I think we pay too little attention to the value of meditation, a principle of devotion. In our worship there are two elements: One is spiritual communion arising from our own meditation; the other, instruction from others, particularly from those who have authority to guide and instruct us. Of the two, the more profitable introspectively is the meditation. *Meditation is the language of the soul.* It is defined as "a form of private devotion, or spiritual exercise, consisting in deep, continued reflection on some religious theme." *Meditation is a form of prayer.* We can *say* prayers without having any spiritual response. We can say prayers as the unrighteous king in *Hamlet* who said: "My words fly up, my thoughts remain below: Words without thoughts never to heaven go . . . "
> *Meditation is one of the most secret, most sacred doors through which we pass into the presence of the*

201

Lord (In *Conference Report,* April 1946, p. 113; italics added).

When I was a young man and somewhat loathe to speak in Church, my father gave me some timely advice. He advised me to enter the chapel quietly, to take my seat promptly, to assume a reverent mood, to meditate about spiritual things, and to determine what I would say if called upon to speak. By doing so, he promised, I would be prepared to participate in the service if and when the invitation were extended; but, if not called upon, I would have heard at least one valuable sermon—the one I had outlined in my own mind.

Home and Church

As mentioned previously in this book, parents have the responsibility to teach their children to pray and to walk uprightly before the Lord. They fulfill this awesome responsibility through a combination of many things, including the blending of home and church worship.

At home, family prayers are said, family home evenings are held, scripture reading is encouraged, and other worshipful activities are conducted. These activities help to build character and to keep the lives of both parents and children ever Godward. Yet most families need additional assistance in teaching and caring for the spiritual welfare of children. Such assistance is obtained through Church officers and organizations. It is not intended that Church leaders and programs replace parents and home influences. To do so would be an abdication of duty on the part of the parents and an intrusion of others upon the prerogatives of the home. But bishoprics, quorum leaders, auxiliary officers, Sunday School presidencies, home and visiting teachers, and other groups of people are included in the Church organization to help parents with the needs of family members.

The Savior gave us a pattern to follow in correlating home and family worship. After his resurrection, Jesus visited the

Nephites and taught them doctrine that he perceived they could not fully understand. He therefore instructed, "Go ye unto your homes, and ponder upon the things which I have said, and ask of the Father, in my name, that ye may understand, and prepare your minds for the morrow." (3 Nephi 17:3). Elder Bruce R. McConkie elaborated upon this pattern by saying:

> We come together in congregations, seeking the guidance of the Holy Spirit, studying the revelations, reading the scriptures, and hearing expressions of doctrine and counsel given by those who are appointed. These teachings ought to be delivered by the power of the Holy Spirit. They ought to be received by the same power. And if they are, then the speaker and the hearer will be mutually edified, and we will have true and proper worship.
>
> Then when the meeting is over, the amen should not end it. We should go to our homes and to our families and to our circles, and we should search out the revelations and find out what the Lord has said on the subjects involved. We should seek to get in tune with the Holy Spirit and to gain a witness, not solely of the truth and divinity of the work in which we are engaged but also of the doctrines that are taught by those who preach to us. We come into these congregations, and sometimes a speaker brings a jug of living water that has in it many gallons. And he pours it out on the congregation, all that the members have brought is a single cup and so that's all they take away. Or maybe they have their hands over the cups, and they don't get anything to speak of.
>
> On other occasions we have meetings where the speaker comes and all he brings is a little cup of eternal truth, and the members of the congregation come with a large jug, and all they get in their jugs is the little dribble that came from a man who should have known better and who should have prepared himself and talked from the revelations and spoken by the power of the Holy Spirit. We are obligated in the Church to speak by the power of the Spirit. We are commanded

203

to treasure up the words of light and truth and then give forth the portion that is appropriate and needful on every occasion (BYU Address, "The Seven Deadly Heresies," BYU Devotional Address, June 1, 1980).

By employing the pattern for home and church worship set by Jesus and as described by Elder McConkie, stewardships are honored and participants are strengthened. How could it be otherwise when parents take the lead and friends in the faith work cooperatively in teaching and guiding the young and the old? Under this inspired arrangement, the home is the launching and landing pad, with parents at the controls; the Church and its programs and programmers are the guidance systems provided as helps to the parents in guiding children along the right path.

Full Purpose of Heart

Said President John Taylor: "When we do meet to worship God, I like to see us worship him with all our hearts. I think it altogether out of place on such occasions to hear people talk about secular things: these are times, above all others perhaps, when our feelings and affections should be drawn out towards God. If we sing praises to God, let us do it in the proper spirit; if we pray, let every soul be engaged in prayer, doing it with all our hearts, that through our union our spirits may be blended in one, that our prayers and our worship may be available with God, whose Spirit permeates all things, and is always present in the assemblies of good and faithful Saints" (*The Gospel Kingdom*, sel. G. Homer Durham [Salt Lake City: Bookcraft, 1943), p. 228).

We sometimes use the expressions "out of tune" or "in tune" in reference to people and worship services. The first expression describes those who drag the world into sacred settings and attempt to pay their devotions to God with half of their mind in Babylon and the other half in Zion. Since they are "double-minded" men and women, their actions are unstable and their words are contaminated. On the other hand, those who are "in tune" come before the Lord at home or at church with humble spirits and eyes upward. They have blocked out the lesser things of the world and are ready to receive instructions from on high (see James 1:8).

I like what President Spencer W. Kimball said about "true worship":

> The best choir, the best speaker, the most noted lecturer, cannot bring true worship into your soul. It must proceed from within, out of a deep sense of love and devotion and dependence and humility. . . .
>
> We do not go to Sabbath meetings to be entertained or even solely to be instructed. We go to worship the Lord. It is an individual responsibility, and regardless of what is said from the pulpit, if one wishes to worship the Lord in spirit and in truth, he may do so by attending his meetings, partaking of the sacrament, and contemplating the beauties of the gospel. If the service is a failure to you, you have failed. No one can worship for you; you must do your own waiting upon the Lord (*The Teachings of Spencer W. Kimball,* ed. Edward L. Kimball [Salt Lake City: Bookcraft, 1982], pp. 514–15).

An Attitude of Reverence

In our materialistic and sometimes raucous world, there is a danger that we will become too accustomed to the noises about us. Such noises, if not controlled, may rouse savage instincts and feelings and bring out the worst in you and me. So, there are times when we must "be still and know that [there is a] God" (D&C 101:16). I speak of times when we sweep away the mundane things around us, cast away idle thoughts, and allow the intents of our hearts to center upon Him who is the discerner of the thoughts and intents of our hearts (see Hebrews 4:12). I speak of times when we assume a reverent posture and worship our Father in Heaven.

Worship and reverence are inseparable. Such was the contention of a modern prophet, President David O. McKay, who spoke often of reverence. In one conference setting, he declared:

> Inseparable from the acceptance of the existence of God is an attitude of reverence. The greatest manifestation of spirituality is reverence; indeed, reverence is spirituality. Reverence is profound respect mingled with love. It is a "complex emotion made up of mingled feelings of the soul." Carlyle says it is "the highest of human feelings." If reverence is the highest, then irreverence is the lowest state in which a man can live in the world. Be that as it may, it is nevertheless true that an irreverent man has a crudeness about him that is repellent. He is cynical, often sneering, and always iconoclastic.
>
> Reverence embraces regard, deference, honor, and esteem. Without some degree of it, therefore, there would be no courtesy, no gentility, no consideration of others' feelings or of others' rights. Reverence is the fundamental virtue in religion. It is one of the signs of strength; irreverence, one of the surest indications of weakness. "No man will rise high," says one man, "who jeers at sacred things. The fine loyalties of life must be reverenced or they will be foresworn in the day of trial." . . .
>
> If there were more reverence in human hearts, there would be less room for sin and sorrow, and there would be increased capacity for joy and gladness. To make more cherished, more adaptable, more attractive this gem among brilliant virtues is a project worthy of the most united and prayerful efforts of every parent, every officer, and every member of the Church (*Conference Report*, April 1967, pp. 86–87).

A Shared Responsibility

One other aspect of worship, a how-to, if you will, should be mentioned. This appendage to the subject is best labeled "joint-preparation" or "shared responsibility." It can be introduced by a story that is now a part of LDS folklore. A rather harried mother awakes from a deep sleep on Sunday morning and anticipates the demands and expectations of the day. Through her mind races thoughts of meals, children, baths, dresses, and all the other trimmings of the day. She nudges her husband, who is snoring peacefully at her side, and brings him back to a state of consciousness. Then, she announces, "Honey, you wake up the children, give them a bath, clothe them, feed them breakfast, and do all else to get them ready for Church. I'll go sit in the car and honk the horn until you all arrive."

Too frequently, I suspect, the burdens of preparing for worship at home or church are strapped upon the back of the mother. Consequently, there is not much rest or refreshment in the Sabbath Day or the family home evening for her. Fathers and children must assume their fair share of the responsibility for family worship and help with the preparations. No one should sit and honk while others are engaged in needful work, attempting to do things with an eye single to the glory of God.

Conclusion

We read the scriptural accounts of the daughters of Onitah and the Hebrew sons who refused to worship gods of gold or wood or stone, even at the peril of their own lives, and we marvel at their moral integrity (see Abraham 1:11; Daniel 3:18). These young spiritual giants were determined not to pollute their worship or offend the living God. At the same time, we wonder why so many of our modern youth walk in their own way, after the image of their own god, "whose image is in the likeness of the world, and whose substance is that of an idol" (D&C 1:16). Is it possible that too few parents are planting and cultivating the "pecan tree" practice of true home and church worship?

We read of the ancient Zoramites who engaged in a false worship service one day of the week. Their rote and boastful prayers were misdirected and Satan-oriented. Their hearts were lifted up in pride and centered upon gold, silver, and all manner of fine goods. Moreover, after the set prayers had been spoken, "they returned to their homes, never speaking of their God again until they had assembled themselves together again to the holy stand" (Alma 31:23). Such practices seem repulsive to most of us. But, once again, we wonder why so many of our people, young and old, fail to worship God in an acceptable manner and fail to carry Sabbath teachings and spirit with them throughout the week and into the home. Would this be the case if the "pecan tree" practice of true home and church worship was growing in our family gardens?

One of our basic tenets is, "We claim the privilege of worshipping Almighty God according to the dictates of our own conscience, and allow all men the same privilege, let them worship *how, where,* or *what* they may" (Eleventh Article of Faith; italics added). Worship is a personal matter; it is a wonderful privilege, and all of us should be guardians of this inalienable right. But is it not our responsibility to help others, especially our children, "worship God, in whatsoever place [they] may be in, in spirit and truth"? (Alma 34:38). In the words of Alma, "their souls are precious . . . therefore, give unto us, O Lord, power and wisdom that we may bring these [our children] again unto thee" (Alma 31:35). Let us plant the "pecan tree" practice of home and Church worship, and

let us nourish it with great care, that it may get root, that it may grow up, and bring forth fruit unto us (Alma 32:37).

TEMPLE ACTIVITY AND WORSHIP

Come ye, and let us go up to the mountain of the Lord, to the house of the God of Jacob; and he will teach us of his ways, and we will walk in his paths (Isaiah 2:3).

"Temple worship [can] do more for an individual in all facets of his Church life than anything else," said Thomas Bell, former president of the Washington, D.C., Temple (LaRene Gaunt, "A Day in Heaven," *Ensign*, December 1991, p. 36). If this is true, and I believe that it is, no subject is more worthy of our consideration as we plant the last tree in our family grove of "pecan tree" practices.

On more than one occasion, President Ezra Taft Benson has spoken tenderly of the family and temple. I especially enjoy the following account:

> Since my earliest childhood memory, the spirit of the temple has blessed our home. I remember as a little boy seeing my mother bending over the ironing board pressing long strips of white cloth, with beads of perspiration on her forehead. I asked her why. She answered, "These are temple robes, my son. Your father and I are going to the temple in Logan." She then put the old flatiron on the stove, drew a chair close to mine, and told me about temple work. I learned how vitally important it is to go to the temple and to participate there in sacred ordinances. Every time my par-

209

ents returned from a visit to the temple, the experience
brought renewed love and strength to our family circle.
I love the temple with all my heart and soul. Nearly
every week, my beloved wife, Flora, and I receive the
ordinances in the temple for a loved one.

The temple is an ever-present reminder that God
intends the family to be eternal. We should share with
our families our love of our forebears and our gratitude
to be able to help them receive the saving ordinances,
as my parents did with me. As we do so, increased
bonds of appreciation and affection will develop within
our families (*Come unto Christ: Through Temple Ordinances and Covenants* [Salt Lake City: The Church
of Jesus Christ of Latter-day Saints, 1987], p. 2).

I am not certain whether President Benson's mother realized the importance of that day with her ironing board, flatiron,
and inquisitive son. But it is certain that she made the most of
a precious teaching moment and instructed her son when his
interest was high and his attention was undivided. There was
nothing contrived or staged about this object lesson. It happened spontaneously, as a loving mother planted truths in a
future prophet's mind and stirred a desire for temple activity
and worship that never waned.

Related Concepts

Whenever I think of the *family*, I think instinctively of the
temple. Why? Because the temple is the birthplace of the eternal
family unit. Whenever I think of the *house of the Lord*, I think
of my own house. Why? Because "only the home can compare
with the temple in sacredness" (*Bible Dictionary*, p. 781).
Whenever I think of the family and the temple, I think of the
Holy Priesthood. Why? Because it is through the power of the
priesthood that the family receives in the temple the crowning
blessings of the gospel of Jesus Christ.

I have always appreciated the significance and the inter-
relatedness of the family, the temple, and the priesthood. Such

concepts are keystones in the gospel arch that spans heaven and earth. However, I have gained fresh and added appreciation for this trio of saving principles through an experience with an unusual couple.

A Full Man

I had traveled to a distant place on a stake conference assignment. My first order of business was to interview a man to see if he was worthy and prepared to receive a restoration of blessings. The man explained to me how he had rebelled in times past, become estranged from the Church, suffered through a divorce, and, finally, found his present wife.

He said he had married his second wife after a short, whirlwind courtship. She was not a member of the Church at the time and knew nothing about her husband's past. A few weeks after their marriage, he awakened one morning out of a deep sleep and was startled to see his wife sitting next to the bed staring down at him. He wondered what was wrong. The conversation went something like this: "Joe, I love you, but sometimes you frighten me." She added, "There are times when I see in you absolute greatness, and there are times when I see nothing. You seem to be two persons — one with unlimited possibilities and one with ordinary talents and abilities. Please explain to me," she begged. "Why do I feel this way?"

After some thought and reflection, he responded: "Honey, you really don't know me at all. I am a Mormon."

"What is that?" she asked.

He then related the basics of his faith and previous Church activity. She listened intently. He said, "I am a high priest and hold the Holy Melchizedek Priesthood."

His wife replied, "What does that mean?"

Again, he gave an explanation. On and on the conversation continued until he had fully revealed himself to his sweet wife. The last subject he addressed was temple sealings and the eternal nature of the family. This subject melted her heart and caused her to weep openly.

When all the questions had been asked and the man's past had been fully disclosed, the woman inquired, "What would you have to do to bring all of the goodness you have mentioned back into your life so that it will remain and bless both of us?"

"Oh, it would be too long and too painful. I would need to find a stake president, confess my sins, and subject myself to Church discipline," was his reply.

The determined woman threw the telephone directory into her husband's lap and cried, "Find a stake president! Whatever is required, we will do it, and we will begin today."

They did find a stake president. The man's records were obtained, and disciplinary action was taken. Then the man began his long climb toward full fellowship in the Church. In the meantime, the wife was taught the gospel, received baptism, and became a very active Latter-day Saint.

The couple's story touched my heart and convinced me that the man's repentance had been complete, and I restored his blessings in accord with approved policies and procedures. Once the amen was pronounced, a beautiful and wonderful thing happened. The wife threw herself into her husband's arms and sobbed over and over again, "Now I have my full man. Now I have my full man."

I shall never forget the lesson taught by this unusual woman. She reminded me that without family, temple, and priesthood, I am only a shell of a man. With these concepts and related powers, however, I do have unlimited possibilities, and I can become a *full man* — even a "man of Christ" (see Helaman 3:29). She also reminded me that I must not take for granted or place in jeopardy those blessings and privileges that are more precious than life itself.

In planting the "pecan tree" practice of temple activity and worship, and in striving to become full men and women in

Christ, we should remember that family refers to *a people*, temple to *a place*, and priesthood to *a power*.

As I discuss each of these concepts, consider, if you will, each one as a root of the plant, with the Spirit serving as the taproot or occupying the central position in the line of growth. Moreover, keep in mind that this "pecan tree" practice has the potential of doing for you what it did for President Benson, who testified, "[Each] visit to the temple . . . brought renewed love and strength to our family circle."

A People

Those who believe in the true and living God and who have sought to obey his commandments have been called by many names. In ancient times, such true believers were referred to as a "peculiar treasure," "a kingdom of priests," "an holy nation," and "a special people" (see Exodus 19:5–6; Deuteronomy 7:6). In the meridian of time, followers of Christ were not only designated as "an holy nation" and "a peculiar people" but also as "Christians" and "a royal priesthood" (see 1 Peter 2:9; Acts 11:26). In our modern day, the following expressions have been used: "a light unto the Gentiles," "a pure people," "salt of the earth," and a light or standard to the world (see D&C 86:11; 100:16; 101:39; 115:5). Common to all of these dispensations, however, is the term *Saints,* meaning those " 'free from blemish' whether physical or moral" (see *Bible Dictionary*, p. 768).

A search of holy writ reveals that people who have entered into a covenant with God have been known as "Saints" from the days of ancient Israel to the present. Such a lofty title is not presumptive or something to boast about. It is a means of identifying those who are striving to become sanctified through covenant-making and covenant-keeping (see D&C 125:2). It refers to those who live with this thought uppermost in mind: "The natural man is an enemy to God, and has been from the fall of Adam, and will be, forever and ever, unless he yields to the enticings of the Holy Spirit, and putteth off the natural man and becometh a saint through the atonement of Christ the Lord, and becometh as a child, submissive, meek, humble, patient, full of love, willing to submit to all things which the Lord seeth fit to inflict upon him, even as a child doth submit to his father" (Mosiah 3:19).

To attain the measure of saintliness outlined in this scripture, we live in family units where truth is taught and modeled; we attend Church regularly and grow in the gospel of Jesus Christ; and we keep ourselves pointed for the temple, where the crowning blessings of the priesthood are received. No wonder the world regards us as a family-oriented, churchgoing, and temple-building people. If only they and we understood more perfectly the saving and exalting role of dedicated temples, perhaps all of us would accelerate our efforts to gain entrance into the house of the Lord and to become Saints in the full sense of the word.

The Psalmist declared: "Who shall ascend into the hill of the Lord? or who shall stand in his holy place? He that hath clean hands, and a pure heart; who hath not lifted up his soul unto vanity, nor sworn deceitfully. He shall receive the blessing from the Lord, and righteousness from the God of his salvation" (Psalm 24:3–5).

In my mind, "clean hands" suggests a cleanliness of body; a "pure heart" suggests a purity of motive; a soul not lifted up unto vanity is one who retains humility; and one who has not sworn deceitfully is one who enters the temple honorably and fully qualified to receive the blessings of the temple.

President Spencer W. Kimball adds this insight and warning about mechanical temple activity and worthiness: "All these ordinances are futile unless with them there is a great righteousness. . . . Sometimes people feel if they have complied with the more mechanical things that they are in line. And yet perhaps their hearts are not always pure. . . . With hearts that are absolutely purged and cleaned, and living the more me-

214

chanical things, we are prepared to come into the holy temple" (*The Teachings of Spencer W. Kimball*, ed. Edward L. Kimball [Salt Lake City: Bookcraft, 1982], pp. 536–37).

One who enters the temple under false pretenses or engages in ordinance work like a robot is little better than the moneychangers who desecrated God's house and were routed from the premises by the Savior (see Matthew 21:12–13).

A few years ago, my wife and I attended an afternoon session in the Salt Lake Temple. The company was small, consisting of no more than a dozen men and a dozen women. I scanned the group, casually noting that all were strangers to me except my wife. We were instructed in the first room and then moved to the next. As we took our seats in the second room, there was a slight commotion. I looked about to see what was wrong. In doing so, I saw a woman leave the room. All of us assumed that she was ill or had perhaps forgotten a piece of clothing. The interruption was brief and the instruction resumed. It was a refreshing temple experience for us, and we returned home rejoicing.

The next day I received a very unusual telephone call. My secretary came to my office door and said, "A woman wants to speak with you, but she won't give me her name."

I picked up the phone and announced myself. The caller promptly asked, "Elder Asay, what do you know about me?"

"How can I answer your question," I responded, "when you haven't even given me your name?"

She continued, "You were in the three o'clock temple session yesterday, weren't you?"

"Yes," I answered, "I was there."

She said, "Do you remember someone walking out of the second room?"

"Yes," I replied.

"It was I who walked out of the temple yesterday. Elder Asay, what do you know about me?"

At this point the conversation was becoming a bit tedious,

and I said, "My dear, please don't play games with me. Unless you tell me who you are, how can I respond to your query?"

Almost totally ignoring what I said, the woman confessed: "It was I who left the temple room yesterday before the instruction began. I did so because you looked at me with a searching look, and you made me feel as though I was unworthy to be there." Once again, she asked, "What do you know about me?"

I said: "Well, if you attended the temple worthily yesterday, I apologize for how I may have looked at you and for how I may have made you feel. However, if you were there unworthily, I make no apology."

There was a long silence and then soft sobbing over the telephone. Finally, the woman confessed: "I have committed a serious sin, and I attended the temple yesterday under false pretenses. However," she added, "I visited my bishop last night, and I will follow his counsel and advice."

This unusual experience reminded me of the words of Moroni:

> Will ye longer deny the Christ, or can ye behold the Lamb of God? Do ye suppose that ye shall dwell with him under a consciousness of your guilt? Do ye suppose that ye could be happy to dwell with that holy Being, when your souls are racked with a consciousness of guilt that ye have ever abused his laws?
>
> Behold, I say unto you that ye would be more miserable to dwell with a holy and just God, under a consciousness of your filthiness before him, than ye would to dwell with the damned souls in hell.
>
> For behold, when ye shall be brought to see your nakedness before God, and also the glory of God, and the holiness of Jesus Christ, it will kindle a flame of unquenchable fire upon you (Mormon 9:3–5).

It is most significant that the woman judged herself through my eyes in the house of the Lord. She verified in part the truth that "no unclean thing can dwell with God" or abide his holy

216

presence (1 Nephi 10:21), for "the piercing eye of the Almighty God" sees all (Jacob 2:10).

Nothing escapes his view, whether it be done in public or in private. Therefore, we should be consistent in our righteousness and strive to reach that state of goodness whereby we feel comfortable in his holy house—the place where he manifests himself to his people (see D&C 109:5).

Perhaps we should regard each visit to the temple as a time to examine and prove ourselves, whether we are planted firmly in the faith and whether we are the type of people we should be.

The discussion of temple activity and God's "peculiar people" would be incomplete if reference were not made to the ongoing temple expectations for Church members. I refer to those essential actions taken by the Saints to fulfill the duties specified by scripture and the teachings of priesthood leaders. They are:

• Study the principles of the gospel relating to temples and temple covenants and ordinances and teach them to your children and others.

• Obtain and retain a valid temple recommend, for it is a certificate of worthiness and serves as a shield against temptation.

• Receive personal endowments and honor the covenants made in the house of the Lord, including the proper wearing of the garments.

• Engage in family history and family research activities, thus welding one generation to another.

• Perform vicarious ordinances for ancestors and seek to become a Savior on Mount Zion (see Obadiah 1:21).

• Keep the family united in the gospel and the Church with the doors of your "tent" pitched always toward the temple (see Mosiah 2:6).

If temple activity and worship is to serve as an edifying "pecan tree" practice for members of the Church, it must not be performed in a perfunctory or mechanical manner. A superficial approach to the ordinances received in the house of the Lord mocks and offends God. It is also imperative that we meet temple expectations and ascend into his holy place with clean hands, pure hearts, and honest intent. Otherwise, our offerings to God may not be acceptable, nor will we be numbered among his chosen flock or known as "a pure people."

A Place

God's house, the temple, is a very special place. It has been referred to as a holy sanctuary, a refuge from the cares of a troubled world, an island of godliness in a godless sea, and as a place where God, his Holy Spirit, angels, and mortals mingle. In a dedicatory prayer, the Prophet Joseph Smith described the temple as "a house of prayer, a house of fasting, a house of faith, a house of learning, a house of glory, a house of order, a house of God" (D&C 109:8).

Another revelation contains this enlightening description: "A place of thanksgiving for all saints, and for a place of instruction for all those who are called to the work of the ministry in all their several callings and offices; that they may be perfected in the understanding of their ministry, in theory, in principle, and in doctrine, in all things pertaining to the kingdom of God on the earth, the keys of which kingdom have been conferred upon you. Yea, and my presence shall be there, for I will come into it, and all the pure in heart that shall come into it shall see God" (D&C 97:13–14, 16).

In summary, "a temple is literally a house of the Lord, a holy sanctuary in which sacred ceremonies and ordinances of the gospel are performed by and for the living and also in behalf of the dead. A place where the Lord may come, it is the most holy of any place of worship on the earth. Only the home can compare with the temple in sacredness" (*Bible Dictionary*, pp. 780–81).

Many ask, Why a temple? In addition to the answers given

above, we respond, "That the Son of man might have a place to manifest himself to his people"; and, so that his people may feel God's power and feel constrained to acknowledge that the Lord has sanctified it, and that it is his house, even a house of his holiness (see D&C 109:5,13). Furthermore, in the words of President Ezra Taft Benson, "The temple is the house of the Lord. Our attendance there blesses the dead and also blesses us, for it is a house of revelation" (Ezra Taft Benson, "A Sacred Responsibility," *Ensign*, May 1986, p. 78).

One cannot read section 109 of the Doctrine and Covenants without knowing that the prayer given by the Prophet Joseph Smith at the dedication of the temple in Kirtland, Ohio, was indeed given to him by revelation. This scripture is packed with truths that could come from only one source — God. For example, there is one short verse, consisting of only *thirty-one* words, that cites four reasons for temple building and temple attendance. Though these four reasons may not be all-inclusive of the many reasons for going to the temple, they are insightful and deserving of further comments: "That they [1] *may grow up in thee*, and [2] *receive a fulness of the Holy Ghost*, and [3] *be organized according to thy laws*, and [4] *be prepared to obtain every needful thing*" (D&C 109:15; italics added).

"That they may grow up in thee." In many respects, the temple is a school of the Saints. Initially, attendees are much like children in a grammar school. They know little about the covenants, ordinances, and related instructions. But as they return again and again to the temple, they learn line upon line and precept upon precept until they reach higher grades of knowledge and understanding. Then, in due time, they find added meaning in the temple procedures and gain deep insights into the plan of salvation. Gradually, they grow in obedience, devotion to duty, and other aspects of gospel living, thus gaining a maturity of faith. All of this is done in harmony with this divine injunction: "Seek ye diligently and teach one another words of wisdom; yea, seek ye out of the best books

words of wisdom, seek learning even by study and also by faith" (D&C 109:7).

Said John A. Widtsoe: "Men grow mighty under the results of temple service; women grow strong under it; the community increases in power; until the devil has less influence than he ever had before" ("Temple Worship," *Utah Genealogical and Historical Magazine,* April 1931, p. 51).

"[That they may] receive a fulness of the Holy Ghost." The Holy Ghost is manifested both as a power and as a gift. The power comes to us before baptism as a convincing witness that the gospel is true. The gift comes only after proper and authorized baptism: "The gift of the Holy Ghost is the right to have, whenever one is worthy, the companionship of the Holy Ghost." Such companionship "acts as a cleansing agent to purify a person and sanctify him from all sin" (see *Bible Dictionary,* p. 704).

We are told that we can speak with the tongue of angels when under the influence of the Holy Ghost (see 2 Nephi 31:13). We read that people are sealed with the Holy Ghost or the Holy Spirit of Promise (see Ephesians 1:13). We know that those who are wise receive the truth and take the Holy Spirit for their guide (see D&C 45:57). Hence, those who go to the temple and partake of its saving ordinances are endowed with power from on high, even the fullness of the Holy Ghost.

"[That they may] be organized according to [God's] laws." God is a God of law and order. His house is a house of order (D&C 109:8), his work is a work of order (D&C 20:68), his power or priesthood is referred to as the order of the priest-hood (D&C 94:6). Of a surety, he is not a God of confusion, nor does he walk in crooked paths.

It is reasonable that the God of order would instruct his children thus: "All who will have a blessing at my hands shall abide the law which was appointed for that blessing, and the conditions thereof, as were instituted from before the foundation of the world" (D&C 132:5).

220

Elder Richard L. Evans taught, "One of the greatest blessings of life is law.... Without law, commandments, standards, discipline, we would be utterly loose and utterly lost."

Anyone who understands the workings of the Lord will agree with Elder Evans's statement and conclude that every "thou shalt" and every "thou shalt not" is an expression of God's love for us. If he did not love us, he would not provide us warnings and directions, nor would he pronounce laws and promised blessings. But since he is our loving Father in Heaven, he commands and invites us to receive the protection and goodness associated with his laws.

Whenever we attend the temple, we are reminded of God's laws, including the laws of the gospel, sacrifice, consecration, chastity, and other holy requirements. Moreover, we are reminded of the blessings and destiny promised those who are obedient. And if we live in accord with temple commitments, we do become organized.

"[That they may] obtain every needful thing." Speaking of the temple endowment, President Brigham Young declared: "Your endowment is, to receive all those ordinances in the House of the Lord, which are necessary for you, after you have departed this life, to enable you to walk back to the presence of the Father, passing the angels who stand as sentinels, being enabled to give them the key words, the signs and tokens, pertaining to the Holy Priesthood, and gain your eternal exaltation in spite of earth and hell" (*Journal of Discourses* 2:31).

Additional understanding about the temple endowment can be obtained from the writings of James E. Talmage. He wrote:

> The Temple Endowment, as administered in modern temples, comprises instruction relating to the significance and sequence of past dispensations, and the importance of the present as the greatest and grandest era in human history. This course of instruction in-

cludes a recital of the most prominent events of the creative period, the condition of our first parents in the Garden of Eden, their disobedience and consequent expulsion from that blissful abode, their condition in the lone and dreary world when doomed to live by labor and sweat, the plan of redemption by which the great transgression may be atoned, the period of the great apostasy, the restoration of the Gospel with all its ancient powers and privileges, the absolute and indispensable condition of personal purity and devotion to the right in present life, and a strict compliance with Gospel requirements (*The House of the Lord* [Salt Lake City: The Church of Jesus Christ of Latter-day Saints, rev. ed. 1976], pp. 83–84).

A master list of "needful things" obtained by the Saints through temple activity includes: the fulness of the priesthood is received; the patriarchal order is conferred upon men; men and women are sealed as husband and wife for time and for all eternity; the family unit is made eternal; the members perform vicarious ordinances in behalf of their kindred dead; members are taught how to gain eternal life; washings, anointings, and other saving ordinances are performed; and members are endowed with power from on high.

While serving as a bishop, I was requested to perform several civil marriages in the homes of Church members. In each instance, the people involved attempted to dignify the occasion and to make it as spiritual as possible. Usually the home was sparkling clean and decorated with fragrant flowers. All seemed intent upon making the experience special and memorable, especially for the more sensitive bride. But in every instance, I felt somewhat uncomfortable in performing the ceremony. I knew that I was properly authorized to speak the required words and to pronounce the couple man and wife. I knew that all was being done within the requirements of the law and in fulfillment of social expectations. At the same time, however, I knew that the ceremony included two restrictive clauses: (1) "as long as you both shall live," and (2) "legally and lawfully wedded for a period of your mortal lives." Such restrictive clauses made me feel as if I was not completing the job or doing all that God would have me do. I knew that the couple was not receiving the crowning blessings of the Holy Priesthood. I knew of a better way.

In recent years, I have been privileged to participate in the creation of new Church units, such as wards and stakes. Each of these occasions has been very rewarding, for I rejoice when observing the marvelous growth of the Church. However, none of these creations has brought me the joy and satisfaction that I feel when I seal a man and woman in the temple and create a new family — the most important unit in time or eternity. Though the unit begins with only two persons, I know that I am sealing a potential king and queen who will eventually rule over a kingdom of many subjects.

Celestial marriage is soul-satisfying because no restrictive clauses are spoken; participants are required to be morally clean and pure; the sealing is performed under the watchful eyes of God, angels, and living witnesses; a power to seal on earth that which is sealed in heaven is exercised; and vows exchanged are binding for time and for all eternity.

Temple activity encompasses work for both the living and the dead. The living receive endowments, participate in sealings, and do other things for themselves that bring blessings into their lives. But not until they become involved in vicarious ordinances in behalf of the dead do they become Saviors on Mount Zion. Such temple activity welds families together and enables participants to gain deep understanding of this scripture: "How knoweth a man the master whom he has not served, and who is a stranger unto him, and is far from the thoughts and intents of his heart?" (Mosiah 5:13).

What parent does not want his or her children to grow up in God, to receive a fullness of the Holy Ghost, to become organized according to God's laws, and to obtain every needful thing? What parent does not prefer celestial marriage over civil marriage? And what parent would not want a son or daughter to become a Savior on Mount Zion? All of this and more can be received by our children if we guide their feet toward the temple—a most sacred place.

A Power

Some may regard Latter-day Saints as a presumptive people when they speak of a power to baptize in behalf of the dead or to seal a couple together for time and all eternity. Such critics are unfamiliar with the restored gospel and the Church of Jesus Christ, else they would know the truthfulness of the following statement: "It may seem to some to be a very bold doctrine that we talk of—a power which records or binds on earth and binds in heaven. Nevertheless, in all ages of the world, whenever the Lord has given a dispensation of the priesthood to any man by actual revelation, or any set of men, this power has always been given. Hence, whatsoever those men did in authority, in the name of the Lord, and did it truly and faithfully, and kept a proper and faithful record of the same, it became a law on earth and in heaven, and could not be annulled, according to the decrees of the great Jehovah" (D&C 128:9).

We must not forget that the Savior instructed his disciples, "I will give unto thee the keys of the kingdom of heaven: and whatsoever thou shalt bind on earth shall be bound in heaven: and whatsoever thou shalt loose on earth shall be loosed in heaven" (Matthew 16:19).

The record states that the disciples went forth under Christ's commission or charge and "preached every where, the Lord working with them, and confirming the word with signs" (Mark 16:20). Like the Master, they healed the sick, performed baptisms, cast out evil spirits, and engaged in vicarious services for the dead (1 Corinthians 15:29). All of this was done in the name of Christ and in behalf of his holy cause.

Malachi, the last of the Old Testament prophets, prophesied that Elijah would return to the earth "before the coming of the great and dreadful day of the Lord." The purpose of his coming was to restore lost powers and "turn the heart of the fathers to the children, and the heart of the children to their fathers, lest [God] come and smite the earth with a curse" (Malachi 4:5–6).

As forecasted, Elijah did return and restored through the Prophet Joseph Smith certain keys pertaining to the restoration of the priesthood and "the great work to be done in the temples of the Lord" (see D&C 27:9; 110:14–16; 128:17; 138:47–48). Since that memorable day, the spirit of Elijah has wrought upon the Saints and prompted significant family history and temple activity.

Speaking about the spirit of Elijah, Elder Boyd K. Packer wrote: "When a member of the Church comes under its influence, it is a powerful, compelling force which motivates him with a desire to be attending to genealogical and temple work. It leaves him anxious over the well-being of his forebears. When that spirit comes, somehow we desire to know more about those forebears—we desire to know them" (Boyd K. Packer, *The Holy Temple* [Salt Lake City, Bookcraft, 1986], p. 210).

One cannot think of the spirit of Elijah, the holy priesthood, and the temple without reflecting upon the "power of godliness," as described in the revelation on priesthood: "This greater priesthood administereth the gospel and holdeth the key of the mysteries of the kingdom, even the key of the knowledge of God. Therefore, in the ordinances thereof, the power of godliness is manifest. And without the ordinances thereof, and the authority of the priesthood, the power of godliness is not manifest unto men in the flesh; For without this no man can see the face of God, even the Father, and live" (D&C 84:19–22).

Let me add some words of a modern apostle: "The work

225

done in the temples of the Lord represents the culmination of the obligations, privileges and blessings of the Priesthood. No man has completed — nor a woman with him — the Priesthood cycle until he has received the blessings that the temple has to offer" (John A. Widtsoe, *Conference Report*, April 1943, p. 37).

The dispensation of the fullness of times was ushered in through the instrumentality of the Prophet Joseph Smith. He and others have been privileged to receive the power and authority to act in the name of God and to perform saving ordinances for and in behalf of the living and the dead. Hence, there is nothing presumptive about temple activity sponsored under the leadership of a living prophet, for he holds the keys of the kingdom and uses them to unlock the doors of the temple and related ordinance work. And how blessed we are to share that priesthood power and to exercise it in behalf of ourselves, our families, and others.

Concluding Words

A number of years ago, I attended a session in the Manti Temple. I recall that the company was large and the proceedings rather long and drawn out. The rooms were crowded and very warm, making it difficult for me to stay awake and to keep my mind from wandering. At a moment when I was relaxed in thought, I heard a speaker quote the words of the Savior: "And this is life eternal, that they might know thee the only true God, and Jesus Christ, whom thou hast sent" (John 17:3).

All of a sudden, I felt a spiritual nudging and became very alert. A voice within me seemed to shout, "That's it! That's why I am here! I am here in the Lord's house to become better acquainted with the only true and living God and his Son — the Savior of mankind." Then the voice in my mind asked, "Is there a better place than the temple to learn of God and his holy purposes?"

No one can really know another unless he has seen him

in his home and visited with him in familiar surroundings. In intimate settings, pretenses are dropped, things are seen as they really are, and true perspectives are obtained. So it is with friends or neighbors in their homes, and so it is with God in his place of abode—the temple.

Each time I visit the Lord's house, I reflect upon that experience in the Manti Temple, and I am reminded of my continuing need to know my Maker and to seek eternal life. I feel privileged to be a guest of Deity in the temple. I feel humbled in his presence. And I come away hoping and praying that I might be acceptable to him and ever worthy of his divine love.

I repeat once more: family (a people), temple (a place), and priesthood (a power). These complementary concepts constitute the roots of the "pecan tree" practice of temple activity and worship. God bless you to

> plant this word in your hearts [that ye may try the experiment of its goodness], and as it beginneth to swell even so nourish it by your faith. And behold, it will become a tree, springing up in you unto everlasting life (Alma 33:23; 32:41).

THE LAW OF THE HARVEST

Be not deceived; God is not mocked: for whatsoever
a man soweth, that shall he also reap. *For he that
soweth to his flesh shall of the flesh reap corruption;
but he that soweth to the Spirit shall of the Spirit reap
life everlasting. And let us not be weary in well
doing: for in due season we shall reap, if we faint
not (Galatians 6:7–9; emphasis added).*

"Don't plant a hundred-dollar tree in a ten-dollar hole!" was
the horticulturist's advice to the customer. "The roots of the
tree," he added, "must have room to expand and to absorb
the nutrients from the soil. Moreover, the tree must be embed-
ded in the ground deeply enough so that the roots can finger
their way into the soil and eventually provide the plant with
needed stability."

The horticulturist also counseled the customer to water
the tree regularly and deeply so that the water would seep
into the root system. "You must not depend upon the sprinkling
of the lawn as the means to nourish the tree, nor must you
consider the casting of fertilizer on the grass surrounding the
plant as adequate feeding," said the expert. "Otherwise, the
tree will flourish for a short season, then waste away."

And so it is with the planting of the "pecan tree" practices
discussed in this book. Each practice should be regarded as a
hundred-dollar tree, and each must be planted in a hundred-

228

dollar hole, for each is a vital plant in your "grandchildren grove" and requires attention and nourishment.

Words of Warning

Those who initiate the practices of prayer, scripture reading, family home evenings, and all the other performances in a casual manner place something very sacred in a ten-dollar hole. They do not provide adequate space or time in their lives for the things that matter most. Things of lesser importance are allowed to take priority over things of eternal value. And in the absence of proper foresight, planning, and resolve, the practice is followed for a short time and then dropped. The "pecan tree" practice eventually dies of neglect or is blown aside by some wind of opposition.

Those who engage in priesthood blessings, names of significance, or personal interviews only sporadically never get the water down into the roots. A rhythm of observance is never established; a habit is never formed. In due time, the practice is starved and permitted to wilt away. What might have taken root, grown, and made fruitful is replaced by pressures of the moment or whatever comes easiest.

One man discussing "pecan tree" practices with me said, "I've planted those practices many times, but I have never practiced them consistently." He acknowledged that family histories, family organizations, family traditions, and so on are important. At the same time, however, he admitted his own weakness in cultivating "the precious plants" in his family garden. Perhaps he, like many others, forgets from time to time the blessings associated with each practice. So, he is forever planting and replanting and never harvesting the fruits of his labors.

"Let George Do It"

I fear that too many parents have the "let George do it" attitude. They think that the Church or community or some other agency will step in and do the family planting and harvesting for them. Those who harbor such thoughts fail to understand the limitations of programs sponsored by outside groups. Can an outside agency sponsor home worship? Can an outside organization foster family traditions? The answer is an emphatic, "No, not as they should be sponsored." Only the parents have the power to plant these practices properly. Others, in and out of the Church, may give parents some assistance with the pruning and spraying of the "pecan tree" practices. But there are no fit substitutes for loving parents, a congenial house, and home-spun activities.

Every parent should read and re-read this inspired counsel given by Elder A. Theodore Tuttle:

> The Lord fixed families to give parents more influence on children than all other agencies combined. There is safety in this arrangement. It provides *parents* the privilege, the awesome privilege, of molding the life and character of a child, even though outside agencies have influence . . . .
>
> We have been counseled to become self-reliant and independent temporally. It is as important spiritually! Suppose conditions changed. Suppose you could not receive all the services to which you have become accustomed. Suppose that much more responsibility were placed on your shoulders to care for the spiritual welfare of your family. Surely you cannot study the scriptures without knowing that perilous times are coming. Will you be unaffected?
>
> Prepare now! Take steps now to strengthen your family. Spend time together. Establish and maintain family traditions that build happy memories. Maintain a discipline with fair rules and regulations. Express unconditional love to one another through word and act. Develop within each one self-esteem and self-respect by loving and believing in him and having him belong. Provide security that children need. These are the values of which life is made. Establish these, and

then we won't need to worry about the frills (*Ensign*, November 1979, pp. 27–28).

Parents are urged to plan and plant wisely each "pecan tree" practice, knowing that each is important to family members. Once the practice is planted, persistence must become the watchword. Habits are not formed overnight, nor are living patterns created in a single doing. Perfecting and exalting habits are formed slowly as such good things as family worship and temple activity are repeated day by day, week by week, and month by month.

Too Much?

It is regrettable when parents look upon the "pecan tree" practices as onerous tasks or burdensome expectancies. I ask of such people, "Where is your faith? How much do you love your children? Do you want to leave your grandchildren a snarl of scraggly, unproductive plum branches? Or, do you want to leave them the substantial shade and sweetmeated nuts of the more enduring pecan trees?"

We all know that a negative attitude, much like the casual approach, is lethal when it comes to actions requiring selflessness and a liberal investment of personal time and energies. A negative attitude kills enthusiasm and stifles the spirit associated with all activities. Worse still, the negative attitude makes the gift of the practice stick to the fingers of the givers (the parents) and raises doubts in the minds of the receivers (the children).

In one of the Apostle Paul's epistles we read these words: "The letter killeth, but the spirit giveth life" (2 Corinthians 3:6). All of us should be intent upon keeping the commandments and in following the counsel of Church leaders. But we should not become so caught up in the mechanics and routines of the law that we forget purposes and run roughshod over people, particularly members of our family circle. The Lord, we are told, expects obedience to his will, yet he also requires "the heart and a willing mind" (D&C 64:34).

How very wonderful it is when parents become converted to the "pecan tree" practices and catch a vision of what each can do to bless the lives of family members! Such parents plant with faith and nourish each "pecan tree" with care. Every effort is made to give each practice lively thought, refreshing variety, and stimulating action, thus guarding against routineness or staleness. In the end, they create an orchard of productive trees that bear precious fruit.

One Step at a Time

I suspect that some, especially the newlywed or single parent families, will read what I have written and wonder whether they can do all that is suggested. My response to these young heads of households is "No, you cannot, and you shouldn't expect to do so overnight. The planting of the sixteen 'pecan tree' practices should occur step by step and as circumstances will permit. You should, however, start with one or two or three and grow into the others. All should be kept in mind and planted and cultivated in its proper season or as the opportunity presents itself."

"Be ye therefore perfect," said the Savior, "even as your Father which is in heaven is perfect" (Matthew 5:48). The Joseph Smith Translation of this same verse reads, "Ye are therefore commanded to be perfect . . . " (JST Matthew 5:50). To some, this command establishes an overwhelming, perhaps even impossible, expectancy. But, when we understand that "perfect" might mean complete, finished, or fully developed, as the Greek text suggests, the task doesn't seem quite so difficult. All of us can become "complete" in our bestowal of significant names upon our children; all of us can "finish" a personal or family history; and all of us can become "fully developed" in our preservation of cherished memories.

The Law of the Harvest

The law of the harvest has always been understood and taught by servants of God, for it is an eternal law. Said Job, "They that plow iniquity, and sow wickedness, reap the same" (Job 4:8). A Book of Mormon prophet quoted the Lord as saying, "If my people shall sow filthiness they shall reap the east wind, which bringeth immediate destruction" (Mosiah 7:31). In his interpretation of the parable of the sower, the Savior promised, "He that received seed into the good ground is he that heareth the word, and understandeth it; which also beareth fruit, and bringeth forth, some an hundredfold, some sixty, some thirty" (Matthew 13:23).

All of these quotations from the scriptures and many more remind us of a simple but profound truth: "Whatsoever a man soweth, that shall he also reap" (Galatians 6:7).

We may apply the harvest law in a variety of ways. For example, the faithless person might say, "The law is harsh and full of risk, so I will not plant at all." Such persons are "they [who] sow not, neither do they reap" (Matthew 6:26). And those lazy souls at the time of harvest may not be as fortunate as the ravens or other fowls of the air who are fed by someone else. Malnutrition and possible starvation may nip at their heels throughout life.

Then there are those who are careless in the selection of their seeds. They neither read the labels on packages nor take the time to inspect the seed that will be placed in the ground. Consequently, they inadvertently and otherwise sow filthiness and later reap the chaff thereof in the whirlwind (see Mosiah 7:30). Perhaps these wanton planters are surprised occasionally by a sweet fruit or two, but bitterness is generally associated with the fruit of careless efforts.

Still others plant cautiously, as if the seed would sprout better in their scrip than in the soil. They ignore the appendage to the law of the harvest taught by the Apostle Paul in these words: "He which soweth sparingly shall reap also sparingly;

and he which soweth bountifully shall reap also bountifully"
(2 Corinthians 9:6). Ofttimes, those who sow sparingly do so
grudgingly and with selfish interests in their hearts. Their view
is toward self, and their minds are blinded to the needs of
children and future generations.

The appeal voiced by this book is simple and direct: *Exercise faith, select the right seeds, and plant the "pecan tree" practices in your heart and in your family circle.* Allow the seeds or practices to swell, sprout, and grow into perfecting and exalting performances. In due time, you will acknowledge the goodness of the seeds because they will get root, grow up into productive trees, and bring forth delicious fruit.

All to Grow

A group of farmers planted five seeds in each hole, as they
sang:

One for the blackbird,
One for the crow,
One for the cutworm,
Two to grow.
(David Grayson, *Adventures of Friendship* [Frederick, Colo.:
Renaissance House Publishers, 1989], p. 63.)

I admire the generosity implied in this jingle. How kind
of the farmers to feed the blackbird, crow, and cutworm. At
the same time, however, I deplore the submissive attitude of
the farmers. They apparently acquiesced to the enemies of
their crops and attempted to plant around them — an expensive
and wasteful method of farming.

As I review the sixteen family performances proposed
within the covers of this book, I see none that is superfluous.
I see none for the birds or worms. All should be planted,
watered, cultivated, and guarded carefully. No power or influence should be allowed to enter our gardens that would uproot
these edifying performances or others of comparable worth.

God Gave the Increase

The Apostle Paul wrote: "I have planted, Apollos watered; but *God gave the increase*. So then neither is he that planteth any thing, neither he that watereth; but *God that giveth the increase*. Now he that planteth and he that watereth are one: and every man shall receive his own reward according to his own labour. For we are labourers together with God: ye are God's husbandry, ye are God's building" (1 Corinthians 3:6–9; italics added).

These words of Paul and his apt analogy remind us of the need to plant and water, for we are a part of God's husbandry and building. At the same time, however, we are reminded that God determines the harvest. It is he who gives the increase; he is the "Lord of the harvest" (Alma 26:7). So, knowing that blessings are predicated upon obedience to law, we should strive to do our utmost in fulfilling those laws or commandments pertaining to family and home, placing ourselves in a position where God will shower goodnesses upon us and our posterity (see D&C 130:20–21).

Welding Links

I repeat a scripture cited previously in this writing: "It is sufficient to know . . . that the earth will be smitten with a curse unless there is a welding link of some kind or other between the fathers and the children. . . . For we without them cannot be made perfect; neither can they without us be made perfect" (D&C 128:18).

Many welding links exist between parents and their offspring, bonding them together as a closely knit organization. For some, it may be sports or outings that tie the group together. For others, it may be family business interests and the prospects of making money that bridges the generation gap. These and similar bonds can be fragile and tenuous depending upon the ebb and flow of relationships. The more prevailing welding links, however, that should be established between fathers and sons, mothers and daughters, are those that are not easily disturbed by time and circumstance. I speak of the welding links founded upon love, related to the gospel of Jesus Christ, and centered in saving principles and ordinances.

Earth and all of its inhabitants are cursed by broken families and estranged children. Of a certainty, the progress of both parents and children is slowed or altogether dammed when the linkage between the young and old is missing. It is incumbent upon all parents and children to weld the family together. Such can be done by courting the spirit of Elijah, searching out our kindred dead, writing family histories, performing temple ordinances for ourselves and others, establishing strong relationships within our families, and taking especial care of our children.

Love of God, Love of Children

Father Lehi saw in vision the tree of life. This tree "was a representation of the love of God" (1 Nephi 11:25). In a similar manner, I regard the "pecan tree" practices discussed in this book as representations of the love of parents for children. Each practice planted, cultivated, and allowed to grow within the family garden declares to the children, "We care; we love you." Each practice, if understood and employed,

> *shall be as a tree planted by the waters, and that spreadeth out her roots by the river, and shall not see when heat cometh, but her leaf shall be green; and shall not be careful in the year of drought, neither shall cease from yielding fruit (Jeremiah 17:8).*

THE LATTER-DAY SAINT CONCEPTS OF FAMILY

1. *Families on earth are an extension of the family of God.* Every person is a child of heavenly parents as well as mortal parents. Each individual was created spiritually and physically in the image of God and Christ (Moses 2:27; 3:5).

2. *Marriage is ordained of God.* "Whoso forbiddeth to marry is not ordained of God, for marriage is ordained of God unto man" (D&C 49:15). Marriage of the kind sanctioned by God provides men and women with the opportunity for complete fulfillment of their divine potentials.

3. *The family can become an eternal unit if sealed by the power of the priesthood.* Worthy members can be married in the temple for time and eternity. At the time of their marriage, both husband and wife enter an "order of the priesthood [called] the new and everlasting covenant of marriage" (D&C 131:1–4).

4. *The power to create life is a gift from God; therefore, chastity is sacred* (cf. Jacob 2:28). Sexual purity is spiritual and mental, as well as physical and emotional. Jesus said, "Whosoever looketh on a woman, to lust after her, hath committed adultery already in his heart. Behold, I give unto you a commandment, that ye suffer none of these things to enter into your heart" (3 Nephi 12:28–29).

5. *Procreation is a commandment of God.* Through the sexual experience, husbands and wives enrich their marriage

and create physical bodies for spirits to come to earth to achieve divine purposes. Latter-day Saints strive to create a homelife dedicated to fulfilling those purposes.

6. *Parents are responsible to teach their children the Gospel of Jesus Christ.* "Inasmuch as parents have children ... that teach them not to understand the doctrine of repentance, faith in Christ the Son of the living God, and of baptism and the gift of the Holy Ghost ... the sin be upon the heads of the parents ... And they shall also teach their children to pray, and to walk uprightly before the Lord" (D&C 68:25, 28).

7. *An environment of light and truth is necessary for rearing children.* "Light and truth forsake that evil one" (D&C 93:37). The spirit of a righteous home is love. The Lord said, "Thou shalt live together in love" (D&C 42:45) — love of heavenly parents, the Lord Jesus Christ, and the Holy Ghost; of husband and wife; of parents for children, children for parents, and siblings for each other.

8. *Making one's home a place of peace and joy requires consistent planning, prayer, effort, and cooperation.* The Church encourages families to hold weekly home evenings in which all members of the family study eternal principles and ordinances and do things together that bring them joy.

9. *Given these principles worthy family members look forward with faith and hope to eternal family relationships both with their earthly families and with ancestors and descendants.* They expect to live again with loved ones who have died. They become those "who received the testimony of Jesus, and believed on his name ... and are sealed by the Holy Spirit of promise, which the Father sheds forth upon all those who are just and true" (D&C 76:51, 53).

10. *All righteous individuals who maintain their own worthiness, love, and faithfulness are promised the riches of eternity, including the eventual blessings of being sealed to those family members who qualify for celestial blessings.* (Adapted from Reed H. Bradford, "Family," *Encyclopedia of Mormonism*, pp. 486–88.)

Ten Commandments for Successful Family Living

Thou shalt meditate therein day and night, that thou mayest observe to do according to all that is written therein: for then thou shalt make thy way prosperous, and then thou shalt have good success (Joshua 1:8)

1. Thou shalt conduct family prayers regularly, both morning and night (Alma 34:18–27; 37:36–37).

2. Thou shalt pray before each meal, expressing gratitude for blessings received and requesting the Lord to sanctify and bless the food (Psalm 55:17; Daniel 6:10).

3. Thou shalt hold a planned family home evening every Monday night or other designated night of the week (D&C 68:25–28; 93:40–48).

4. Thou shalt keep the Sabbath Day holy and attend church meetings as a family unit (Exodus 20:8–11; D&C 59:9–14).

5. Thou shalt observe the law of the fast by abstaining from eating and drinking for two consecutive meals on the first Sunday of each month and by giving generously to the fast-offering fund (Matthew 6:16–18; Isaiah 58:6–12).

6. Thou shalt pay tithing faithfully, honestly, and willingly (Malachi 3:8–12; D&C 119:1–7).

7. *Children,* thou shalt love, honor, respect, and obey parents (Deuteronomy 5:16; Proverbs 6:20–23). *Parents,* thou shalt

love, respect, and care for the temporal and spiritual needs of each child (Ephesians 6:4; Deuteronomy 6:7–9).

8. Thou shalt search the scriptures daily and live in obedience to the laws, principles, ordinances, and teachings of the gospel of Jesus Christ (John 5:39; D&C 1:37–39).

9. Thou shalt learn how to serve others by sharing household responsibilities, such as washing dishes, cleaning floors, making beds, weeding the garden, picking up clothes, and doing other helpful jobs around the home (Mosiah 2:14–24; Matthew 25:34–40).

10. Thou shalt obtain a spirit of harmony and oneness in the family by speaking kind words, performing deeds of kindness, and living for the companionship of the Holy Ghost (John 13:34–35; D&C 121:45–46).

"I have no greater joy than to hear that my children walk in truth" (3 John 1:4).

FAMILY PERFORMANCE CHECKLIST

Directions: Study carefully each item listed below and check the response that best describes your behavior. Afterwards, draw a line down the page connecting the responses given from item #1 to item #10. This line will provide you a graphic representation of your family performance. Regard "always" as a celestial behavior; "sometimes" as terrestrial; and "never" as telestial. Repeat the exercise periodically and strive to get all responses into the "always" column.

In our family:

	Always	Sometimes	Never
1. We conduct family prayers regularly, both morning and night.	☐	☐	☐
2. We pray before each meal, expressing gratitude for blessings received and requesting the Lord to sanctify and bless the food.	☐	☐	☐
3. We hold a planned family home evening every Monday night or other designated night of the week.	☐	☐	☐
4. We keep the Sabbath Day holy and attend Church meetings as a family unit.	☐	☐	☐

	Always	Sometimes	Never

5. We observe the law of the fast by abstaining from eating and drinking for two consecutive meals on the first Sunday of each month and by giving generously to the fast-offering fund. □ □ □

6. We pay tithing faithfully, honestly, and willingly. □ □ □

7. The children love, honor, respect and obey parents, and the parents love, respect, and care for the temporal and spiritual needs of each child. □ □ □

8. We search the scriptures daily and live in obedience to the laws, principles, ordinances, and teachings of the gospel of Jesus Christ. □ □ □

9. We learn how to serve others by sharing household responsibilities, such as washing dishes, cleaning floors, making beds, weeding the garden, picking up clothes, and doing other helpful jobs around the house. □ □ □

10. We obtain a spirit of harmony and oneness in the family by speaking kind words, performing deeds of kindness, and living for the companionship of the Holy Ghost. □ □ □

Characteristics of Effective Mormon Families

In 1987 data was gathered from 200 strong LDS families on the characteristics of effective Mormon families. Here are some of the things that were discovered:

1. Almost 100% of the families are full tithe payers, attend all of their meetings regularly, and always accept a job or position in the Church.

2. These families have very clear goals as to what they want for their children. Virtually 100% said their goals included having their children marry in the temple, get a good education, develop a strong self concept, be active in the Church, develop a strong sense of family unity, and have children go on a mission. (We also found that the less-effective families did not have these clear goals for their children.)

3. In effective families, 73% said they always or usually held daily family prayer.

4. Two-thirds of these families said they always or usually held regular weekly family home evening. The other one-third also held family home evening, but not as regularly.

5. These families did not identify movie stars or sports figures as family heroes. They most often said the heroes in their families were Church leaders or other older family members.

6. Husbands and wives work at having a good personal relationship in their marriages. On a scale of 1 to 10, the average family was at 8.5 in terms of feeling the marriage was strong and good.

7. Ninety-six percent said they most often would do things together as a family. Ninety-two percent said they always went as a family to activities where another family member performed or was in a game or activity.

8. These families are not free from adversity. Eighty percent said they had some real adversities in their lives (illness, death, problems with children, etc.) but they worked as a family to deal with problems. The family was the first line of defense in times of adversity. They worked things out together as much as possible.

9. Over 80% said they daily express affection physically to other family members.

10. These families on the average watch TV only 1/3 as much as the average family in America.

11. Effective families tend to see themselves as somewhat stricter than other families. They had rather few rules but very high expectations. They expect a lot from their children.

12. They tend to reward their children more by giving praise or some special treat, rather than giving money.

13. These families spend a great deal of time talking together. Almost 100% said they talk regularly as a family and also to each child individually on a regular, almost daily, basis.

(W.G. Dyer and P.R. Kunz, *Effective Mormon Families* [Salt Lake City: Deseret Book Co., 1986].)

CHECKLIST: HOW IS YOUR FAMILY DOING IN BUILDING CHARACTERISTICS OF AN EFFECTIVE MORMON FAMILY?

1. Does your **Church Activity** include: • Being a full tithe payer? • Attending all Church meetings regularly. • Always accepting a job or position in the Church.	Low 1 2 3 4 5 High Low 1 2 3 4 5 High Low 1 2 3 4 5 High
2. Have you identified **Family Goals** such as: • Children marrying in the temple. • Good education. • Developing a strong self-concept. • Activity in the Church. • Developing a strong sense of family unity. • Having children go on missions.	Low 1 2 3 4 5 High Low 1 2 3 4 5 High Low 1 2 3 4 5 High Low 1 2 3 4 5 High Low 1 2 3 4 5 High Low 1 2 3 4 5 High
3. **Family Prayer**–Do you hold a daily family prayer?	Low 1 2 3 4 5 High
4. **Family Home Evening**–Do you hold regular weekly family home evenings?	Low 1 2 3 4 5 High
5. **Family Heroes**–Does your family hold family members as heroes?	Low 1 2 3 4 5 High
6. **Marriage Relationships**–Do you have a good personal relationship in your marriage?	Low 1 2 3 4 5 High
7. **Family Activities**–Do you do things together as a family?	Low 1 2 3 4 5 High
8. **Adversity**–Are you able to deal with adversities within your family, such as illness, death, problems with children, etc?	Low 1 2 3 4 5 High

9. **Affection**–Do you daily express affection to other family members?	Low 1 2 3 4 5 High
10. **Television**–What is your family's television viewing habits compared to the average family in America?	Low 1 2 3 4 5 High
11. **Discipline**–Do you see yourself as somewhat stricter than other families?	Low 1 2 3 4 5 High
12. **Praise**–Do you reward the children more by giving praise or some special treats, rather than giving money?	Low 1 2 3 4 5 High
13. **Communication**–Do you talk regularly as a family and also to each child individually on a regular, almost daily, basis?	Low 1 2 3 4 5 High

(This checklist is an adaptation of ideas taken from a research study by Dr. William G. Dyer and Dr. Phillip R. Kunz on the characteristics of effective Mormon families. (See W. G. Dyer and P. R. Kunz, *Effective Mormon Families* [Salt Lake City: Deseret Book Co., 1986].)

INDEX

McConkie, Bruce R., on true worship, 203–4
McKay, David O.: on family home evening, 47; on need for love at home, 47; on meditation, 201–2; on reverence, 205–6
Means not to be confused with ends, 83–84
Meditation, 201–2
Memorabilia boxes, 123–25
Memories: fallibility of, 85–87; of home, 86; as security blanket, 86; and Enos, 87–88; Alma recalls, of sins, 88; evoked by Moroni's Title of Liberty, 88; positive use of, 88; and models, 90–91; suggestions for creating, in family, 95–96
Memory: and mood, 87–88; as colored window, 87–88; in obtaining testimony of Book of Mormon, 89; and testimony, 89–90; poem about, by Christina Rossetti, 91; and thoughts, 91–93; and you, 93–94
Mind, capacity of, 86–87
Missionary: receives inspired phone call from mother, 153–54; receives letter from repentant father, 155–56; whose service blessed family, 185
Model: in effective prayer, 15; and memories, 91; need for worthy, 91
"Moisture" as characteristic of humor, 98
Monson, Thomas S., on service, 177–78
Mood and memory, 87–88
Moroni: knew Joseph Smith's name, 74–75; interviews Joseph Smith, 76; and Title of Liberty, 88
Mosaic law, "dryness" of, 78
Mosiah, King, purposes of, in reading records to people, 118–19

Mother: poem about, who read to child, 27–28; prompted to call missionary son, 153–54

Name: young woman who hated, 64–66; importance of, in scriptures, 66–67; story of George Albert Smith and, 67–69; of Asay daughters, 69–70; in blessing of children, 70–71; giving, to children among Africans, 71; need for care in choosing, 72; of Joseph Smith prophesied, 72–73; of Christ, among Nephites, 73–74; God knows our, 74–75; of Joseph Smith known by God, 74–75
New Year's Eve in Asay family, 140–41
Nightcap in scripture study, 38–39
Note, supportive, to Carlos E. Asay from wife, 155

Oaks, Dallin H.: on family history, 112; on encouragement to keep histories, 125
Obedience, blessings predicated upon, 59–61
Oral histories, 123
Organization and temple worship, 220–21
Osler, William, on reading scriptures, 29

Packer, Boyd K.: on family home evening, 45–46; on leaving briefcase at office, 45–46; on method of writing personal history, 124–25; on spirit of Elijah, 226
Parents: obligations of, 5; duty of, to teach children to pray, 14; First Presidency on responsibility of, 53; power of example of, 157–58; unity among, 158; prayer of, 160–61; responsiblity